SANTARÉM—RIVERBOAT TOWN

SANTARÉM

—

RIVERBOAT TOWN

A Gringo's Own Account of Tourism on
The Brazilian Amazon and Tapajós Rivers

Steven Winn Alexander

MISSOURI PARTNERS PUBLISHING
2007

ISBN 978-0-9795643-0-7

Missouri Partners Publishing
229 Gentry Hall
Columbia, Missouri 65201

http//www.mo-para.com

CONTENTS

FOREWORD

Steve Alexander has done a most useful service in highlighting the many wonderful biological and cultural attributes of the Santarém area of the Amazon. I have been going to and from Amazonia for thirty-six years, and have lived there for various stretches, and I would agree with Steve that Santarém and environs is really a jewel when it comes to tourism possibilities.

Where else on earth do two mighty rivers collide with such drama— on the one hand a relatively clear river (the Tapajós), and on the other the creamed coffee Amazon which carries some ten times the water of the Mississippi. The Tapajós itself dwarfs the Mississippi and it meets the much larger Amazon right in front of Santarém. Two great aquatic ecosystems with different plants and fish are therefore at Santarém's doorstep.

The lower Tapajós is sort of a tropical fjord, except its valley was scoured down by water rather than a glacier. During the Pleistocene (from roughly 1 million years ago to 10,000 years ago) much of the earth's freshwater was tied up by huge ice sheets. None of these ice bulldozers ever reached the lowland tropics, but seawater dropped by about 100 meters during each major glaciation, and this allowed the rivers to dig their beds deeper. As the last of the great ice sheets melted 10,000 years ago, the Amazon and its tributaries backed up. The waters of the lower Tapajós formed what looks like a great lake and the Amazon, because it carries so much sediment from the Andes, formed a huge floodplain with its myriad side-channels and lakes.

Santarém is therefore a marvelous stepping off point to see the wonders of the Amazon. From the generous floodplain of the Amazon itself with its huge lakes stocked with fish and colorful birds to the clear water Tapajós and black water Arapiuns, the latter two

7

rivers famous for their extensive sandy beaches festooned with wild cashew trees, and to the majestic bluffs of the planalto behind Santarém with their tall forests teeming with unusual plants and animals, the area around Santarém is a nature wonderland. No wonder famous nineteenth-century naturalists tarried in Santarém, such as the Yorkshire botanist Richard Spruce, to observe and report on the exuberant plant and animal life.

Santarém and its vicinity is also a fascinating place to learn about the way of life of people who eke a living from the waters and forests of this bountiful laboratory of evolution. Long before the arrival of Europeans, numerous cultures have come and gone along the middle Amazon. At least 10,000 years ago, hunters and gatherers had set up shop at the foot of massive sandstone hills near Monte Alegre on the opposite side of the Amazon from Santarém. One of Steve's tour options is to see the painted rocks near Monte Alegre and it is well worth a visit to imagine who these people were who left their red handprints and fantastic geometric patterns on the sun-bleached rocks so long ago. Some 8,000 years ago, people were making pottery at Taperinha, about 50 kilometers downstream from Santarém, another one of Steve's tour options. Shell mounds mixed with bones and pieces of pottery are testament to their long vanished lifestyle.

When Francisco Orellana, the Spanish explorer, passed down the Amazon in front of present-day Santarém in 1542, the area was densely settled by the Tapajó nation, a proud warrior people with extensive villages, intricate pottery, exquisite wooden carvings, and women who enjoyed braiding their hair. Vast areas of black earth with pieces of pottery and the occasional stone axe for cutting down trees or chisel for woodcarvings can be found in many parts of Santarém and its vicinity. Although the Tapajó nation is no more, the indigenous cultures have left their mark on the present-day population, which during the colonial times received an influx of Portuguese and Africans. One of the most rewarding parts of any visit to Santarém and its vicinity is to interact with the people who, as Steve points out in the book, are so friendly, helpful, and eager to

8

show you aspects of their daily lives, whether it be making baskets to fishing and gathering forest fruits. Steve's book and guide services are a marvelous way to begin your adventure in Santarém and other parts of the Amazon.

Nigel Smith
Professor of Geography
University of Florida

PREFACE

The Amazon River begins its 4000-mile journey as a trickle high in the Andes Mountains. More than a thousand tributaries join its passage to the Atlantic Ocean. I live on one of these confluences, the Tapajós River.

Our city, Santarém, is appropriately called the "Pearl of the Tapajós." Tourism began here with the Spanish and the Portuguese explorers in the early 1500s, and prior to them, indigenous people, who arrived in the region more than ten thousand years ago. Regardless of who has come and gone, you still have the pleasure of visiting one of the most beautiful places in the world without facing large numbers of fellow travelers. While you reap the benefits of being one of the few to discover this part of the world, it is only fair to recognize that there are certain inconveniences associated with traveling in areas where few go. Most are linked to minimal infrastructure or experience on the part of those receiving you. One example is the lack of information about what to do and see during a visit. Today's fast-moving traveler has little or no time for digging out encoded or cryptic travel plans. They want to know what options are available, on the spot. One purpose of this book is to provide precisely that, to give you an inside view of Santarém and the Tapajós region.

I have also identified some of the common flora and fauna of the region. Most visitors encounter an unfamiliar world upon arriving in the Amazon and find little educational materials to help them sort out the unknowns, including the history and culture of the region. While the scope of this edition cannot include detailed information, it is intended to give some orientation to the wonders that will surround you.

Acknowledgments

It is only appropriate to direct my first statement of appreciation to fellow travelers. Some have spent days and weeks with me on the Amazon River, under every circumstance conceivable—and their images are forever etched in my memory. Many were with me for shorter periods of time, and it is only understandable that some names and faces have faded into oblivion, in a similar way as the Tapajós River and other tributaries dissipate into the muddy waters of the boundless Amazon. Regardless of the duration of our encounters, each was unique and always a pleasure.

I am grateful to clients who have shared special skills with me. Robert Stein, retired professor of biology at Buffalo State College, sparked my interest in birding from the beginning of our many tours together. Truthfully speaking, I did not know a cattle egret from a white-necked heron the first time we went out in 1989. Others have shared their knowledge, far too many to mention names. Then there were those who sparked my curiosity for research by the way of well-put questions, which I could not answer at the time.

Appreciation goes posthumously to Captain William Wheeler of Dunedin, Florida, for sending me a clever piece of equipment called a laptop computer. Never having used one of these gadgets before, I decided to take advantage of it to revise a small booklet called *Alexander's Guide to Santarém*. The awesome 20MB of hard disk made the logistics of writing so easy, I could not stop. I soon became addicted to writing and computers.

One does not write a book without taking incalculable time away from home affairs, so I thank my wife, Áurea Lúcia, and sons, Steven David and Arthur Daniel, for allowing me to do so.

I am also grateful to friends who have helped me edit earlier versions of the text. Special thanks go to Julie Maris, Sharon E. McGladdery, Alice Stein, Walter Stein, Elaine Trump and Daniel Weiss.

Last, but not least, I thank the Brazilian people of the Amazon for having received me and my fellow travelers. We are surely privileged to have passed your way.

Steven Winn Alexander

MEN AND CLAMS MAKING HISTORY —
HISTORICAL NOTES

Geological History

South America was once part of Gondwanaland, a super continent that began to break up about 150 million years ago. After drifting westward for approximately 50 million years, it encountered another landmass coming from the opposite direction and the upshot of this tectonic encounter was the Andes Mountain Range. The Amazon River, which had been flowing westward, found itself blocked by the mountains and thus formed a gigantic lake system covering large portions of Northern Brazil. The last ice age, which peaked around 18,000 years ago, lowered ocean levels by 100 meters (328 feet), and triggered the inclination necessary for the river to flow eastward into the Atlantic Ocean. After the draining streams picked up speed from the lowering ocean levels, they cut very deep channels into the riverbeds, creating one of the deepest rivers in the world. As the ice age declined, ocean levels came back up.

Distant Relatives — First Human Inhabitants

A clamshell is just a clamshell to most of us, but the mounds of them at Taperinha, a ranch site located on Igarapé de Maicá, just east of Santarém, reveals much more about the significance of this shy shellfish. The first time I visited Taperinha, I did not realize that this had been an important archeological site for establishing dates and lifestyles of the first human inhabitants of this region. This was January of 1991, and my stop was an impromptu one to satisfy the curiosity of my clients who were infatuated by the forest, the old colonial house and the beauty of the Amazon floodplain. We were received with some apprehension by the caretaker of the ranch, but managed to convince her that our visit was with good intentions and that we would advise the owner, Graciela Hagmann, of our visit when we got back to Santarém. The house was completely abandoned at

13

that time, but just a glance around at piles of dusty old books, manuscripts and weather instruments was enough to convince us that the former occupants had not been typical ranchers of the region. Built by the Baron of Santarém, Miguel Antônio Pinto Guimarães, in the 1800s, the house was later sold to Godofredo Hagmann, a zoologist at the Emilio Goeldi Museum in Belém. Rumor has it that Hagmann was with President Theodore Roosevelt the first time he set eyes on the property, but I have not seen documentation to confirm it. Regardless, the ranch is still in the hands of the Hagmann family and they are very selective in giving permission to visit the place. Excavations of the clam middens (scientific term for garbage pile), which are located a hundred meters back of the main house, by archeologist Anna Roosevelt and her colleagues at the Emilio Goeldi Museum, indicate that Native Americans were living in that area more than 6,000 years ago.[1] Nelsí Neif Sadeck—civil engineer, teacher and self-taught anthropologist from Monte Alegre—tells me that indigenous cliff and cave paintings near his hometown date back at least 11,000 years. Research there, also conducted by Anna Roosevelt in 1995-1996, testifies this to be true, placing them among the oldest cave paintings in the Americas.[2]

The last ice age provided easy access for human occupation of the Americas and the fabulous network of waterways in the Amazon made for very rapid tribal settlement. The new generation of anthropologists and archeologists believe there was a much greater occupation of the Amazon floodplain than that of the highland forests. Rich soils and waters filled with fish, turtles and other wildlife made the floodplain a much better choice for livelihood than the *terra firma* forests. Only after European occupation of the Amazon did the surviving tribes move up inaccessible tributaries to get away from the onslaught of the new inhabitants. It is estimated that there may have been between six and nine million Indians in the Amazon in the early 1500s, when the first Europeans arrived. Today there are fewer than 120,000 survivors.[3] The non-Indian population, on the other hand, has increased from a handful of explorers to more than 12 million today and is growing fast.

European Exploration and Colonization

Vicente Yáñez Pinzón, a Spaniard who had sailed with Christopher Columbus on his first voyage to the Americas, reached the northern coast of what is today Brazil in January of 1500. He then sailed northwestward, where he discovered the fresh water of the Amazon.[4]

Captain Francisco de Orellana, also Spanish, was the first European to travel most of the distance downstream, in 1542. The voyage of eight months had not been planned, but resulted from Orellana's split from a larger exploration party organized by Gonzalo Pizarro to exploit natural resources along the Napo River in Peru. Orellana's charge in separating from the leader of the expedition was that of finding food, not an easy task. Some historians speculate that he took advantage of the situation to make off with some booty, but in any case, he continued downstream to the point of not being able to go back.[5]

Based on my experience as a tour leader on the lower half of the Napo River, it is easy for me to believe that, in fact, Orellana found himself beyond the point of easily returning to Pizarro's group. On every visit to Explorama's Napo Inn, we make it a point to travel by motorized canoe upstream for quite a distance and then float back down while bird watching. I am always impressed by how fast we get back to our starting point. The flow of the current is considerable and I can well imagine the distance Orellana must have gone in four days on the river. On another Napo River episode, I was also reminded of the story of how Orellana and his band of 53 men ended up eating their leather footwear in order to repress their hunger. We were on one of Explorama's new speedboats, which have reduced the traveling time between Iquitos and the Napo Inn from approximately eight hours, via the old motorized canoes, to about three hours. Somewhere on the Napo River we were startled by a terrible noise that brought the powerful diesel engine to a dead stop. It may have been a broken drive shaft, but in any case, it was not reparable and we found ourselves drifting back down the river. The Napo River has the reputation of being dangerous—not only because of the strong current, but also because of submerged sandbars and lodged debris.

15

Half submerged trees are the most dangerous because of the violent impact of a canoe crashing into the sweeping limbs. Our circumstance brought to mind Alaska days when it was common to hear of persons zipping off to great distances on their high-speed snowmobiles in 40° below temperatures with no provisions for mechanical breakdowns. Our high-technology boat, likewise, had no provisions for the situation in which we found ourselves. No radio, no food, no water, no spare parts, not even a paddle. Our driver quickly came up with an old broom, which at least steered us away from major obstacles. To make a long story short, we were eventually rescued by two Indians in a dugout canoe and, much later caught a ride to Napo Inn in a small outboard canoe.

It was on Orellana's journey, near Terra Santa on the Nhamundá River (west of Santarém), that Orellana reported being attacked by the legendary one-breasted women warriors, thus coming up with the name *Amazonas*, borrowed from Greek mythology. In fact, the Spaniards stopped at Santarém itself, but a very large Indian population sent them on their way downstream.[6]

The Amazon region is immense. It takes nearly a one-hour commercial jet flight between Belém and Santarém, another hour between Santarém and Manaus, nearly another hour between Manaus and Tefé, and yet another hour to Tabatinga, on the border with Columbia. Flying on towards the Andes Mountains, it is yet another hour to Iquitos, Peru, and there remains a lot of river southwest of Iquitos before getting to the Andes. The Amazon is large enough that few travel companies, if any, offer trips that cover the breadth of the region. One person, who took on the river, almost in its entirety, was Pedro Teixeira. Teixeira, Portuguese, began his trip from Cametá (located on the Tocantins River, 149 kilometers from Belém) on October 28 of 1637, arriving almost one year later in Quito, Ecuador. The return expedition from Quito began on February 16, 1639, and terminated on December 12 of that same year.[7]

Even though the vast majority of the Amazon region belonged to the Spanish, as delineated by the Treaty of Tordesillas (1494), the Portuguese dominated exploration of the region with very little resistance from the Spanish, who were much too occupied with the riches of the Andes to worry about endless waterways surrounded by impenetrable jungle. The settlement of the area by the Portuguese and protection of it against the French and Dutch explorers guaranteed their dominion over most of the Amazon.

Obviously, the conquest and pacification of the Indian populations were top priorities for the Portuguese in their effort to settle the Amazon. Santarém was strategically important in this regard, given its large indigenous population and its location at the confluence of the Amazon and Tapajós Rivers. Regional domination by the Indians changed dramatically in 1639, when they were forced to surrender to the Portuguese provincial government.[8]

Santarém became an official Portuguese settlement in 1661, when the Jesuits established a mission at the site. Within the next century the Indian population was reduced incredibly to a handful of individuals who eventually resettled to other parts of the region.

Economy
Almost from the beginning of colonial times the raising of livestock became a major economic activity in the Amazon Basin. The Portuguese had been successful in this venture on the Azores and Madeira Islands and, by 1680, large herds of cattle roamed the natural grasslands of Marajó Island, where the Jesuits and later the Mercedarian priests were responsible for administration of Indian labor.[9] Asian buffalos were introduced to Marajó Island in 1893. Rich, fertile soils of the Amazon floodplain and natural grasses of high nutritive value made ranching one of the most popular business enterprises and remains so to this day. One can travel from one end of the river to the other and hardly ever get out of sight of a ranch.

Among other economic endeavors, including ranching, harvesting of cacao, timbering, subsistence farming, hunting and fishing, none has been as dramatic as that of rubber extraction. Rubber trees are native to the Amazon, and thousands of years before the arrival of the Europeans, the Indians used latex for making rubber balls, figurines, bottles and a number of other products. It was not until the 1770s, however, that the Europeans found a use for rubber—as erasers ("rubbers," in European English).[10] By 1800, Brazil was exporting large numbers of rubber shoes and eventually the raw material made its way to the raincoat and rain hat factories in the United States. In 1888, John Dunlop invented the rubber tire, and the rubber boom intensified. Because Brazil monopolized the world's production of industrial rubber, the Amazon had a key role in the country's economy.

The rubber boom ended almost as dramatically as it started, and Santarém played a major role in that history. Richard Spruce, a British botanist who lived in Santarém (1849-1850) conducted studies on a variety of rubber tree species in South America and came to the conclusion that the best one was *Hevea brasiliense.* Furthermore, he advocated that the rubber from the Tapajós River Valley was of higher quality than other regions. *Acre fino*, from the State of Acre, later proved to be of superior quality to that of the Tapajós;[11] nonetheless, Santarém became the departing point for 70,000 rubber tree seeds that ended up in Kew Gardens in England. Richard Spruce, ironically named after a conifer himself, did not take the seeds out of Brazil. This came about several years later, in 1876, when another Englishman, Henry Wickham, who was living in Santarém at the time, collected and transported them to Kew Gardens. The question of whether or not the seeds were actually "smuggled" out of Brazil may be controversial, but Wickham to this day is known as an industrial spy. By 1913, the Oriental plantations, where the seedlings were taken after leaving Kew Gardens, were producing as much rubber as the Amazon. In the late 1930s, Brazil had lost the market almost entirely. World War II brought a brief but very intense revival of the Brazilian rubber market to assist the Allied Forces in improving the quality of synthetic rubber. Following the war, however, the market subsided again. Henry Ford made an attempt to establish his private plantations in Fordlândia and Belterra (also in the Santarém area) between 1928 and 1946, but finally determined that production was not economically feasible, mainly due to the high cost of producing trees resistant to leaf blight disease, *microcycous uli*.

I was surprised to learn that Henry Ford never once set foot on his gigantic, modern rubber tree plantations in Fordlândia and Belterra. When clearing operations got started on the 2,500,000 acre site at Fordlândia in 1928, Ford Motor Company was already celebrating 25 years of existence and the famed Model-T had by this time been discontinued—with over 15 million units sold. Historians and technicians may debate the practicable aspects of a project of this magnitude in the middle of the Amazon forest without extensive feasibility studies, but nobody can negate the fact that Henry Ford could well afford to take the risk of losing several million dollars to continue his tradition of not wanting to be dependent on anyone for anything, including rubber for tires.

Ford Motor Company's venture on the Tapajós River was long before my time, but I had the pleasure of learning a bit more about this important piece of Brazilian/American history by way of a special client, Alfred Weeks (now deceased), attorney of law from Georgia. Alfred had come to Santarém in 1996 to make final arrangements for a riverboat to take him and his son, Jim Weeks, to Fordlândia, where he had lived for a year back in 1931. He was fifteen years old on his first visit to Fordlândia and had come to visit his father, Archie Weeks, who was Ford's chief engineer for construction at the project. Alfred tells me that Ford believed in promoting people within the organization rather than bringing them from outside. He believed in self-educated men, as opposed to graduate-degree types. Archie, himself, was such an individual, having little formal education, but lots of experience from the school of hard knocks, including credentials as an exultant saloon boxer and several years of seasoning as Ford's construction engineer in Michigan. Jim recounts that his

19

grandpa was by no means an uneducated man. Archie studied building and civil engineering on his own through correspondence courses and books were always part of his life. He, indeed, was a self-educated man, as Henry Ford liked them. As to the boxing matches, Jim says that these events were normal in his grandfather's day and that matches were always organized. Although not a brawler, he was prepared to use his skills outside the ring if necessary. Archie Weeks' father was an immigrant from England, a contractor who sank mine shafts in Pennsylvania. Archie was only in the sixth grade when his father died, but he went right to work as a breaker boy in the coalmines, where he quickly became foreman of his crew. Jim reflects, "From that time on, Grandpa was a 'boss' for the rest of his life." On our 1996 visit to Fordlândia, Alfred rightfully seized control of my tour to reminisce over the year he spent there with his father in 1931 and what the project was like in those days. Memories included minute details of his family home at the *Vila Americana*; his classroom at *Escola Princesa Isabel*, the state-of-the-art machine shops, the high-rise sawmill and kilns, the 125 bed hospital, employee housing, docks, the public water system, ice and electrical generating plants, and other sophisticated infrastructure no longer found in Fordlândia today.

In 1933, Ford Motor Company shifted the emphasis of its project to Belterra, where terrain and soil conditions were more suitable to the planting of rubber trees. Archie Weeks moved to Belterra to head up construction at that location, and as Alfred best remembers, his father was one of the last American employees to leave the project when Ford Motor Company pulled out in 1946. Not at all surprising, Archie Weeks made several return visits to this region after retirement, mainly to visit friends, including an American, Chet Coleman. Coleman, (pronounced locally as "Kolamann"), is still very much a household word among many residents of Santarém. Chet arrived in Fordlândia in December of 1928, at 19 years of age, employed as a baker onboard one of the Ford Motor Company ships, *Lake Ormoc*. He decided to stay on with Ford in Brazil, and stay he did, residing in the Tapajós region the rest of his life. When I arrived

20

in Santarém in 1979, I was frequently asked if I knew "Senhor Kolamann." As a matter of fact, I remember having met him only once, a brief encounter that took place shortly before his death in 1982, when I chanced upon his broken-down vehicle, a Ford Willys, on the narrow, sandy road connecting Belterra and Aramanaí. Someone on our public health team made the introduction under the hot noon sun and we exchanged a few words. I remember his remarking that he was surprised he could still speak English. Coleman did, however, make visits to the United States occasionally and it was on one of these trips, at the home of Archie and Alfred Weeks, that he received word from Santarém that his 11-year- old daughter, Lenore (named after Alfred's sister), had died of hemorrhaging following a tonsillectomy operation.

Alfred and Jim Weeks made a return visit to Santarém in September of 1997, accompanied by Martha, Alfred's wife; Martha's daughter Toni Hardy and her husband Darrell; and friends, Ted and Margaret Smith. On the riverboat trip to Fordlândia, I made a stop at Aramanaí to show my guests the small rubber tree plantation owned by Francisco Coimbra, and Chet Coleman's old house, located right on the sandy beach of the Tapajós River. Serendipity was, indeed, with us that day because I learned from "Sr. Maneco," president of the village, that Dona Jorgina, Coleman's widow, was visiting the old homestead that day. We made the introductions and I had the pleasure of serving as interpreter for Alfred Weeks and Dona Jorgina Coleman, both in their 80s and both full of emotional memories of times and people so common to their lives.

The Confederates
Another interesting piece of Brazilian/United States history was the immigration of approximately one hundred Confederate families who came to Santarém in 1867. These families were part of a larger group of North Americans who were recruited by the Brazilian government in an effort to upgrade agricultural skills in the country. Most went to the State of São Paulo and were quite successful in their economical endeavors. Even today there is still a very large community of

American descendants, called *Confederados*, living in Americana, Campinas, and other cities in São Paulo[12]. In the Santarém region, farming proved to be very difficult and, as today, there was a lack of infrastructure to get produce to market. Thus, many of the original families who came did not do well and returned to the United States within a few years. There were, nevertheless, several families who persevered in Santarém to become involved in ranching, farming and other successful enterprises. Family names, some of which still exist today, included Hennington, Jennings, Vaughan (now spelled Waughan/or Von), Steel, Riker and Rhome.

Golden Days

As you ramble around the streets of Santarém, you may see a number of shops dealing in gold (*ouro*). The big gold "strikes" occurred in the Amazon between 1959 and the late 1980s. Serra Pelada, located in the southern part of the State, was the richest find of that period and the one that got the most attention from the international press. We all remember seeing pictures of thousands of workers hauling out sacks of pay dirt from the open-pit mine. Closer to Santarém, there were said to be more than 350,000 *garimpeiros* (miners) working the upper Tapajós River region. Nobody knows exactly how much gold was extracted there during those years, but guesses are calculated in tons per year. Santarém's population exploded at the time and gold became the center of economic activities throughout the region. The "boom" crashed in 1991, mainly because most of the richer sites had been mined exhaustively, but also because of a concurrent economic recession. Inhabitants of the region are still optimistic that someday the international price of gold will rise sufficiently to bring back the prosperous era of the past.

"THE FISH IS OUTSTANDING" — REGIONAL/NATIONAL FOODS

In looking back over the years of travel with friends and clients, I can report that they consider Brazilian foods superb in every way. I would, therefore, like to introduce some foods and drinks typical of the Amazon, plus a few more that are relished everywhere in Brazil.

Farinha

No other food item is more basic to the Amazonian diet than *farinha*. Bread might come close, but only in the larger cities. *Farinha* is a by-product of *mandioca (Manihot esculenta)* and, for the most part, represents the fiber of the root after it has been processed and toasted. It is produced in a variety of textures, from fine to the much coarser grounds appreciated in the rural areas. *Farinha* can be yellow like corn meal or white and may have different tastes, as determined by the species of manioc and the mode of preparation. *Farinha* is normally mixed with servings of beans, rice, fish or other foods.

The *mandioca* plant has been cultivated by the Indians for thousands of years and may have been introduced from Central America. The Portuguese settlers and successive generations of Brazilians learned to appreciate the virtues of farinha and today it is eaten daily all over the country. When times get tough, we can be sure that farinha will be the last holdout in the local larder.

Farofa

If you did not like farinha the first time you tried it, fear not; it takes some practice. Besides, there is a better version of it, called *farofa*, which is *farinha* finely ground and fried in butter with a touch of salt. The farther south we go in Brazil, the fancier the *farofa*. Some include bacon-bits, fried eggs, sliced olives and other ingredients. *Farofa* is very tasty and can be prepared in short order, sort of a local "fast food."

23

Pirão

This is a thick porridge made of *farinha* cooked in fish broth, normally served as a side dish with fish and rice. I have never met a visitor who did not like *pirão* on the first try. Watch your waistline; it is full of carbohydrates. Most by-products of *mandioca* fall in this category. Rarely do we see a "hefty" Brazilian, but that can be credited to other factors, like physical activities.

Tucupi

This yellow liquid is extracted from the *mandioca* mash prior to toasting. The prussic acid content makes it highly poisonous in its unprocessed form, but once boiled or fermented, it takes on very appetizing and consumable properties. *Tucupi* is used in a variety of regional dishes, some of which are described in this section.

Pato no Tucupi

Duck in *tucupi* is a traditional dish of the Middle and Lower Amazon. Seldom will you find *pato no tucupi* on restaurant menus because it is prepared mainly for celebrations and special events, such as birthdays and major holidays. If you are not fortunate enough to be present for one of these occasions, ask the manager of your hotel to prepare this delightful dish for you. Please make the request at least one day in advance, since it takes considerable time to purchase the ingredients and prepare it. In Belém, we find *pato no tucupi* on a regular basis at the *Lá Em Casa,* a restaurant within easy walking distance of the Hilton Hotel. The basic ingredients include roasted duck, chopped up and added to the *tucupi* juice, *jambu,* a spinach-like plant with anesthetic properties, and *tucupi.* At home we normally prepare *pato no tucupi* two or three times a year, mainly for special occasions. We make enough that we can enjoy eating it over the next couple of days. As many people observe, the dish is even better on the second day.

Maniçoba

Maniçoba is an indigenous food made of finely ground *mandioca* leaves, cooked slowly over two to three days. Pork sausage is added towards the end of the preparation. This dish may demand an acquired taste. In the beginning, I did not care for it at all, but now find myself jumping at the opportunity to dine on this old Indian recipe. On tours I try to provide an opportunity for people to sample some of our regional foods, which most people appreciate greatly. Nevertheless, I am aware that maniçoba is the least appreciated of the many dishes.

Tapioca

Tapioca is the starch of the *mandioca* root and is used for making a variety of foods, including a pancake-like delight called *tapioquinha*. Some of the better hotels in the Amazon and the northeastern part of Brazil serve *tapioquinhas* as part of the breakfast menu. The best ones are served right out of the frying pan onto your plate, but be prepared to stand in line for a "few" minutes with people tripping over their tongues. Some special-order cooks add slices of buffalo cheese before folding the tapioquinha over. Need I say more?

Farinha de Tapioca

This is another version of the above, but in bead consistency. It is the same ingredient used in tapioca pudding in less equatorial climes. The most popular way of eating *farinha de tapioca* is to add it to hot milk, coffee and lots of sugar.

Tacacá

Tacacá is a thick gel-like soup made of *tucupi, jambu, goma* (a liquid form of *tapioca* starch), and shrimp. *Tacacá* is traditionally served on the street, rather than in restaurants, and is sipped from a *cuia*—a bowl made from half of a calabash gourd. On a late afternoon walk around town, we see many women serving this traditional dish from their sidewalk tables.

Macaxeira

This form of "sweet *mandioca*" can be cooked and eaten like potatoes or yams. It does not contain prussic acid, as in other varieties of *mandioca*. Try fried *macaxiera*. Most people like it much more than French fries.

Fish

Do not leave Santarém without sampling the much-esteemed fish of the region. Most restaurants offer a variety of fresh fish prepared in various ways. The most popular ones are *tucunaré, pirarucú, tambaquí* and *surubim*. Traditional methods of preparation include *na brasa* (barbecued over charcoal or wooden coals), assado (baked), *escabeche* (covered with sauces) and *muchica* (a thick porridge of shredded and roasted fish, spices and farinha).

Açaí

Açaí is the thick dark-purple pulp extracted from the fruit of the *açaí* palm, normally served cold with *farinha* and lots of sugar. In Belém, capital of the *açaí* world, it is traditionally served with salted shrimp. *Açaí* has always been a favorite in Santarém and Belém and is now becoming a real fad in the larger cities of southern Brazil. *Açaí* ice cream pleases the taste of everyone, nationally and internationally.

Bolo de Macaxeira

Bolo de macaxeira, a delicious, sweet, heavy cake made of shredded *macaxeira* root (*Manihot aypi),* the non-poisonous variety of *mandioca*, sugar, eggs, coconut and butter.

Feijoada

Brazil is famous for its black beans with pork. This delicious Afro-Brazilian dish did not originate in the Amazon but is, nevertheless, a favorite food throughout the region, especially for Saturday luncheons. Ingredients include black beans and a variety of smoke-dried and salt-cured pork, all cooked together for several hours. Side dishes consist of rice, *farinha, couve* (collard greens finely cut and fried in butter and garlic sauce) and freshly peeled oranges. The favorite drink to accompany feijoada is *caipirinha* (refer to the regional-drinks section). Before sitting down to this highly recommended lunch, please hang your hammock in a cool, shady spot and reserve an hour or so for some fine snoozing.

Having eaten *feijoada* at our home or on a tour, many people ask me for the recipe. Readers may wonder why anyone leaving Brazil would want a recipe requiring so many Brazilian ingredients. Believe me, you can have your friends licking their "chops" when you invite them over for your slide show of the Amazon. There was a time in my life when I spent roughly an equal amount of time in the United States and Brazil. I remember distinctly the joy of having American and Brazilian friends over on Saturdays for my own adaptation of the recipe. You may use the following *receita* but make your own changes, as you see fit. Your best bet for finding ingredients will be in grocery stores catering to *Latinos*. An ethnic-food grocery store for Brazilians would be even better. Who knows? You may even find a bottle of Brazilian *cachaça* on the shelf.

Ingredients for feijoada:

> 1 kilo (2.2 pounds) of black beans
> 1 kilo of salted/or smoked pork ribs
> ½ kilo of salted/or smoked pigs feet, ears and tails
> ½ kilo of assorted smoked sausages
> ½ kilo assorted non-smoked sausages
> 1 kilo of lean, fresh ham
> 3 large onions, chopped up
> 2 bay leaves
> 4 garlic cloves, diced
> pepper and sauces to taste
> 3 teaspoons of olive oil
> salt to taste
> 5 large tomatoes, chopped

***Cooking instructions*:**
Remove small stones and other debris from the beans, if present. Add water and bay leaves and cook in a large kettle or pot—very slowly. Some black beans are harder than nails and require lots of soaking prior to cooking. Although I need to get up three or four times to add water to the pot, I prefer to cook the beans very slowly overnight (Áurea threatens to throw me out of the house because of the smell). Depending on the type and quality of beans, some cooks simply soak them for an hour or two and then make up the difference with a pressure cooker. On some occasions, black beans are simply so hard that they cannot be cooked in anything! In this case, we look for another source of beans or wait for another shipment to come from Southern Brazil, as they do not grow well in the Amazon. Alternatively, we can resort to using other types of beans, including white ones. *Feijoada* does not taste any the worse because of bean substitution.

After the beans are well cooked, the next step is to cut up all the sausages into about half-inch slices and the remainder of the pork into 2-4-inch sections. Boil all the salted cuts in water for approximately ten minutes and drain off the brine. Rinse in fresh water until excess salt has been removed. Add pork to the beans and cook slowly for approximately two hours. Then fry the onions, garlic, tomatoes and other seasonings in the olive oil and add to the *feijoada*. Cook for another 30 minutes or so. Add salt and pepper, as you think essential. Serve with rice and *farofa* (if you cannot find real *farinha*, try the supermarket version made of wheat, or even toasted breadcrumbs), and peeled oranges. This recipe will provide good-sized servings for up to 15 happy people.

Vatapá
The State of Bahia claims fame for having concocted *vatapá*, but this tasty Afro-Brazilian shrimp dish is also prepared in the Amazon for many special events. Ingredients include shrimp (the more the better), dendê oil (from the dendê palm, *Elaeis melancocca*) and a

thick sauce made of flour or bread. Add a touch of hot pepper to suit your taste. It is usually served with rice.

Churrasco

The Amazon is a major producer of cattle and buffalo, so it should be no surprise that barbecue ranks high on the list of favorite foods. Nothing arouses a *Santareno's* appetite quite like an invitation to eat *churrasco*. These are customarily weekend events taking place in a friend's back yard or at a *sitio* outside the city. A variety of meat cuts are barbecued on spits over wood-charcoal, and the servings are normally communal rather than individual. Restaurants that specialize in barbecue cut slices of meat directly from the spits onto your plate. This way, the meat is always hot and you can choose your favorite cut of meat. Pork and chicken are also part of the barbecue menu.

The Gaúchos, people from the southern state of Rio Grande do Sul, are noted for their superb skills at preparing churrasco. Consequently we are never surprised to see one of these big strong European-looking men wielding a heavily laden spit and a sharp knife over our plates.

Condiments and Food Coloring

Most visitors are pleasantly surprised that Brazilian foods are not spicy-hot. They are even more puzzled that they never find a peppershaker on the table, knowing that Brazil is one of the largest producers of black pepper in the world. Here in the Amazon the most popular pepper is *pimenta de cheiro,* which translates into "smell pepper." These are the small round peppers found in all the market places. Some are red and some are yellow, and they all emit a very agreeable smell when broken open. The favorite way of serving *pimenta de cheiro* is to mix both mashed and whole peppers in *tucupi,* the aforementioned extract of the *mandioca* root. People who like pepper simply add a spoon or two of the liquid to their food. Then there are those who enjoy searing their tongues by eating the whole pepper. I think it only fair to warn my guests of the consequence of such foolishness, but not everyone listens to the voice of experience.

Such was the case of a client who bit into a *pimenta de cheiro* at Lá em Casa restaurant in Belém. I pretended not to notice her turning all colors of the rainbow, but her fellow travelers demanded attention when they saw smoke coming out of her ears. On another occasion, in the same restaurant, I was ready to call in the fire department as I watched a veteran pepper eater from Wilmington, Delaware, chew up five of the peppers, one right after another—without batting an eyelash. Later I discovered that he grew up in Tucson, Arizona, where he learned his fire-eating techniques from the Mexicans. It is only fair to mention that most Brazilians in this region do not eat pepper at all and, should you be so inclined, you will need to ask the waiter to put it on the table.

The hottest pepper concoction I ever tasted in the Amazon was one that an ex-neighbor on Avenida Rui Barbosa prepared for me. He simply asked for the smallest glass bottle I could find at home, filled with olive oil. To this he added a dozen or so *pimenta de malagueta* (the tiny red peppers) he had plucked from a bush in his back yard. "Put a bottle cap on it and let it sit for a few days," he said, without letting on what was coming up. I prayed that some of my Korean friends would visit me, because I could not begin to do justice to that pepper. Just one drop of the olive oil would send me running for the cold water. The bottle kept getting shifted around from place to place over the years and became downright dangerous to handle. Strange, but it never arrived at our new residence on Travessa Turiano Meira.

Condiments
The ones most used for cooking here in Santarém are salt, garlic, onion tops and a coloring agent called *corante*. The latter is what cooks use to make their rice and spaghetti dishes red. It is taken from the seed pulp of the *urucu* plant (*Bixa orellana*), the same dye used for body paint by indigenous groups. Some people refer to it as the "lipstick plant." The use of it in food is solely that of coloring, since it has no special taste or nutritive value.

Vinagrete

Along with the standard meal of rice, farofa, fish, chicken or beef, you can usually expect to find a sauce bowl of a relish called *vinagrete*, which is a salty mixture of finely chopped onions, tomatoes and onion tops in vinegar. Add it to your rice or *farofa* in the quantity that suits you.

Sorvete

A wide variety of tropical fruit-flavored ice creams, homogenized and pasteurized, can be purchased locally. Most people savor *castanha de Pará* (Brazil nut), *cupuaçu* (*Theobroma grandiflorum*) and *açaí* (pulp of the açaí palm, *Euterpe olerçea*). Nido and Kibon ice cream parlors are the best ones.

Some of the regional foods described, for example, *vatapa, maniçoba, bolo de macaxeira* and *tacacá,* may be appreciated at Casa de Vinoca (Travessa Turiano Meira, 367, near the intersection with Avenida Mendonça Furtado). This is a home-style setting. The hosts do their own cooking, and they serve a very dedicated and select clientele, almost to the point of making it a private affair. Servings are considered a late afternoon snack or a light dinner. *Casa de Vinoca* opens mid-afternoon and closes early evening, depending how long it takes to get to the bottom of the bright, shiny aluminum pots and pans lined up on the main table.

Pass the beans: *Feijoada* is traditionally served at the Amazon Park Hotel and the Mascote Restaurants on Saturdays from mid-day to late afternoon.

Cultural contrast: What do lemons, pineapples and cucumbers have in common? Well, actually not much, except as figures of speech. In English, at least the American version, we use the word "lemon" when referring to something less than desirable. For instance, after purchasing a repair-prone car, one may say, "I bought a lemon." In Brazil the expression would be, "I bought a pineapple." *"Comprei um abacaxi."* Similarly, the word for cucumber in Portuguese, *pepino,* denotes something or a situation not appreciated. For example, "*Ela deixou um pepino*" ("She left us a cucumber") means that she left some difficult problem to resolve.

"MAIS UMA CAIPIRINHA, FAVOR!" —
REGIONAL & NATIONAL DRINKS

Cachaça

Sugar cane rum is unquestionably the most-consumed alcoholic beverage in Brazil with many brands available. Supermarkets, corner grocery stores, and almost any place you go sell *cachaça* at prices starting at $1.25 a bottle. Maybe that explains why it is the most popular alcoholic beverage.

Caipirinha

Although many *macho*-men prefer to drink *cachaça* as it comes out of the bottle, the most popular cachaça drink is *caipirinha,* which is prepared individually with sliced and crushed lime, a tablespoon or two of sugar, one or two shots of *cachaça* and crushed ice. It is generally served in an old-fashioned glass or in a gourd bowl, and customers are quick to order a second and a third. F*eijoada* fans find a *caipirinha* in perfect harmony with their meal.

Batida

Batida is another *cachaça* drink and includes any variety of blended fruit juices. Tired of orange juice in your screwdriver? Try one of the tropical fruit juices listed in this section. A word of warning! *Batida* is nothing less than a punch, which means you do not know how much liquor is in the drink. Go slowly until you get a feel for reactions. Most restaurants and bars are not too liberal in terms of how much liquor they put in a drink, but on occasions like parties, play it on the safe side. Personal experience tells me to never drink more than two or three *batidas,* or *caipirinhas,* in one sitting. *Perigoso!*

Cerveja

Beer is what most people *really* prefer to drink in the Amazon. In a tropical climate where one loses a lot of body liquid through perspiration, a *louro* (one of many slang words used to describe beer) is always a welcomed sight. Due to its alcoholic content, beer can be chilled well below the freezing point of water—and that makes it taste even better. Serving warm beer in the Amazon is not considered appropriate behavior. It is politely called "politician's beer," since a little bit goes a long way. Very seldom do you ever hear of anyone ordering beer without accentuating the words *bem gelada* (ice-cold) to the waiter. That explains why most bars use freezers instead of refrigerators. A smart barman/host knows exactly when to take the bottle out of the freezer before it turns into ice. If there is any doubt, pick up the beer by the bottle-cap, without touching the bottle. Otherwise, you may see the contents crystallize before your eyes. Antarctica, Brahma, Skol and Cerpa are by far the most accepted brands throughout the Amazon and most customers prefer the large, 600-ml bottles. Cerpa was more popular in other parts of Brazil than its own home state, Pará, at least up until 1997, when the company came up with a new brew, called Cerpa Draft Beer. It is now making a big comeback. Cerpa Export (Cerpinha), sold only in small bottles, is considered of excellent quality anyplace in the world. Newcomers to Brazil are quick to recognize good beer on the first sip, but are often taken aback by the size of the 600 ml bottles. When ordering the first round, they inevitably ask the waiter to serve a whole bottle for each person, and then are surprised to see the size of the *garrafa* (*bottle*). "I can't drink all of that" is a common reaction. Brazilians typically share the contents of a single bottle, thus keeping a "cold one" on the table at all times. Some foreigners go into culture shock with this custom because they like to keep tabs on what they personally consume.

Speaking of *cerveja*, most foreigners are impressed with the unique coolers used by the Brazilians to keep the open bottles icy cold, even under tropical temperatures. These Styrofoam holders can be bought at most supermarkets and stores around town, and make for excellent, lightweight gifts for friends back home. Most are adorned with popular brand names of beer companies and soccer teams.

If you do not have "empties" (the bottles cost about the same price as the contents), canned beer, *cerveja em lata*, is available at most supermarkets, bakeries and bars. It is more expensive per ounce than bottled beer and does not compare at all in taste. Nonetheless, it is very convenient for long trips. "Cans only" is generally the rule for public events, for instance rock concerts, thereby excluding the danger of "flying bottles."

Fruit Juices
The Amazon produces many tropical fruits from which delicious juices are made. Fruits have their own seasons, so you may not find a great variety at certain times of the year. Among others are *caju, carambola, cupuaçu, goiaba, graviola, jenipapo,* mango, *maracajú* (passion fruit), *muruçí,* orange, pineapple and *taperebá.* Tony Rocha, an international consultant now living in Macapá, counts off more than 120 varieties of popular fruits from the region and says that most are seasonal and require some type of processing or special preparation before they can be consumed. I am sorry to report that there is no living off the fruit of the land without some work. Actually, for us city slickers, some of the more popular *sucos* are now available year around, prepared from frozen pulp, or bottled concentrates.

Guaraná
Guaraná fruit *(Paullinia cupana)* is the main ingredient for making a popular Brazilian soft drink commercialized under the same name. In recent decades *guaraná* has gained international recognition for its energetizing and aphrodisiac properties. Most of Brazil's production comes from the State of Amazonas, west of Santarém. Several brand names of *guaraná* soft drinks exist, among them Antarctica and Taí, and all taste a bit like ginger ale. Most visitors agree that those brands with lesser amounts of sugar are the best. The pure *guaraná* in powder or stick form (*bastão*) may be purchased at most of the arts

and crafts stores in Santarém. Remember that the pure product has not been decaffeinated, as in the case of soft drinks. *Guaraná* has about five times more caffeine than coffee, which may explain why some people consider it an aphrodisiac. I assure you that you will not do any sleeping after a cup of this tea. The *bastão* form of *guaraná* can be ground with an ordinary cheese grater, but if you want to do it in local fashion, use a dried *pirarucú* fish tongue—removed from the fish, of course. They are for sale in local markets, but expect to pay up to $20 or more for this unique kitchen tool.

Coffee

The customary manner of drinking coffee throughout the day in Brazil is that of the *cafézinho,* a strong, sweet coffee served in a demitasse. Breakfast coffee is generally served in a large cup with a greater percentage of milk and sugar than coffee. Cream is not used in coffee here, but milk can be used as a substitute. Most hotels and restaurants make artificial sweeteners available to their customers. Ground decaffeinated coffee can now be found in most supermarkets in Santarém but it is expensive and seldom used. Instant decaffeinated is not available. If you like coffee, plan on staying "wound up" while in the Amazon.

Cultural Contrasts

Restaurants and hotels accustomed to serving foreigners understand that some people like a large cup of black coffee, and without sugar. The waiters may not even bat an eyelash when we request a second or third cup. In other circumstances, we may get that look of "Should I call a doctor?"

A local custom that gets some visitors upset early in the morning is that of not making coffee available until all the breakfast foods are on the table. The practice of sipping on hot coffee before breakfast is a hard one to explain to Brazilians. I have often made recommendations to ecological hotels and other hosts that coffee be made available starting at daybreak, but to no avail. Since morning coffee is served traditionally with a lot of milk and sugar, it is looked on as food, rather than drink. On a six-day riverboat tour in 1998, I came to realize that I had gone "native" in this regard. In the beginning of the trip I joined my guests topside early in the morning, and we all waited patiently for the cook and her assistants to get breakfast ready. I noticed that everyone was keeping an eye on the staircase leading to the kitchen, but little did I realize that all seven of my clients had only one thing on their minds, *coffee*. At last came breakfast—first the fruit, then the bread, then the oatmeal, then the cheese—last of all came, the *coffee*! On the third morning, as I climbed the stairs to the upper deck, I was ambushed by one of my caffeine-deficient friends, who warned me that the kitchen staff might be on the warpath. An emissary had been sent down to the kitchen to ask if it were possible to serve some coffee before breakfast. The word for coffee in Portuguese is "*café*," as is the word for breakfast. Never dreaming that the request was for coffee, our cook and crew, always wanting to please our visitors, put themselves into "full speed ahead" to get breakfast on the table early. When I got to the kitchen, nearly everything was ready, except for; you guessed it, the coffee. Not wanting to hurt anyone's feelings, I asked them to hold off on the food until everyone had a cup of "café." Ever since that day, my crew has acquired the strange, but much appreciated behavior of serving coffee before *café*.

Looking for gifts to take back home? Try some of the small packages of ground coffee found in any supermarket. Café Amazônia is my favorite because it is ground and toasted in Santarém. At home you can program your electric percolator to make that fresh cup of Brazilian coffee, as early as you like. Likewise, *guaraná* is an excellent gift, since it is something exclusive to this region, and easy to pack in your baggage.

More Cultural Contrasts
At home Brazilians usually have a very light breakfast, a heavy meal for lunch and then a snack for dinner. Eating out may call for a change of pace, but these occasions are not everyday affairs. Local restaurants also tend to open for businesses much later in the evening

than we are used to in other countries, so do not plan on dinner before 7:30 PM. Most travelers arrive early at the restaurant to find that they are the only customers, which can raise concern over the quality of the restaurant chosen. Good service, good food, and drink quickly calm such anxieties. Such "early bird" patrons may end up paying their bills before the first Brazilians start dribbling in for dinner. By 11 PM the waiters are running around like *doidos* (crazies) trying to keep up with a full house.

Travelers subtly comment about another cultural oddity around the dinner table, that of napkins. To be more specific, they are referring to the size of napkins. Classy restaurants normally set their tables with standard cotton-linen napkins, but other establishments use the paper versions, which are to be expected, except they are tiny and non-absorbent. By the end of the meal everyone has a pile of used napkins next to their plates, and nobody is really pleased with the results. One could say that this is a mere cultural oddity, but surely there is some rational explanation back of it. Are Brazilians less messy with their food than other nationalities, thereby justifying smaller napkins? Or is it just a question of tradition on our part to use big, absorbent napkins? Large paper *guardanapos*, by the way, are available in some supermarkets. I remember once buying a package of them thinking that I would allow my dinner guests the pleasure of wiping their lips royally. After everyone was at the table, I discovered that our maid had cut each napkin into four individual pieces, thereby reducing them to the "normal" size.

Another cultural oddity at mealtimes is the absence of salt and peppershakers. Have you ever sat down at a table in North America or Europe without facing the ubiquitous salt and peppershakers? Here, in the Amazon, you will probably need to ask the waiter or the host for extra salt or pepper, and the chances are good that when they are put on the table, they will be in a saucer, not in shakers. Come to think of it, I never remember seeing shakers here at home, or on the boats we use for our tours. Plainly put, it is not a day-to-day habit to put *sal* and *pimenta* on the table and, therefore, we forget to do so.

Cultural oddities have cultural explanations: ground pepper is used sparingly for cooking food, but it is not relished as a doctor-it-up condiment. In place of a peppershaker, we may find a bottle of pepper sauce, normally *pimenta de cheiro* in tucupi juice, at least in popular restaurants here in the Amazon. Most Brazilian food is prepared with abundant or even too much salt, so it is not needed on the table. Besides, have you ever seen salt come out of a shaker in an environment where the average relative humidity is in the high 80s? When served on the table, it is mainly served on a dish, and one applies it with a pinch of the fingers.

HAVING A GOOD TIME — THE WAY BRAZILIANS LIKE IT

Privileged are those of us who have the opportunity to participate in the social life of Santarém. Brazilians know how to have a good time, and there is always something going on like birthday parties, dinners, anniversaries, religious celebrations, live shows, professional engagements and, of course, just friends getting together. Rest assured that music and song are of key importance to these frequent gatherings.

On a personal and somewhat "flat" note, I plead guilty to having zero aptitude for music and voice. At birthday parties I more often than not rush off to the bathroom or make some excuse not to be close to the cake when it comes time to sing *Parabéns Para Você*. I hate those occasions when friends ask me to sing "something American." When they discover I am tone-deaf, they end up singing a repertoire of American songs *for me*. It would certainly be an over generalization on my part to say that all Brazilians sing, play the guitar and dance carnival for three days and nights without resting their blessed bones, but it *does* seem that way at times. And while not being able to prove it, I am willing to bet that they are indeed much more talented in this regard than most non-Brazilians. One visit to Brazil should be sufficient for you to come to a similar conclusion.

If you are the average wayfarer, your stop in Santarém will be a short one, and the chances are good that you will spend most of it in sightseeing activities. Few eco-tour enthusiasts express an interest in going to nightclubs or even cultural events, especially those beginning late in the evening. Our travel schedules have a tendency to be quite demanding, and most clients prefer to have an early dinner and return to their hotels for some "down time" and a good night's sleep. This is not to declare a lack of interest in such matters, but a question of time and convenience. Nevertheless, many opportunities present

40

themselves for listening to Brazilian music and getting involved in cultural events in Santarém, and you will not be sorry for having made the effort.

Folk Music

Folk music, song and dance are traditional to Santarém, and the month of June is by far the best time to hear such presentations. *Festas juninas* are animated by many diverse folk-groups, all of which are quite competitive with one another in dress, performance and interpretation of pieces. These events take place at schools, public presentations and private parties. Many events feature stiff competition for trophies. Just to show the variety of dances and themes, here are names of a few of the more popular pieces: *Boi-Bumbá* (Dance of the Bull, which is the most popular of all); *Cavalo Manco* (Lame Horse); *Dança do Ariramba* (Dance of the Kingfisher); *Dança da Formiga* (Dance of the Ant); *Dança do Tipiti* (Dance of the Tipiti, an indigenous press for extracting liquid from the *mandioca* root); *Passaro* (many dances representing different birds, e.g., kiskadee, egret, oriole blackbird, etc.); *Pastorinha* (Little Shepherd); *Dança do Boto* (Dance of the Dolphin) and *Quadrilha* (Square dances).

Typical foods served at *festas juninas* parties include *munguzá* (a sweet porridge of hominy), *bolo de tapioca* (tapioca cake), *bolo de macaxeira* (macaxeira cake), *canjica* (pudding of cornmeal, coconut and cinnamon), *pé de moleque* (peanut brittle), popcorn and some of the other regional foods and drinks described earlier.

Santo Antônio (St. Anthony), São João (St. John) and São Pedro (St. Peter) celebrations occur on June 13, 24, and 29 respectively. Should you be in Santarém on any of these days you will witness hundreds of bonfires burning along the streets during the early evening.

Another significant event, specific to the village of Alter do Chão, is *Sairé* (*Çairé*), a folklore festivity drawing thousands of people from all over the state. The dates for this weeklong event have been changed recently in an attempt to match up the festivities with the time most convenient for the public, which, in this case, means vacation time and beach availability. Early September is now officially the opening date. A reasonably good paved road from Santarém, plus an ever-growing number of weekend residents, guarantees a large turnout for the occasion. The dates may have changed, but not the enthusiasm, dedication and humility of the local community for presenting their local dance, song and music.

The Bulls — Garantido and Caprichoso
Wherever one goes in the Amazon, and whatever the occasion, the conversation eventually turns to *Boi*—or "bull." You may say that is "a lot of you know what," but I am referring to one of the biggest and most elaborate folklore festivals in Brazil, the Parintins Festival, which takes place in June of every year. The central theme of the event, the competition between two rival bulls—Garantido and Caprichoso—has never changed since the celebration started more than 30 years ago. One can only compare the festival to the celebrated Rio de Janeiro carnival. Literally thousands of participants work the entire year preparing for the weeklong event in order to defend their favorite bull, Garantido or Caprichoso. Parade themes, music, dance, special effects and costume are all part of the competition. What has changed in recent years is that the *Boi* festival has gained national and international fame, and along with it, many more visitors. Government and private sponsorship of the event, so I am told, approximates six million dollars a year.

Carnival
Some travelers schedule their visit to Santarém before or after carnival in order to catch the best events in Rio de Janeiro, Salvador or Recife. But if you happen to be here at that time of the year (pre-Lenten days fall in either February or March), do not miss the chance to celebrate carnival. Unlike the cities mentioned above, Santarém street festivities are quite modest. A few *blocos* (organized groups) take to the streets, but the numbers are small, and they seldom attract

a lot of attention. Endless delays between each presentation take some of the fun out of the show.

Most *Santarenos* prefer to dance carnival at private clubs, and I recommend the same alternative for travelers. Private clubs always offer tables to non-members, and they are very receptive to outsiders. Check with your hotel manager or tour operator for details. Like nearly all dances, carnival parties start quite late, around 11:00 PM, and last most of the night. No early-morning tours, please.

Strike up the Bands

With so much musical talent around, it is no surprise that Santarém boasts several bands, the most famous ones being *Banda Sinfônica Wilson Fonseca* and *Banda Filarmônica Professor José Agostinho*. A good time to hear them is on national holidays or on other special celebrations. Maestro Wilde Dias Fonseca and other family members contribute most of the leadership in this area. Wilde is also a local historian and director of several choral groups.

Hall of Fame

Santarém's most famous composer was Wilson Dias Fonseca, who composed, published and recorded nearly two thousand musical numbers. "Isoca" Fonseca's creations range from classic to folk music.

A Guitarist by the Name of Tapajós

Sebastião Tapajós was born on a riverboat one day's traveling time from Santarém, but he has every right to call Santarém his hometown. Since he is a guitarist and composer of international acclaim, Santarém would have it no other way. Should you not catch one of his many presentations here in Santarém, you can do so in London, Madrid, Munich, New York or one of the other many cities in the world where he performs quite regularly. Do not miss the opportunity. The first time I went to one of his presentations I expected to see an intense, lean, long-fingered character come out onto the stage to uphold the legend that comes with his name. To my surprise, I discovered that he is young, somewhat bald, slight in build and not at all endowed with the "fingers" of a *jaçanã* (a long-toed bird described in the bird section of this book); and, most impressive of all, he is the picture of total tranquility playing an array of music ranging from classic to local folk themes. He seldom ever looks down at the strings of his guitar and never once gives the impression that he is doing anything at all difficult. In fact, more than once I had to remind myself that he was producing the unbelievable sounds being broadcast out to his very appreciative audience at a full house (actually over-flowing) presentation at the *Casa de Cultura*. Sebastião has dozens of recorded albums to his name.

Flutes Everywhere
Whenever I parked in front of the SANCLIN Hospital (now closed) on Avenida Borges Leal, I was impressed with the number of children passing by with flutes in hand, all wearing Fundação Carlos Gomes tee shirts and a proud look on their faces that indicated that they were going somewhere important. As a matter of fact, these kids were on their way to music classes at the *Casa de Cultura* (Culture Center), where they study under the direction of Maestro José Agostinho da Fonseca Neto, son of the aforementioned "Isoca" Fonseca. More than four hundred children study music at this state- and municipality-supported school. They first study flute; then, other instruments.

The name José Agostinho ("Tinho") da Fonseca is a household word in Santarém, but my first encounter with the professor was only in March of 1998, at the home of Hélcio Amaral, then Secretary of Culture for the Municipality of Santarém. Clutched tightly in the maestro's hand was a telegram inviting his *Banda Sinfônica Wilson Fonseca* to perform in São Paulo, with all expenses paid, plus a $10,000 honorarium! The cost of an airplane ticket to São Paulo is equivalent to one to the United States, representing a considerable investment on the part of the host. This is the proof of the pudding that Fonseca knows what he is talking about when he says that Santarenos have an unusual aptitude for music. He should know—or does it also reflect an unusually gifted teacher? Amaral told me that this was actually the second telegram from São Paulo. The first had gone unanswered for some reason, maybe in disbelief. A second invitation offered a considerable increase in honorarium. I jokingly remarked that maybe the maestro should delay a bit more in responding.

Cultural Contrast — Private Invitations and Events

Brazilians tend to be much more formal than North Americans when it comes to opening up their homes for visits. I believe this decorum comes from wanting to treat their guests in the very best manner possible. One would never extend invitations without an undue amount of planning and attention to such matters as cleaning, painting and polishing up the house and premises. Then, too, the old North American habit of asking, "What can I bring?" is not a very common occurrence here, unless the get-together is a very informal one among close friends. The host is automatically expected to foot the bill for all the costs, which can be considerable. This is not to insinuate that only the affluent throw parties. To the contrary, the poorer are much more inclined to spend everything they have and more, to celebrate birthdays and other esteemed occasions. Some of the best parties I have ever attended were in the back yards of friends who had absolutely no means of providing anything beyond a *batida* (rum with fruit juice) and a piece of cake. Generosity was extended to the fullest.

Regardless of whether the host is barbecuing an entire cow or offering a simple plate of *vatapá*, a party is never without music. My favorite professional group, often playing for larger affairs, is *Paulinho Produções*. The group is made up of Paulinho, keyboards and voice, a guitarist and normally two other singers, including Luiz, who just returned from a 15-year "performance" in Japan. I have heard them many times over the years, but the most memorable occasion was at a Christmas party in 1994, when Edilson was still lead singer for the group. Áurea and I had gotten off to a late start in joining her health-department colleagues at the beach home of Antônio Machado, and I guess in the rush neither one of us had paid much attention to directions on how to get there. As it turned out, we should have

45

followed someone because once we got off the main road we encountered a number of unfamiliar turnoffs. After half an hour of driving over narrow, blistering-hot sandy roads and always on the verge of getting stuck, we were ready to call it quits and return to the city. "Turn off the motor," Áurea whispered. "I think I hear music." Sure enough, in the far distance was a droning beat. In little time we were at the party, where at least 200 people were dancing to the sounds of Paulinho and his group. People were dancing on the beach, in the waters of the Tapajós River, and on the picnic tables. Whole families were dancing together. Our exuberant host, Antônio Machado, was dancing behind the bar. He never missed a beat as he served cold beer and soft drinks to surgeon Sérgio Castro and his health department team. It was one of those parties that could have gone on all night had it not been for an electrical failure that left Santarém and the surroundings in dark silence.

Informal encounters with friends are always the best of social affairs in Santarém. We stop by the home of Hoiama Miranda and his wife, Eliane, from time to time on Saturdays. These are not "eat, drink and run" affairs. They begin around noon and may not end until midnight. Without any advance notice, nor invitation, close friends come and go during the course of the day. Some contribute to the barbecue pit and beer reserve and others will chip in the next time. It is rare that any of the men prepare a plate of food for themselves. The etiquette is that of *catando* (picking at) the food as an on-going variety of barbecue fish and meats appear on the table of the machos. It is a way of extending companionship and conversation over the day. Hoiama and Eliane are also hosts to a number of musicians and dance groups, including the famous *Garantido* and *Caprichoso* rivalries from Parintins. Stopping by occasionally are my favorite singers, João Otaviano and Everaldo Martins, both local physicians and polished politicians. Hoiama is a walking dictionary when it comes to discussing Brazilian music, and he and Eliane are both members of Ilha do Governador carnival group in Rio de Janeiro.

Other resident hosts and hostesses offering exceptional hospitality to their guests, including us, are Edivar Macedo, his wife Dona Luzia, and their son Sávio. Paulo and Zilma Pimentel, in the neighboring suburb of Mararú, also receive their guests with class. All are hosts and friends *par excellence*.

TRANSPORTATION — AIR, RIVER AND LAND

The Fast Lane — Up in the Sky

Someone passing through Santarém erroneously commented that the breadth of South America at the equator is greater than the length of the continent itself. Even though it is not true, the Amazon Basin is large enough that most visitors prefer to fly between major cities, rather than using up all their vacation time traveling on riverboats.

VARIG (Viação Riograndense): Once the reference point for travel to Brazil, this airline suspended flights to Santarém in 2005. Nonetheless, it is still an option for international travel to Rio de Janeiro and São Paulo with interconnecting flights to Manaus and Belém.

One of the best travel bargains going for passengers coming from outside Brazil is VARIG's Brazil Pass. It costs around $450 and allows for five stops anywhere in Brazil during a three-week period. The major disadvantage to the Brazil Pass is that you must schedule all stops in advance, or pay additional fees for making any changes along the way.

In October of 2001, TAM Brazilian Airlines made its debut in Santarém with connecting flights to Manaus, Belém and other points in and outside Brazil. The TAM option has facilitated travel to and from Santarém greatly. Most international passengers coming to Santarém now choose TAM, since they only need to deal with one airline. RICO Airlines is yet another company providing jet service to and from Santarém via Manaus and Belém.

Santrém's airport is 13 kilometers (8 miles) from town. Airport taxi service, as well as public bus service is available. Our airport is noted for its beautiful landscaping, and passengers take pleasure in walking on solid ground between planes and the terminal building. If you have extra time after getting checked in, enjoy the shade of the flamboyant and jumbeira trees in front of the terminal. Silver-beaked tanagers, kiskadees, tropical kingbirds and spotted tody flycatchers fly in and out of the trees all day long. Swallows and martins, more often than not, decorate the electrical lines along the parking lot area. If you have a lot of time before your flight, you might want to venture across the parking lot and soccer field to look at the *cerrado* (tropical savannah) forest. A couple of years ago on one of these little outings, I spotted a beautiful pair of toucans just 100 meters from the terminal.

Back inside the terminal building, try the tropical flavored *sorvetes* (ice creams) at the small candy shop just to your right as you come in the front door. They are outstanding. Another tip: the shop next to the embarkation door is one of the few places in Santarém where you can buy semi-precious stones.

It is very important to reconfirm your upcoming flight at least a day ahead of time. Ask for a computer printout, just in case you need to prove that you have actually reconfirmed. The fact that your ticket is marked "okay" will not get you a seat if seats are at a premium. Reconfirmation is especially important during the months of July and December when nearly all flights are booked well in advance.

Getting to the airport at the recommended time is also important since latecomers can find their seats taken by passengers on the waiting list. It does not happen too often, but occasionally flights are canceled due to mechanical problems, weather conditions, heavy smoke (during the dry season) and overbooking.

If your ticket was issued outside of Brazil, check to see if the local airport taxes were paid with the cost of the ticket. This tax varies according to the classification of the airport. Whatever you do, do not forget to reserve money for the international airport tax on leaving Brazil. It is between $35 and $45, depending on the airport.

Surveillance of baggage and carry on items is not overly stringent in Santarém, but you should use common sense in packing your bags. Pocket knives or any other items classified as possible security risks should be put in your checked luggage. Manaus is the most restrictive of all airports in the Brazilian Amazon and many passengers complain of excessive security measures taken there prior to embarkation. Some "benign" souvenir items, like blowgun darts, decorative knives and toy spears will not be a problem when you go through customs back home, but they will not pass surveillance at the Manaus airport if you try to carry them on board personally. Play it safe; put these things in your checked suitcases. Should you be traveling on to the western reaches of the Amazon, prepare yourself for even more scrutiny. In Iquitos, Peru, you must accompany your checked-in baggage to a closed cubicle where you open your bags in front of an armed guard. Then you return to complete airline check-in, pay airport taxes and proceed to embarkation, where you pass through x-ray units and open your hand luggage for a visual inspection.

The first time I went through all these procedures, at the end of a Nature Expeditions International tour, I entered the air-conditioned embarkation room thinking to myself, "God, it's good to get through all that bureaucracy. At last, a chance to relax from the heat of the day." I used the bathroom, had a cold beer and sat down to await announcement of my flight to Leticia. As I looked out through the blinding glare of the large glass windows, I noticed several purple martins and fork-tailed flycatchers in flight around the eves of the airport building. "Well, bird watching is good to the end," I muttered to myself, remembering of all the fine observations we had made over the last fifteen days of our tour. As I lowered my binoculars to the ground, in front of the small, 35-passenger Russian jet being readied for the one-hour flight to Leticia, I unexpectedly came to realize that security checks were not yet over. There was our baggage, all neatly lined up on the ground—along with two German police dogs trained for drug surveillance. They smelled out every bag, before being walked back to wherever they were kept. Our baggage was then promptly put on board, and we were called for embarkation. As I was about to enter the plane, a security officer asked me to open a plastic bag I had acquired at the airport gift shop. After a quick glance inside, he motioned for me to enter the plane and we were off—about half an hour later. By the time we got up into the air we were all baked medium rare and the plane showed no sign of cooling off until we got up into the higher atmosphere. Less than an hour later we landed at Leticia, Colombia, where we went through a thorough baggage inspection and then it was taxi ride to Tabatinga, Brazil, for immigration procedures with the Federal Police. As you might guess, my belongings went through another security check at the airport in Tabatinga prior to the flight to Manaus. Every single item in my pack went through a hands-on-inspection, including toothpaste, medicines, books and binoculars. I mean to tell you, passing through security of three Amazonian countries in one day is something to remember. The blow-by-blow details are not to give the impression that airport security in the Amazon is more of a hassle than other places in the world. It is simply a price we pay for added safety.

Swinging in a Hammock — on the River
The oldest and still the most common mode of travel in this region is by boat, as evidenced by better than 7,000 vessels operating in the Municipality of Santarém. Depending on the destination, one may choose among a variety of boats, ranging from canoes to modern riverboats. Larger boats and ships use the deep-water pier (*Docas do Pará*), located on the western end of the city. Up until the end of 1998, smaller passenger boats docked along the city waterfront, but due to structural problems in the riverbank wall, they have been rerouted to improvised docking areas. Many of us yearn for the day when this problem will be solved because we miss the coming and going of boats and passengers in the picturesque downtown area. Clearly, restaurants and stores also promote the same concept.

Booking for Manaus and Belém may be made with one of the ticket venders located outside the security area at the deep-water pier. Departures occur almost daily. Most boats destined for Manaus or Belém offer a limited number of private cabins, but they should be reserved as early as possible. If you plan on sleeping in a hammock, you should get on board at least three or four hours early in order to secure a spot. Many travelers report that cabin beds are much too small for their liking, and the cabins tend to be "smelly" and hot. More often than not they use their cabins to lock up their belongings and then sleep in a hammock out on the main deck, like most others. In all fairness, cabins look much better after the riverboat is underway. The high RPM of the motors cools down the cabins soon after getting underway, and a bit of privacy can be precious. A recently inaugurated boat with several first-class cabins, operating between Belém-Santarém-Manaus and return, is the *"N/M Santarém."* Paulo Corrêa, the owner of the vessel, has the foresight of preparing schedules one year in advance, thus making it easier for travel agents to work out travel schedules for international clients well ahead of time. The price of boat tickets always includes meals, which are generally very adequate. Traveling time to Manaus or Belém is approximately two to three days. Soft drinks, mineral water and beer may be purchased from the boat bar. Travelers are often disappointed in not being able to see more from the public boats, but all agree that the trips are great for socializing. It is not uncommon to find newly made friends getting together in Santarém for dinner, a cold beer, or even a tour following one of these trips.

Visitors are let down to learn that most riverboats going to villages in the region travel at night, which makes it impossible to see anything during the course of a trip of twelve hours or less. Most folks resolve this problem by arranging private tours during daylight hours.

"Oh, My Aching Back" — *Traveling By Road*

Travel by road, whether it is by car or bus, is not one of the best options to consider in this part of Brazil. Road conditions are terrible, to say the least. When talking about highways, I like to tell the story of a former state health official, who in 1995 made a three-day trip over a stretch of the Transamazônica in order to resolve some bureaucratic problem at a health station. The day after he returned to

Santarém he found himself unable to get out of bed. X-rays revealed an out-of-place vertebra from all the bouncing around in the government vehicle. Barely escaping surgery, he was back to work some three months later. A colleague of the same physician actually returned with a broken arm from a similar trip.

The only road connecting this part of the Amazon with the rest of the country is the Santarém-Cuiabá Highway, BR-163, which is paved only the first 100 kilometers. Beyond that short distance, expect anything, especially during the rainy season. A hard rain can destroy a relatively good dirt road in a matter of hours and there are times of the year when the road becomes impassable due to gigantic mud holes and washed out bridges. And there are also a lot of segments where bridges should have been built but, due to economical constraints, were not. These are filled in with dirt, and as you might guess, erosion is a serious problem.

Construction of BR-163 (Santarém-Cuiabá Highway) began in January 1971, by the 8th Army Corps of Engineering and Construction (8^0 BEC). The extension of the road, which connects Santarém with the Transamazônica Highway, was inaugurated in August of 1972, and the remaining portion, to the city of Cuiabá in Mato Grosso, in October 1976.[13] The distance between Santarém and the Transamazônica Highway, as mentioned, is 215 kilometers (about 135 miles). Santarém to Cuiabá is 1,774 kilometers (1,099 miles), just to give you an idea of the magnitude of road construction and maintenance. This is to say nothing of BR-230, the Transamazônica Highway, which stretches across the breadth of the Brazilian Amazon.

The conclusion of the Santarém-Cuiabá and the Transamazônica Highways has always been the dream and obsession of the regional population. All political campaigns, including presidential elections, make use of this issue to the maximum, and promises are never lacking. Over the years we have heard rumors over and over again of congressional appropriations for paving the roads, but such reports eventually vanished into the realm of rumors and fantasy, following elections, of course. Only in 1997-98 did we begin to see some additional road building activity on BR-163, under the command of the 8^0 BEC (Eighth Army Corps of Engineering). Politicians again pledged that the remaining distance to Rurópolis was guaranteed within the next few months. It never happened, of course. During the rainy season of 2000-2001, it often took days to drive that short distance of 215 kilometers! I can verify this because a friend, who worked at the Bank of the Amazônia (BASA) in Rurópolis, tried to commute back home to Santarém on the weekends. During the rainy season, it became nearly impossible. The most promising proposal of paving the highway comes from a conglomerate of government and private enterprises made up of the soybean producers. Brazil is the largest exporter of soybeans in the world and second largest producer after the United States. The transportation of this grain to seaports, mostly in the State of São Paulo, is nothing less than a nightmare because of poor roads and outdated port facilities. The opening up of the Santarém-Cuiabá Highway to the port facilities of Santarém on the Tapajós River will reduce transportation costs from central Brazil considerably and relieve congestion from current avenues of exportation. By 2004, I was convinced that final construction of the road was about to begin but the following year reports were spreading that soy prices had dropped due to a large production in the United States and that the private sector was backing off.

Bus service is available on a regular basis to Itaituba and on most occasions to Marabá (around 45 hours by bus, during the dry season), from where one can make connections to other points in the country. There is now bus service once or twice per week to Cuiabá. There have been years when this bus route was suspended totally because of road conditions. For all practical purposes, the government has abandoned both the Transamazônica and the Santarém-Cuiabá Highways. Many of the thousands of homesteaders placed by the federal government along the Transamazônica have abandoned their lands because getting produce to market was impossible. Somewhat ironically, the most important events taking place on the road today are the long-distance, international endurance rallies, the Camel

Trophy being one of them. We are abruptly reminded of this fact when we see a convoy of four-wheel vehicles arriving in town. Tired, red-eyed drivers squint through layers of yellow mud on their windshields as they search for the Amazon Park Hotel, where they hang out for two or three days getting ready for another adventure on the "road." Some folks want just that. I remember a French client and his teenage son who hired me to take them to Rurópolis, which is on the junction of the Santarém-Cuiabá and the Transamazônica Highways, some 215 kilometers from Santarém. After driving for a few hours I discovered that they were not in the least interested in trees, plants, birds or anything else, just an adventure on the road. On getting to Rurópolis on the last traces of gasoline, we filled up, downed a Coke with a package of cookies, and we were back on the road to Santarém. At the end of the sixteen-hour tour, I dropped the pair off at their hotel. The father was absolutely ecstatic that he had provided a challenging experience for his son. I was much too tired and distracted to catch much of what he said as we parlayed our good-byes, but I think I heard him refer to former times on the Paris-Dakar race.

Another highway leaving Santarém for the southern part of the municipality is the Curuá-Una Highway. It has an extension of approximately 80 kilometers (50 miles) and was built for the purpose of constructing the Curuá-Una Hydroelectric Dam, from where Santarém received most of its electrical energy up until 1999. Future road construction will connect the Curuá-Una and the Transamazônica Highways, which will shorten the distance between Santarém and Altamira by 174 kilometers. My dentist friend, Dr. Otávio Gomes, drove the makeshift road in December of 2005 in his four-wheel Toyota pickup, along with friends in two similar vehicles. It was so bad they decided to return to Santarém from Altamira via the Santarém-Cuiabá Highway.

"WOW! THAT'S A LOT OF RIVER!"
SOME NOTES ABOUT THE AMAZON

Loren McIntyre, famed writer, photographer and lecturer on South America, calculates that the Amazon River may discharge up to one-fifth of the earth's continental runoff annually. The volume of water is so great that it invades the salt water of the Atlantic Ocean for more than 160 kilometers (100 miles). Even though the Amazon and the Nile Rivers are about the same length, the Amazon transports 60 times more volume.

The Amazon River flows across almost the entire breadth of South America. The river begins at a small mountain lake on a tributary of the Apurimac River at 5,250 meters (17,220 feet) in the Andes, only 200 kilometers (120 miles) from the Pacific Ocean. The distance from that point to the mouth of the river is more than 6,500 kilometers (4,000 miles). Larger than you might ever imagine, the mouth is around 322 kilometers (200 miles) wide.

Writers have pointed out that we can navigate the entire length of the Amazon River without ever passing under a bridge (discounting a few rope footbridges on the Apurimac). Going a bit further, one can also observe that there is not one tunnel under the river, not a power line crossing it, nor one dam built on it. It is one of the true wonders of the world.

Few "large" cities are to be found on the Amazon River. Belém (population of about 1.7 million) is located on the Guamá River and

Baía do Guajará. The main channel of the Amazon River flows north of Marajó Island. Santarém (population 262,000) is located almost entirely on the Tapajós River. Only in recent years have suburbs grown up along the shores of the Amazon River east of the main city, where the Tapajós and Amazon rivers mix. Manaus (population close to 2 million) is the largest city in the Amazon and for the most part it is located on the Rio Negro. Only a small portion of the industrial section of the city has sprawled down to the muddy waters of the Amazon. Iquitos, Peru (550,000 population) is the largest city actually situated on the Amazon River. Macapá (population 350,000), near the mouth of the Amazon, makes claim of being the largest Brazilian city on the mighty Amazon. Smaller towns along the river include Óbidos, Parintins, Tefé, Tabatinga and Leticia.

"The river gives and the river takes away" is an adage that came to mind one day when I was walking on the banks of the Amazon River just east of Iquitos. Our outboard motor had broken down and rather than wait around for help, we decided to walk two hours back to Explorama Lodge. This was in August of 1994, low water season, and we found ourselves high up on the bank, tiptoeing along the edge for fear that it would give way at any time because of the erosion. The circumstance reminded me of a lot of glaciers and their "calving" attributes. It is quite common that several meters of land are lost every year to the river in some areas and are being built up in other locations. Our local guide at Explorama Lodge showed us an island that must have been at least three kilometers long, all of which had been created over the last few years. Another example is the island right in front of our own Santarém. It did not exist at all when I arrived in 1979. Christovam Sena at ICBS (Instituto Cultural Boanerges Sena) has an aerial photograph to prove it. Today several homes and ranches are located on the island and it continues to get larger every year. Local hearsay has it that disputes over ownership already exist. The prevailing wind is from the east, an influence of the easterly trade winds. Winds are particularly strong between August and November and they are more pronounced during the day.

Small and medium-sized boats navigate with great care during this time and it is not uncommon to encounter waves coming over the bow of the boats, or even higher. Since regional boats have very little keel, there is normally a lot of rolling in high winds. Once, on a tour to Monte Alegre, our boat rocked back and forth so much that the grime on the bottom of the fuel tank got mixed up with the diesel fuel and plugged up the filter system. There was no other option for the captain than to turn the motor off to clean the filters. As you might suspect, the free-floating boat then got pounded broadside from the powerful waves. Many of our passengers became "seasick" on this occasion and some had to be transferred from the boat to a hotel when we got to Monte Alegre. It is common for boats to travel at night to take advantage of wind lulls and, in case of imminent danger, head to protected areas. Early European explorers exploited the easterly trade winds to power their ships to South America and up the Amazon River. Descriptions of their travel and their frequent encounters with frightful storms are exciting to read, especially knowing that these same circumstances can be experienced today.

Contrary to what many visitors expect of the Amazon with its vast "rain forest," that precious resource called "rain" can be very scarce during a good part of the year in our region. I call Santarém *Cidade do Sol* because we see sun almost every day of the year. A dark cloudy day is so exceptional, it is something to behold. Weather patterns are very erratic, but the months of August through December are usually the driest and the hottest, and the easterly trade winds roar up the Amazon Basin threatening to make a desert out of the region. Given that Santarém is located on rolling hills of Tapajós River sand, an almost wasteland scenario is created this time of the year. At home we have to water plants every day, or they wither up like grass in the Sahara. Our little patch of grass in the front yard only took on a green appearance after we drilled our own well and declared independence from the non-functioning public water system. I remember one year when the dry season extended into February and another year when it hardly sprinkled during the traditional "rainy season." In 2005, we experienced what might be called two summers, one on top of the other. The hot equatorial sun, super-imposed over cloudless blue skies, along with strong winds, makes for rapid water loss.

"Steve, this is a desert island," remarked one of my guests as we kicked up dust on our walk from the private runway of Fazendas Bomjardim on Marajó Island to the ranch house. This was the middle of November 1995, and indeed everything, except for a few isolated watering holes, was bone dry. Looking at the parched cracked land and the scarcity of grass, one was hard pressed to imagine how thousands of cattle and buffalo could survive the remaining weeks of the season. This was quite a contrast to an earlier visit to Marajó Island in March when it was a luxurious carpet of wet green.

Agricultural production up and down the Amazon River and surrounding *terra firma* is severely limited during the pronounced dry season. Major crops like corn, beans, rice, soybeans and even citrus fruit are restricted to only one harvest a year. Generally speaking, the agricultural cycle calls for cutting of the forest areas between September and November and burning of the downfall towards the end of the year. Then everyone patiently waits for rains, normally in January, before planting. By the end of July, rains are getting sparse or have terminated altogether for the season.

In mid-October of 1997, I remember ordering an ice-cold, green coconut at a small bar in front of the city while I waited for the family to do some shopping, only to discover that all my sucking and slurping on the straws hardly produced a mouthful of water. So I ordered another, thinking that I had gotten a bad one. Disappointed, I repeated the order. "Well, I'd better ask what I'm going to pay for these coconuts before ordering another one," I thought. The waiter told me they were fifty centavos (about fifty U.S. cents at that time) each, but that he was going to "give" me a third one because they had little water. As he explained the circumstances, the intense heat and dryness produces coconuts of this quality, and the same may be said for oranges and limes—little juice.

The burning of agriculture and ranching lands in the Amazon is very intense between October and January. I remember certain years when the Santarém airport was forced to close down due to the excessive amount of smoke in the air. Likewise, riverboat travel by night is greatly impaired or halted altogether under these circumstances.

The lack of rain during the dry season not only affects agriculture and ranching activities, but also the very basics of life. Take, for example, drinking water. Many families in Santarém go for days and even weeks without a drop of *água* (water) flowing through their faucets and are forced to carry water long distances. "I haven't had a good night's sleep in 30 years," one of my neighbors complained. He was referring to the fact that water flows through the water pipes mostly during the night. Residents lose as much sleep as necessary to collect water they need to get through the next day. Another neighbor, a Brazilian federal police agent on temporary assignment in Santarém, looks sadly at the Amazon and Tapajós Rivers down below and comments, "Steve, why is it that we don't have water? Why don't we have a treatment plant in Santarém?" Some neighbors are fortunate enough to live next to someone with a private well. At home, as mentioned, we finally faced the fact that we could not remain dependent on a public water system incapable of pumping water up the hill just ten blocks away from two of the largest rivers in the world. So we ended up drilling our own well 54 meters deep. In the beginning we pumped a lot of water up and down the street for neighbors, mostly by connecting hoses to their far-off water boxes or cisterns. Then the demand got to be too much for our pump and us. We ultimately came to realize that we could not play the role of a local water company. Although we may have hurt some feelings, we are now more conservative in the use of our pump, providing water only to our closest neighbors and gate requests, when necessary. A very kind neighbor who lived across the street had more time, and the patience of Job. She pumped water almost daily to a larger number of families living on the side streets of this area. They lined up in front of her house for hours at a time with buckets, pots, plastic bottles, pans and every other conceivable container, often making dozens of trips back and forth. It was also common for many of these families to take a quick hose bath in her driveway on the last jaunt. Eventually this neighbor moved to another part of Santarém and I heard from one of the daughters that the daily task of providing water got to be too much for their mother. Another neighbor, a block up from us, also assists a large number of waterless people via a faucet rigged up between his water box and the street. During critical shortages of public water there is always a line of people waiting their turn at the connection.

On occasion, to everyone's surprise, the public water company makes a comeback, as happened at the end of 1998. For the first time in my memory, water flowed through the underground pipes of Travessa Turiano Meira during the day. But by October of 1999 neighbors were once again without water and by early 2000, many streets in the area were dry. As of this writing, January 2006, there is once again water, and lots of it, especially at night. During the first few days of recurrence many water pipes burst under the pressure and small creeks could be seen running from many backyards into the street.

Severe droughts in this part of the Amazon used to bring about drastic shortages of electricity to Santarém and neighboring communities served by the Curuá-Una Hydroelectric Dam. Rationing of electricity during peak hours of consumption had gotten to be common over the years, but it reached catastrophic proportions at the end of 1997, when "El Niño" nearly dried up the Curuá-Una Reservoir. This episode caught everyone by surprise, including the public utility company responsible for providing electricity to the state. With very little advance notice, this city of 200,000 inhabitants found itself being rationed to just a few hours of energy per day. The scheme most used for rationing was that of dividing the city into five service units— rotating each with six hours of electrical energy, followed by *twelve* without. This annoying schedule went on for weeks with constant rumors of even more severe cutbacks—like closing the dam altogether. Public outrage was unprecedented in the time I have been in Santarém—with good reason. You can imagine coming home from work at 6 PM to spend the next twelve hours without lights, refrigerator, freezer, television, water pump, street illumination, air conditioning, fans, computer, and other conveniences of life. Aside from the distress of not having electricity, high temperatures and lofty humidity levels make for a terrible night's sleep. Many people just do not sleep at all under these circumstances and move their hammocks out to the backyard in hopes of finding some ventilation. Less fearless people do not want to take a chance on being assaulted in the darkness of the night, so they sweat it out in their private saunas. At 6:00 AM the lights come back on and everyone rushes to collect water, wash clothes and do all the other good things done with electricity, including office work. At midday the lights go off again for another twelve hours. In the early evening, candles are lit, flashlight batteries replaced and everyone goes to bed in the dark. At midnight the lights come back on. Yes, it is time to get up in order to get some things done, because at 6 AM it is another twelve hours without energy. And life continued on this schedule of "six yes and twelve no" for what seemed an unbearable interval.

Under the siege of little or no electricity, old lifestyles are abandoned without choice, much like living in a war zone. You may not face bombing raids, but you risk your life at every major street crossing because traffic lights do not function without electricity. Food is available in small quantities that must be consumed the same day because freezers and refrigerators are constantly in the alarm mode from having been disconnected for extended periods of time. Outbreaks of diarrhea are common and public health officials predict more serious epidemics around the corner.

There was no lack of conjecture on the part of the public as to why we found ourselves in this unfortunate situation. It was always a major topic of conversation wherever people got together, especially in the beginning of the episode. One of the most prevalent theories was that the public utility company had reduced the amount of water in the reservoir by 1.4 meters in order to rescue a pontoon of logs that had gotten stuck downstream on the Curuá-Una River. Another hypothesis was that the turbines were not functioning properly and that the utility company was simply using climatic conditions as an excuse. A further revelation was that the dam had been constructed to take care of electrical demands for only twenty years and that this life span was exceeded several years. Indeed, a power line from the gigantic Tucuruí Dam in the eastern part of the State of Pará was already being constructed and was to reach Santarém by early 1999. Regardless of suppositions, the final verdict was that the Curuá-Una Dam reservoir was at an extremely low level and nothing short of rains could resolve the energy shortage. And rain it did not, at least in this region.

Ron Bertagnoli, Executive Director of Fundação Esperança, facetiously accused unknown powers of holding a gigantic umbrella over Santarém. He may have been right because it was raining in some other parts of the Amazon while we continued to face hot tropical sun and clear blue skies—day after day, week after week—along with winds roaring up the valley. At night the winds died down, assuring everyone a fitful night's sleep. Dust got thicker by the day and the grating sounds of metal water buckets being dragged over a nearby concrete driveway started early in the morning, as lines of people waited for water. Flora on the tropical savanna turned many shades of parched red and brown following brush fires, which gleefully raced from roadsides and agricultural burns right up to the peaks of surrounding hills. On our tours to the rural areas it was common to hear families remark that the fruit trees around their houses were dying—and many did just that, as we witnessed in Belterra and other communities. Closer to home, we lost most of the reforestation seedlings planted at Bosque Santa Lúcia the season before. Isolated trees and palms, not having the benefit of community shade, were the first to die. Farmers lost even the most basic of plants, their mandioca, to the drought.

Following many political evocations, the mayor of Santarém declared a state of public disaster and political pressure was put on the State of Pará to purchase auxiliary generators to compensate for the loss of power at the dam site. Wherever people got together, generators became the subject of day-to-day conversation. The State of Pará purchased six gigantic Caterpillar generators in Miami and smaller private generators were installed by anyone who could afford them. Commercial enterprises were forced to make this investment right away or close down completely. Supermarkets, gas stations, television and radio stations, bakeries, ice plants and other food and drink related industries were in this category. Many offices were soon to follow suit because the heat of a closed environment in the Amazon is unbearable.

I vividly remember a meeting at the IBAMA (Instituto Brasileiro do Meio Ambiente e dos Recursos Naturais Renováveis) office at the beginning of this *novela* (soap opera). A security guard politely unlocked the front door of this large federal agency on what should have been a regular workday and ushered us through a totally abandoned building for an engagement with Selma Melgaço, then director of the Tapajós National Forest. Selma prefaced her orientation very carefully by saying that she was honoring the

64

scheduled meeting with our visiting NASA and U.S. Forest Service dignitaries but, in fact, all IBAMA employees had been given the day off due to the *falta de energia* (lack of electricity) at the work site. As our guests advanced into some rather lengthy discussions, it became unequivocally clear why the employees had been dismissed. *Que calor!* It was obnoxiously hot. The windows facing the Tapajós River were open, but there was zero ventilation passing through the room, putting it in the category of a sauna that could not be turned off. *Graças a Deus* (thank God), I did not have to return to that building again, at least under those circumstances. It is only hoped that this federal agency—equivalent to the USDA Forest Service, the U. S. Fish & Wildlife Service and the Environmental Protection Agency, all rolled into one—was able to install a generator.

A city facing total collapse of this sort prepares everyone psychologically for hearing tales of personal tragedy. So it came as no surprise one day when a merchant friend pulled Áurea and me to the side to tell us of an incident that had occurred just that day. The tale of sorrow involved a five-year-old child who, after taking a shower, accidentally touched a bare electrical wire, which electrocuted the poor thing. Áurea was quick to catch a frail grin on the lips of our friend, betraying his sense of humor. After all, Santarém was without both water and electricity.

Meteorologists and other scientists were certainly correct in forecasting that El Niño of 1997-98 would be one of the most disastrous of this century, provoking exceptional flooding in many parts of the world, and droughts in others, as in the case of the Santarém region. Some quibblers erroneously blame present-day deforestation of the Amazon as a possible cause of *El Niño* antics, but historical records indicate that the "Baby Boy" has flexed his muscles in this vicinity before—and in a much more destructive fashion than the current visit of 1997-98, or even the noted one of 1982-83. Betty Meggers in, *Amazonia—Man and Culture in a Counterfeit Paradise,* cites catastrophic droughts occurring around A.D. 500, 1000, 1200 and 1500, long before anyone ever heard the rancorous roar of a chainsaw.[14]

Our first notable rain during the 1997-98 El Niño occurred on March 8, 1998, almost six months from the time rationing of electrical energy was initiated in Santarém and almost eight months after the last heavy rains of the previous season. While precipitation during the month of March and April was less than normal, the lack of water in the Curuá-Una reservoir came to be a poor excuse for the continued rationing of electricity. By this time everybody recognized that the problem was not merely the lack of water in the reservoir, but also the operational conditions of the turbines and other equipment at the dam site. Rationing, albeit much less radical than the original schedule, continued to be a part of our lives until December of 1998. The construction of the power line from Tucuruí Hydroelectric Dam was completed at the end of February 1999, thus resolving many of our electrical problems!

"I can't take this heat anymore," is a comment I hear from time to time. Interestingly enough, the declaration is not from foreigners, but from Brazilians, who are from other parts of the country, or from Santarenos returning from temporary residencies elsewhere. I suppose we all suffer from tropical temperatures, but we feel it much more when returning from more temperate zones, or even air conditioned environments. The combination of heat and high humidity on the equator during the dry season is oppressive, especially if you are not blessed with shade and ventilation. Nothing substitutes for these two ingredients, I assure you. Temperatures rise to 96-98° Fahrenheit in my office in the afternoon, and the air-conditioning unit is incapable of bringing the temperature below 92 degrees. Then, too, electrical bills have become ridiculously high; I have gone back to using an electric fan. It provides for plenty of ventilation and does a great job of removing perspiration.

Fortunately for travelers, most tours in the Amazon are conducted on the rivers, where cooling winds make for a more amenable environment during *verão* (summer months). After returning from an extended riverboat tour, we always dread the thought of facing the lofty temperatures in the city—a climatic condition brought about by asphalt, buildings and irregular currents of ventilation.

During the dry season our family goes through many liters of refrigerated water daily, to the point that we need to watch our electrolyte balance. I always find it necessary to take oral re-hydration solutions during this time of the year in order to avoid severe dehydration. Then, too, when outfitting boats during the last four months of the year, I must remember to double the quantity of mineral water normally consumed by our clients.

Visitors traveling on the rivers in the Amazon Basin during the dry season witness a scene quite different from the high water interval. At Ariaú Jungle Tower (near Manaus) we find ourselves climbing the equivalent of four stories of stairs just to get to where the boats dock during the high water season. Surrounding lakes and smaller tributaries are inaccessible by November and riverboats used to transport guests from Manaus to Ariaú must transfer passengers to canoes far out on the Negro River. In the event of an extra dry season, it is quite common to see burning of grass and low vegetation in tropical savanna areas. The "high forest" remains relatively green under these circumstances due to the greater shade and, of course, the very high humidity.

In what direction is the river flowing? If one looks out onto the rivers in front of Santarém on a windy day, it appears that the water is flowing upstream. It is actually surface water being blown back by the wind. More than one thousand tributaries feed into the main channel of the river. Included are some of the largest rivers in the world—the Rio Negro, Rio Madeira, Rio Tapajós, Rio Xingu and Rio Tocantins among them.

The Amazon is classified as a "white water" river, referring to the white, muddy color of the water (nothing to do with rapids). This is due to the origin of the river being in a "new" geological formation, the Andes Mountains. The Tapajós River, on the other hand, has its origin south of the Amazon in an area known as the Brazilian Shield. Being a very old geological formation, it provides very little sediment to the river and is, therefore, a "clear water" river. One can only appreciate the difference between the two rivers when returning from a long riverboat tour on the Amazon. The clear blue color of the Tapajós River is indeed very impressive, and welcome, on these occasions. It has been rumored that one of the reasons that cruise ships stop in Alter do Chão is to take on the fresh, clean water of the Tapajós River. It only makes sense.

An important characteristic of the Amazon River is that it flows for almost the entire breath of the continent with very little difference in elevation. Santarém is more than 645 kilometers (400 miles) inland from the Atlantic Ocean, but is only 36 meters (120 feet) above sea level. Manaus, located on the confluence of the Amazon and Negro rivers, approximately 1,500 kilometers (900 miles) inland from the Atlantic, has an elevation of only 93 meters (300 feet). Leticia, Colombia, on the border with Brazil and Peru, is 95 meters. Iquitos, Peru, some 3,000 kilometers (1,850 miles) air distance from Belém, is only 120 meters (380 feet) above sea level. Our well at home is 54 meters deep (177 feet), which means we are pumping water from below sea level.

The Amazon Basin covers an area of some two and one-half million square miles and contains the largest remaining tropical forest in the world. Contrary to popular opinion, little of the forest has been cut.

Best estimates, determined by satellite imagery, conclude that only 15-17% of the primary forest has been destroyed. "Developed" countries of the world often point fingers at Brazil for cutting its forests, but forget that they have ravaged their own, in most cases several generations ago. The bad news is that most of the deforestation in the Amazon has taken place in the last three to four decades. On an even sadder note, the Amazon floodplain, representing the richest soils in the Amazon, has been almost deforested.

The Amazon River has an average width of four to five kilometers (up to three miles), but can vary greatly from place to place. The narrowest section of the river is at Óbídos, just west of Santarém, where it is only two kilometers (a little over a mile) wide. This is also the deepest water of the Amazon, about 100 meters (330 feet) deep.

Except for a few days of the year when it stabilizes, the Amazon River is either rising or falling. Peak flood levels are normally reached by the end of May. Low levels generally occur by the end of November. The old timers tell me, however, that if the season begins late, to count off six months from that point in time rather than the previously mentioned timetable. Regardless, the difference between the high and low water marks is impressive. In Santarém it is around 7 to 9 meters (23 to 30 feet). As one goes west, the difference increases. In Manaus it is about 10 meters (32.8 feet). Even further west, differences between high and low can be as much as 20 meters (65 feet). Floodplain dwellers deal with annual floods by building their homes on the high banks overlooking the river, and they place them on stilts as an added measure of safety. I have noticed, nonetheless, that many homeowners have to move out during the high water season and those who stay are rightfully concerned with fast-moving waters slapping at the floorboards of their houses. If I were conducting a household survey along the river ways, I would certainly plan to do it during the flood season, when one can literally float right up to the door of every home. I was reminded of this in April of 1997, when we sallied forth daily from the *M/S Alla Tarasova* in Zodiacs to look at flora and fauna on the stretch between Iquitos and Belém. We obviously attracted a lot of attention and curiosity on the part of locals as we moved about on a world of submerged pasturelands, farms and backyards, often nudging our rubber boats right up to the porches of homes for more intimate conversations. Larger herds of livestock had been removed to higher lands by this time, but most ranchers kept a few buffalo in elevated corrals for the milking and cheese making. These water-loving animals were allowed to come and go as they pleased, always finding their way back home after long grazing periods on the floating meadows of canarana grass.

Water levels can also change directions very quickly within a season. Once on a tour in the Leticia area, our local guide, Daniel, reported that he could not get very far into one of the local lake systems because the water levels had dropped considerably. Indeed, we saw recent watermarks on trees some two meters higher than the current levels. Knowing that water levels are on the rise that time of the year, I asked Daniel the reason for the drop. Very elementary—it had not rained in two weeks.

The closer one gets to the Atlantic Ocean, the greater the influence of the tides in determining water levels. Incredible, but tidal action can be measured as far west as Óbidos, more than 1,000 kilometers (620 miles) from the Atlantic Ocean.

The Amazon can get cold on occasion. Not so cold that anyone is going to get frostbite, of course, but cold enough that at home we close windows, turn off electric fans and get under a sheet or blanket at night. If you are sleeping in a hammock, it is even colder. Cloud cover, for the most part, determines temperatures in the Amazon, but cold fronts can move in from the Antarctic to leave us all shivering to the bones. The last one I remember was on February 9, 1995. A *frente polar* smacked up against hot summer temperatures in the southern part of Brazil provoking devastating floods in many major cities in the country. The lowest temperature I measured that day, here in Santarém, was 25 degrees Celsius (77 degrees Fahrenheit). It was definitely hibernation weather for those of us used to the sweltering heat of the Amazon.

Though it can vary a lot from year to year, the rainy season commonly begins in January and lasts through May or June. February, March and April are the months with the greatest rainfall. Most rains are of short duration and seldom does it rain over the course of a whole day. The average annual rainfall in the Santarém region, as well as around Manaus, is approximately 2,000 millimeters (80 inches). Belém gets more, around 3,000 millimeters (120 inches). Ranchers on Marajó Island tell me that they get even more rainfall than Belém. As mentioned, the dry season peaks during the months of August through November and a total lack of rain is not uncommon during this time of the year. Bright sunny days and starry nights dominate the weather scene. Add to this scenario some of the finest beaches in the world on the Tapajós and Arapiuns Rivers and you have an explanation of why it is difficult to find anyone at home on the weekends and holidays.

Mark Morgan, professor of tourism at the University of Missouri - Columbia and member of the Missouri Partners of the Americas, visited Santarém and my Bosque Santa Lúcia in November of 2004. He was fortunate in that he was hosted by Frei Leão Brune and Eunice at their cabana on the sandy banks of the Tapajós River, a few kilometers west of the city. Although Mark did not need a hotel while here, as a specialist in tourism, he was naturally curious about the status of them, as well as motels. I laughed out loud when he asked about motels because I no longer associated them as places of lodging. They are in essence a place where people get together for something called love and sex. I dare say mostly sex—and accordingly, one pays by the hour. There are several thriving motel establishments in town and some are more comfortable than the best hotels. They play an important role in this society because the average household offers zero in terms of privacy. Every nook and cranny of the house or apartment is filled with family members and relatives, twenty-four hours a day. Here the Privacy Act is a motel, especially for those having extramarital relationships. Much like our own concept of motels, they are places where guests drive in by vehicle. The similarities end there, for the most part. The entire complex is hidden from public view by brick walls and each room has an attached carport with drawn curtains to conceal the vehicle. Now, having been around here for awhile, it is only expected that I have heard some motel stories from friends regarding their not-so-secret love lives. The most humorous episode was from a person who was getting up in the years at the time of incident. I knew he was going out on a regular basis with a girl young enough to be his granddaughter, but I had not heard about the motel confrontation between him and his beloved wife. I am sure that she suspected something was going on but that she was never able to catch him red-handed, so to speak. The opportunity presented itself one Saturday afternoon when a gossip monger spotted him wheeling into the Hippopotamus Motel on the Santarém-Cuiabá Highway with his young sweet thing. This person immediately called my friend's wife, who grabbed her 38 revolver and hailed down a taxi to pay her dues at the motel. Luckily an attendant was in the office when she arrived, thereby preventing her from invading the motel room. Relentlessly, she stood ground at the entrance/exit gate waiting for her husband and paramour to come out. Considering her state of passing lunacy, it was not clear who she was going to shoot, maybe both of them. The humorous part is that about an hour later she saw the family car coming out of the motel and she nervously raised the revolver ready to fire. To her surprise, her husband was not driving, nor was he even in the car. The old fox had outsmarted her again. The motel receptionist had alerted Mr. X as to what was going on and he quickly called a friend over to accompany his girlfriend out of the motel—in his car, of course! In the meanwhile he sneaked out of a secret door in the back and was relaxing in front of the television when his wife got back home. His story: he had simply loaned his car to a friend who had some intimate business to take care of that afternoon.

"YOU MADE MY TRIP" — THE BEST OF THE TOURS

Finding a tour program in Santarém can be a frustrating experience because the volume of tourist traffic here is small. Very few people visit our region, which means that one cannot expect to find routinely scheduled tours. More often than not we host only one or two persons at a time, which means private tours. That is great for the clients, except prices are much higher because of the small-group situation. As all over the world, tours in the Amazon are tier-priced, meaning the more participants, the cheaper the price per individual. Nobody wants to go bird watching with a large group of people, but even a small group of four to six would help a lot in reducing the costs. Nevertheless, I think you will find that many excursions are within reach, even on a small group basis. Even without a tour group, you will find a number of things to do by striking off on your own. You have come to the right place. It is just a question of sorting out the details.

Santarém is exceptional in that it offers a variety of environments to explore. There is the Amazon River with its muddy waters and myriad channels, lakes, and floodplain. There is the Tapajós River, a clear- water river bordered with some of the most beautiful sandy beaches in the world. Up river, a few kilometers from the banks of the Tapajós, we can still find some high forest. On the other side of the Tapajós River, about four hours by boat, there is the Arapíuns River, which is a clear-water river during the low water season and a black-water river in the flood season. By driving south of Santarém on BR-163, one can be on the *planalto* in minutes. Santarém itself is a city with which most people can identify, making it an excellent choice for an extended stay.

Santarém — the Waterfront

One of the most exciting and convenient excursions you may make is along the city waterfront of Santarém. Walk the entire 3.5 kilometers via the retainer wall bordering this part of town. The levee on which you walk prevents the Tapajós River from invading and washing away some very expensive commercial property. We find an ever-changing scenario here due to the rise and fall of the river system over the span of the year. Should you happen to walk in late November, you will see the river at its lowest level and you will look down on wide sandy beaches being used for outdoor markets, football fields, motorcycle races, improvised snack bars and all kinds of other activities. Coming back to Santarém in May, you will find the water level seven to nine meters (23 to 30 feet) higher—and boats looming over the retainer wall. The difference between the two seasons is astounding.

Regardless of the season, you will always encounter a lot of riverside activity on this stroll. Santarém is the commercial center for the middle Amazon and, as such, serves hundreds of villages in the region. As you make your way across town, you will witness many boats coming and going. They arrive loaded with villagers and their marketable goods—pigs, chickens, fruit, corn, farinha, beans, fruit and rubber. Watch closely and you will notice that most produce is sold within minutes after arrival, right on the boat. Perhaps the villagers sell their goods at a cheaper price to the "hawkers," but in turn they free themselves up for shopping and for taking care of other tasks before making the return trip back home. When we do this stroll during the low-water season, it is always worth the extra walk down to the beach to see the outdoor fish market. Some of the more popular fish are dourado, pescada, pirarucú, tambaquí, curimatá, tucunaré, apapá, pacú, pirapitinga, acarí, jaraquí and surubim.

On the other side of the street from the river, you will observe the commercial section of town. Most business taking place here is related to the basics of subsistence, such as foods, dry goods, equipment and commerce in general. At the western end of Avenida

Tapajós is Mercadão 2000, the largest indoor market between Belém and Manaus. Visitors are always surprised at the quantity and variety of foodstuffs sold there. Near downtown, just across the street from the Rio Dourado Hotel, you will find another indoor market called Mercado Municipal. A third open air marketplace is built over the beach area across from Marcadão 2000. Even though not very large, it has a great assortment of fruits, fish and an unusual collection of medicinal plants, barks and other home remedies from the Amazon. Easy access from river or from land makes for an easy stop before departing on a boat trip.

Meeting of the Waters — a Beautiful Wedding
The encounter of the Amazon and Tapajós Rivers can be seen from almost any point downtown, but the best spot to look at it is from Praça São Sebastião, on the eastern side of town. A bird's eye view can be had from Praça Mirante, a small knoll. The hill is only a few meters back of the waterfront, but in order to get there, one has to approach it from the back side. Walk up the street from the Mascotinho Bar and then turn right on Travessa Inácio Corrêa. Turn right again at the next street, which will take you to the top of the hill. The view is well worth the extra few minutes it takes to get there. Although there is nothing there to call your attention to the fact, the Fortaleza do Tapajós (Tapajós Fort, built by the Portuguese during early colonial days) once capped this hill. Today the site is home of a public school, Frei Ambrósio.

Centro Cultural João Fona
While at Praça São Sebastião, visit the Centro Cultural João Fona, a small, but excellent historical museum. Notice the Pre-Columbian era ceramics, which are typically embellished with intricate, sculpture-like ornaments, a trademark of *Tapajônica* style pottery from this part of the Amazon. Outside, next to the São Sebastião Church, you will find gigantic replicas of the same ceramics. Observe the zoomorphic forms of art on the outer edges of the vases—in particular, jaguars, vultures, frogs, snakes, turtles, monkeys and other animals. Browsing through the collection of artifacts at the Centro Cultural João Fona,

you will also recognize anthropomorphic motifs on some pieces, a style that evolved towards the end of the *Tapajônica* era, depicting a period of permanent highly populated villages governed by powerful chiefs. Sadly, these tribal units were totally wiped out by the Europeans as early as the 1700s, leaving not much more than archeological finds as a reminder of civilizations extraordinarily skilled in ceramic making. Because the vast and rich collections of *Tapajônica* pottery have been sold off to museums in other parts of Brazil and around the world, it is tragic to see how little is left in Santarém. On the positive side, it is pleasing to see the local government taking measures to increase the size of the local collection, as well as investing in secure display cases to better exhibit it.

In March of 1998, I accompanied Hélcio Amaral, and his guest, Laurie Goering, South America Correspondent for the Chicago *Tribune*, on a private visit to the museum. The stop was part of a four-day program that Laurie had set up for covering the archeological research previously conducted by Anna Roosevelt of the Field Museum in Chicago. I suppose what impressed me most about what I saw at Centro Cultural João Fona was the skill of staff members in repairing broken vases, using mere ceramic fragments found at excavation sites. By filling in blanks areas with plaster of Paris, they were able to totally reconstruct ceramic pieces, much like paleontologists reconstruct dinosaur skeletons. When I refer to "excavation sites," I do not mean to call forth images of scientific digs, as we would visualize them from the slick pages of a *National Geographic Magazine* article. As a case in point, on our way to the downtown market place Hélcio pointed out a new building under construction just a few doors from the main post office building. "This is where we found some of those ceramic vases you saw being reconstructed at the museum," he commented. "When the construction crew started digging the foundation," he continued, "I talked with the workers personally, telling them that I'd pay for any Indian artifacts found." Hélcio's hunch of uncovering something important in that location was founded on the knowledge that this part of Santarém, still called *Aldeia* for the word "village," was where the Indian population lived at the time the Portuguese settled in here. According to Hélcio, Native Americans inhabited this locale for several thousand years prior to the arrival of the first Europeans. Even though it is rare that anyone sees an Indian survivor in the streets of Santarém, local residents are adept at recognizing and collecting indigenous ceramics and other artifacts whenever they are unearthed. A local person visited my office in 1997 asking if I were interested in buying a collection of over 200 stone axes his brother had collected, literally a cardboard box full of prehistoric relics. Remembering Centro Cultural João Fona, I mentioned this to Hélcio one day. Too late! The whole lot had been sold to a collector in Manaus. To illustrate how easy it is to acquire some of these collector items, a visiting professor from the University of Brasília called me over to a table of arts and crafts items in Alter do Chão to ask if the items were Indian-made. Glancing quickly at the odds and ends before us, I impulsively declared that the only place to buy true indigenous articles was up the street at the Center for the Preservation of Indigenous Art. Plucking a piece from the table, our visitor, a Russian physicist, skeptically remarked, that the old man had told him that it was more than 400 years old. Wow! I nearly fell over backward when I saw what he was showing me, for it was nothing less than a genuine piece of *Tapajônica* pottery. Swallowing hard and apologizing for my oversight, I confirmed what the vendor had said and went on to tell him that it was one of the sculpture-like protrusions found on the outer edges of vases, diagnostic of *Tapajônica* pottery, in this case, the head of the king vulture. It was nearly three inches in size, so it must have been part of a rather large vase. Seeing no particular interest on the part of the physicist to buy the piece, I asked the vendor how much he was asking for it. After paying less than US$5 to the dealer, he asked me when I was going to be back in Alter do Chão again. "Somebody's going to bring me a stone axe and a pipe," he went on to say. Unfortunately, I did not return to Alter do Chão right away, but I did alert Hélcio Amaral about the fact—and passed on the king vulture relic to him for the museum collection.

Security

Unlike in Belém and some other cities in Brazil, you do not have to be overly concerned with your personal security while walking around Santarém. You will certainly attract some attention as a traveler, but by taking some basic precautions, you will have no problems, even walking alone. Be prudent, though. Like anywhere in the world, there are always those who will take advantage of the careless. Cruise ships seem to attract an undo amount of attention and the risk of harassment and thievery increases greatly on these days.

Exercising

On the lighter side of life, the waterfront is the city's favorite area for exercising. Early in the morning, as the sun is making its debut on the horizon, you will find many people running or walking the entire distance of the sidewalk, and again in the early evening. Local enthusiasts refer to it as their "Cooper," referring to Kenneth Cooper of aerobics fame. The waterfront gets quite congested during business hours; if you exercise this time of the day, go to Praça São Sebastião. It is much quieter and you have two square blocks of sidewalks for working out.

"Meeting of the Waters" — by Boat

The Amazon and Tapajós Rivers meet directly in front of Santarém and flow side by side for a few kilometers before the Amazon inundates the Tapajós completely. Each bears its distinctive color, the Amazon being muddy-white and the Tapajós, clear blue. The contrasting colors occur due to the fact that the Tapajós River drains the Brazilian Shield to the south—an old geological formation now lacking in sediments and organic materials. The Amazon River, on the other hand, comes from the "newly formed" Andes Mountains and is, therefore, heavily laden with sediments. Other factors associated with the side-by-side flow include the warmer water of the Tapajós and the higher density of the Amazon.

Do not expect any routine, ongoing tours to get you out to the "meeting of the waters." You will need to make arrangements with a tour agency or negotiate with a local boat owner. It is not advisable to go out in a canoe, unless it is an extremely calm day—which is not a very common occurrence on the river. The most prevalent type of boat used in this region is wooden and always diesel-powered. Outboard motors are not very popular because of the heavy importation duty placed on them by the government, plus the high cost of gasoline. Nevertheless, you will find a wide array of wooden boats for hire and, if you are lucky, one that has a muffler on the engine. Seeing that it does not take much time to visit the "meeting of the waters," you may want to also include the city waterfront or a longer riverboat ride to Igarapé Açu or Maicá.

Alter do Chão — Caribbean of the Amazon

Not many people leave Santarém without going to Alter do Chão, a small village located on the beautiful, sandy beaches of Rio Tapajós and Lago Verde. It takes about three hours to get to this "little piece of heaven" by riverboat, but I would recommend saving time by taking the road. All 33 kilometers are paved and it takes less than an hour to get there. Public bus service to Alter do Chão leaves from the Avenida São Sebastião, next to Colégio Santa Clara, or from Mercadão 2000. Check with your hotel staff for information on departure times. Better yet, take an organized tour. Nearly all tour agencies offer this trip, some including lunch and a visit to the endless sandy beaches.

If you really want to unwind, plan on staying for a few days in Alter do Chão at the BeloAlter Hotel, or one of the *pousadas* (small hotels). Stretch your hammock out between a couple of trees; swim in the clear water of Lago Verde or the Tapajós River; explore what used to be a major Indian settlement; eat "finger licking good" fish under a mango tree and gawk at "The Caribbean of the Amazon."

Regardless what you may hear, the Center for the Preservation of Indigenous Art is no longer open. This is too bad because it was a major tourist attraction for Alter do Chão and the region. Tribes from the Amazon and other parts of Brazil were represented in an exhibition of more than 2,000 pieces of indigenous art. David Richardson, founder and curator of the Center, was a personal friend. His death and the subsequent closing of the establishment saddened us all.

If you are lucky enough to be in Alter do Chão during September, participate in the annual weeklong *Sairé* (*Çairé*) folklore festival. You will delight in seeing a variety of folk dances performed by the hospitable villagers of this riverside community. Take along your tape recorder to document original songs and folk music presented by the *Espanta Cão* (Scare the Dog/Scare the Devil) Band. In recent years *Sairé* has broadened the scope of presentations by adding the dueling dolphins—referring to the boto (pink dolphin) and the tucuxi (smaller dolphin)—dances rivaling the popularity of the dueling bulls in Parintins in the State of Amazonas. These are beautiful people performing traditional dances with a twist of commercialism. The dance depicting the seduction of a young village girl by the pink dolphin (from Legend of the Boto) is quite sensual and always a favorite among participants of the festival.

Do not take your checkbook to Alter do Chão. You may be tempted to buy a riverside lot to spend the rest of your blessed days. Seduced by the enchantment of the village, the spectacular beauty of the area and the charm of the people, clients often fantasize about buying the whole village. It is one of those places.

Maicá — Looking for Dolphins and Birds

Maicá is a favorite half-day tour, which normally begins with a visit to the "meeting of the waters." The canal is a natural outlet (*furo* or *igarapé*) of the Amazon River and is located just downstream from Santarém, where it meanders over the floodplain. During the low water season (September through January), this whole region is one gigantic pastureland interspersed with vestiges of floodplain forest. Like most other floodplain areas of the Amazon, about 95% of the forest has been cleared to make way for cattle and buffalo ranching. When in low-water season, boats are restricted to the main stream of the *igarapé*. At other times, they can navigate over a larger domain, including entire ranches. Bird watching is one of the highlights of this tour. On any given day you can expect to see many different species of birds, many of which are listed in the "Fauna" section of this guide.

Are you tired of looking at birds? Then try your hand at fishing for piranhas. It is not guaranteed, but you will probably catch a few. Let a crewmember remove the fishhook from the piranha's mouth. Lunch can be a two-way affair.

Another feature of this tour is that of seeing freshwater dolphins, as well as iguanas, almost without fail. In all likelihood you will see monkeys during a stop at one of the forested islands.

Taperinha — an Archaeological Site
This all-day riverboat tour will give you an overview of the Amazon River floodplain and an opportunity to visit Sítio de Taperinha, a private estate built in the mid-1800s by the Baron of Santarém. The trip will begin with a visit to the "meeting of the waters," where the Amazon and Tapajós Rivers come together in front of Santarém. From there it will continue down river to the Maicá Canal, a natural waterway winding through gallery forest and floodplain pasturelands. When water levels are low, boats go to Taperinha via Ituquí, which extends travel time by at least one hour. Regardless of the route, you will have a chance to see freshwater dolphins, many species of birds, iguanas and flora typical of the Amazon floodplain.

The Casa do Barão (Baron's House) was built with slave labor as a retreat for Miguel Antônio Pinto Guimarães, the Baron of Santarém. The Baron eventually joined into a farming partnership with Romulus J. Rhome, an American Confederate, who immigrated to Santarém after the Civil War. Sugarcane cultivation, whose by-product was distilled into rum, was the main business enterprise here. After the Baron's death in 1882, Rhome left Taperinha and the partnership. In the early 1900s, the property was sold to Godofredo Hagmann, a European zoologist associated with the Museu Paraense Emilío

Goeldi in Belém. Taperinha is now owned and managed by the grandchildren of Hagmann.

The feature of the trip to Taperinha is that of visiting the renowned clam middens, located a few meters back of the main house. The archeological excavations, conducted there by Anna Roosevelt and her colleagues at the Goeldi Museum in the early 1990s, indicate that Native Americans had been living at this site more than 6,000 years ago. Optional activities during the stay at Taperinha include horseback riding, fishing, birding and, of course, relaxing.

By making advance reservations, guests may stay overnight at the Casa do Barão. The rooms are plainly furnished, but gigantic, and the local cooking will make you want to stay for several days. This tour may be combined with the Monte Alegre, making for a three-to-four day riverboat tour for travelers interested in South American archaeology.

Bosque Santa Lúcia
Bosque Santa Lúcia (Santa Lúcia Woods) is owned by my wife, Áurea. The land (279 acres) was bought back in 1981 and our objective has always been that of keeping it in forest. The tour is an excellent choice for seeing the biodiversity of native Amazonian flora. This three-to-four hour excursion can be scheduled for mornings or afternoons. Begin the trip at Kilometer "0" of the Santarém-Cuiabá Highway (next to the deepwater pier), the only road connecting this part of the Amazon with other points in Brazil. Pass through the industrial section of town and then on up to the Planalto (plateau) at an elevation of 158 meters (518 feet). On top of the hill at the BEC Army Base, visit an unmarked historical site (Piquiátuba) where Sir Henry Wickham lived prior to smuggling out the famed rubber tree seeds. A few kilometers down the road you will enter a secondary dirt road leading to a small village called Poço Branco. Stops will be made to show the different stages of "slash and burn" agriculture and the effect it has on the forest and land. You will also have a chance to observe mechanized agriculture, which is now

overrunning large tracts of land in the region as rice and soybean farmers from southern Brazil move into the region. At Bosque Santa Lúcia you can choose between more than four kilometers of walking trails for that nature walk you have wanted to take since arriving in the Amazon. As you hike over the trails, you will have the opportunity to see biodiversity at its best. It is estimated that there are more than 400 different species of trees and palms on the Bosque lands, nearly half of which have been identified and labeled for your information. Bosque Santa Lúcia provides most of the characteristics noted throughout the more distant primary forest—that is, widely diversified species of trees and plants making use of nutrient-poor tropical soils. Discover for yourself the secrets of how they survive. While at Bosque Santa Lúcia also visit the small Museum of Woods, where there is an exhibition of wood and lumber, many items representing species found in the Bosque forest.

Visitors may consider the following suggestions when touring the Bosque. Comfortable walking shoes are always important for any nature hike. Tennis shoes are footwear of choice for most travelers coming to Santarém. Boots are also in order, especially during the rainy season. Also, although malaria is not endemic to the area, take insect repellent for occasional mosquitoes and chiggers, which can pester you on occasion. And for photographing forest walks, flash and high-speed films are recommended, especially on cloudy days.

Belterra — of Henry Ford Fame
Belterra is a half-day tour via the Santarém-Cuiabá Highway. Recent paving of the road to the turnoff has reduced driving time to the main village to about one hour, quite a difference from old days when Belterra was an all-day excursion for us. Leaving the main highway there is a small stretch of newly paved road and then it is dirt all the way to the village. It can be quite dusty during the dry season and very muddy or flooded during the rest of the year. Henry Ford, of the Ford Motor Company, established this huge rubber tree plantation in the early 1930s. The company abandoned the project completely in 1946. Some 15,000 acres of planted rubber trees returned to jungle

over the years, but they have been all cut down in favor of crop farming. The main village of Belterra still maintains the appearance of a rural American town of the 1930s. In the outlying areas of the village, as well as the lands bordering the Santarém-Cuiabá Highway, soybean farms occupy immense areas, which were formerly in rubber trees, pasture land and forest. This is now "Gaucho" country, a generic term referring to the soybean farmers, most of who have migrated from the southern part of Brazil. Mechanized agriculture, European-looking homes and people contrast greatly with the traditional "caboclos" of the region.

In 1996, a referendum vote created the Municipality of Belterra, thereby suspending political dependence on the federal government, as well as Santarém. The first elected mayor, Oti Santos, took office in January of 1997, followed by Geraldo Pastana in 2005.

Tapajós National Forest
This trip can be done in six-eight hours. Main entrances to the Tapajós National Forest are at Kilometers 67 and 123 on BR-163, the Santarém-Cuiabá Highway. Since the highway is paved only to Kilometer 100, the road conditions can be muddy during the rainy season and extremely dusty during the summer. Tour prices reflect the wear and tear on vehicles to reach this beautiful primary forest, some 1.5 million acres. The area is administered by IBAMA (Instituto Brasileiro do Meio Ambiente e dos Recursos Naturais Renováveis) and only recently has it been opened to ecotourism. The Tapajós National Forest represents the only accessible primary forest close to Santarém. Tours are conducted only on a prearranged basis. Normally IBAMA permits and fees (paid at the Banco do Brasil) are handled by the tour company.

Longer Riverboat Tours — Hold the Phone Calls
Check with local tour agencies for details on overnight excursions and expeditions of even longer duration. If possible, your group should make tour arrangements before arriving in Santarém so as not to lose valuable time trying to put something together here. Riverboat tours

of up to three days or more require a considerable amount of preparation. The very best combination is to have everything set up in advance. On returning to the city, you should have at least a day or two for cleaning up, packing and, of course, spending time in Santarém, fittingly called the "Pearl of the Tapajós."

Personal Supplies and Equipment

What to bring on a longer riverboat excursion is indeed a matter of personal preference. First, check with your tour operator or guide to see what will be provided as part of the tour package. Basic supplies include a *rede* (hammock), a sheet, a blanket, a towel and a mosquito net for the hammock, the essential elements for setting up a "household" in this part of the world. As I often say, "A hammock on the Amazon is equivalent to a sleeping bag in Alaska. Do not be without one." It is also a good idea to take a pair of long pants, a long-sleeved shirt, hat and sunscreen lotion. Shorts, swim clothes and tee shirts are needed most of the time. Your eyes can get sunburned quickly, so a pair of sunglasses is essential. For that unexpected rain, a lightweight poncho is much more useful than a raincoat. Bring your own, since this item is very difficult to find in Santarém. Insect repellent is a must if you are going to be on the Amazon River. Flashlights always come in handy during the night when the boat generator has been turned off. A pair of binoculars is appreciated by all, whether you are a bird watcher or not, and a personal water bottle is preferable to common glasses. Somewhere in your bag, you may want to stash some candies or other favorite snack food. Peanut butter addicts normally go into convulsions after discovering that it is unavailable in Santarém. The boat's crew (normally two to three on a boat) always appreciate a tip. Most of these fine people really go out of their way to make sure your trip is an enjoyable one, so a *gorgeta* should be considered when calculating your budget.

Fordlândia — by Riverboat

Before traveling up the Tapajós River, visit the "meeting of the waters" of the Amazon and Tapajós Rivers. Arrive in Alter do Chão before midday for a quick visit and then continue upstream to Aramanaí, where you will observe the only active rubber tree plantation in the region. Sleep on board as the riverboat navigates the darkness of night. Arrive in Fordlândia around dawn of the next day. Spend most of the day touring the American Village, the old industrial plant and the local village. Begin the journey back downstream by early evening. The last day of the trip will be spent on the Amazon floodplain. During that evening the boat will moor at one of the beautiful sandy beaches of the Tapajós River for dinner and relaxation. Arrive in Santarém at approximately 7:30 AM the next day. For persons with early morning flights, arrangements can be made for the boat to arrive earlier.

It takes about fifteen hours to get to Fordlândia by riverboat. For visitors wanting to travel upstream from Fordlândia, Itaituba is the next major stop. Traveling time is four to seven hours. Flights from Santarém to Itaituba are available but none to Fordlândia, since the airstrip there has been closed for many years.

"Steve, how far is it to Fordlândia?" asked Sam Johnson, President of Johnson Wax Company on his November 1998 visit to Santarém. My whimsical response of "fifteen hours by riverboat" was not exactly what the industrial billionaire wanted to hear. He inquisitively looked over to the next table at the Amazon Park Hotel restaurant to ask one of his eleven escort pilots the same question. A rapid response, calculated in aeronautical jargon, was yelled back to Sam—and he flew off to Fordlândia early the next morning. The lack of a runway there was no obstacle because Sam was flying a replica of the 1928 Sikorsky S-38 amphibian, a plane that his father, Herbert Johnson, had flown in an adventurous 15,000-mile flight from Racine, Wisconsin, to Brazil in 1935. Sam built the S-38 reproduction to blueprint specifications, since his mission was that of replicating the flight completed by the Johnson patriarch some sixty-three years earlier. Fordlândia was included in the original itinerary of Herbert Johnson because he was researching plantation operations which might be applied to the planting of carnauba palms (*Copernecia cerifera*), the fronds of which produce the carnauba wax. This hard wax was influential in improving the high-gloss quality of Johnson

Wax Company products long before Herbert flew off to Brazil. The palm is better adapted to the dry regions of northeastern Brazil, so it is understandable that the Amazon was never selected as a plantation site. Major plantation efforts on the part of Johnson, none of which reached the level of Ford Motor Company investments in Fordlândia and Belterra, were concentrated in Ceará, where the company continues to produce a carnauba wax to add to its synthetics. Sam Johnson, accompanied by his sons, Curt and Fisk, described his visit to Fordlândia as one of the highlights of their expedition to Brazil.

Combination Tour
This one is called a "combination" tour because in a relatively short period of time you have the opportunity to visit some very diverse environments such as the Tapajós, a clear-water river, the Amazon, a very muddy river with vast floodplains, and *terra firme* with a variety of forest types. On day one, depart from Santarém by riverboat for Alter do Chão on the Tapajós River. Tour this quaint village located between Lago Verde (Green Lake) and the Tapajós River. Continue upstream to the village of Aramanaí. Sleep on board the riverboat. On day two, enjoy an all-day hiking tour into the upland forests. Anyone in the group not in the hiking mood can relax on the boat or walk around the beaches and the village. Late afternoon the boat will begin its return down river. Day three, visit the meeting of the waters (Tapajós River and Amazon Rivers) and spend the rest of the day on the Amazon floodplain for birding, dolphin watching and a stop for piranha fishing. Sleep on board the last night, or return to Santarém for hotel accommodations.

Monte Alegre — by Riverboat
Traveling from Santarém down the Amazon River to Monte Alegre takes from four to six hours. The boat will stay as close to the shore as possible for birding and general sightseeing. By late afternoon you will enter the Gurupatuba River and then on to Monte Alegre, about half an hour traveling time. Tour the lower and upper villages of Monte Alegre and observe the large egret rookery right in the middle of town.

On day two, there will be an early morning departure by vehicle to Serra da Lua, 30 kilometers away. Main attractions during the day are the wind-carved monuments, caverns, and the famous but rarely visited prehistoric paintings dating back 9,000 to 12,000 years of Paituna and Ererê Mountains.

Day three travel to Curuá-Una River for observation of birds, dolphins and other wildlife. Sleep on board or at hotel accommodations in Santarém.

Arapiuns River

The schedule calls for a brief tour of the Santarém waterfront, then a visit to the meeting of the waters. From there the riverboat continues up and across the Tapajós, arriving at the mouth of the Arapiuns River after lunch. This river is different from others in this region because during flood season it is a "black-water" river, much like the Negro River. It may look like a giant cup of tea, but the water is actually very clean and the white sandy beaches make for a natural paradise for swimmers and divers. Your boat captain will make several stops for beach walks, swimming, birding and other activities. That night we will sleep on board at one of the isolated beach areas. Day two, continue upstream. Relax in your hammock, eat typical foods of the Amazon, visit a local village, and enjoy the natural beauties of the Arapiuns. Towards the end of day, arrive at Aruã Cascades, the farthest upstream we can go. Sleep on board the boat listening to the sounds of the cascading water. Day three, begin the journey back to Santarém. We will sleep on board, arriving in Santarém during the early morning to transfer to a hotel or the Santarém airport.

The Amazon — Yesterday, Today and Tomorrow

This tour will take you away from Santarém, as far east as Monte Alegre on the Amazon River and as far west as the Tapajós River, well beyond Alter do Chão. The objective of the excursion is to get you as close as possible to nature and at the same time expose you to the ways of the village people living there. Traveling on a traditional riverboat of the region, you will have the chance to think about what happened in the past, what is going on today and what the future might be.

The first day of travel will take you down the Amazon River to Monte Alegre, a town that boasts upper and lower levels. Spend the night onboard the boat and the next day travel by four-wheel-drive vehicle to the surrounding hills of Serra da Lua, Paituna and Ererê, approximately 30 kilometers away. Visit bizarre sandstone formations and the infrequently visited indigenous cave and wall paintings, which date back 11,000-12,000 years.

Another focus of our trip will be wildlife such as river turtles, side-necked turtles, river dolphins, iguanas, snakes, caiman, monkeys and many species of birds.

On the third day of the trip, you will visit not only the floodplain areas, but also *terra firma*, where are found semi-humid tropical forests like the areas surrounding the Curuá-Una River, which you will visit. Then it is on to the Tapajós, where you will visit and observe the day-to-day life of riverside *Caboclos*, the name given to persons of Indian and European descent. It is intriguing to see their lifestyle, which contrasts so much to our modern way of life. On the afternoon of day four, visit Alter do Chão, commonly referred to as the "Caribbean of The Amazon," and then back downriver to Santarém.

Sandy Beaches — Where you Least Expect to Find Them
Most likely you would never dream of shuffling your feet over sandy beaches while in the Amazon, but it is possible if you pay a visit to this region. Brazilians love their beaches and they automatically associate them with the best of tourism. Rarely does anyone mention flora or fauna when touting the benefits of visiting Santarém and the Tapajós River. But beaches are almost always the theme of any conversation dealing with natural resources, and since the Tapajós River possesses some of the finest beaches in the world, at least part of the year, it only makes sense that they are looked upon as the

potential economic salvation of the region. It has been my experience that visitors do, indeed, enjoy the amenities of hot sun, sand and river water, but few come for that reason alone. Nevertheless, Santarenos cannot be wrong in their assessment of the good things in life, so it does not take long for the newly arrived wayfarer to find himself joining in the fun. It may be just a fast swim that substitutes as a bath on a riverboat trip, or a time to cool off after a very hot trek into the forest, or even a delightful opportunity to mix with Brazilian people. A local saying dictates that when a person wets his soul in the Tapajós River, he/she will never leave. Maybe this aphorism is true because most visitors, after a swim in the Tapajós, make the comment, "I'd like to stay."

When people think of beaches, they immediately picture Alter do Chão and Ponto das Pedras, but there are other beaches even closer. Maracanã, for instance, is only a ten-minute taxi ride from downtown. A variety of beach huts will satisfy your need for drink and food, including cold beer and fried fish. For those of you privileged to be on a riverboat, an untold number of pristine beaches can be found farther up on the Tapajós and Arapiuns Rivers. Note that most beaches are covered by floodwaters during the months of April and May.

Touring the Night Skies
You will have exceptional opportunities to observe stars and planets from this latitude, seeing both southern and northern skies at the same time. Nothing can compete with the splendor of constellations like the Southern Cross, Centaurs, Scorpius, Orion and others on a clear night. One option is to get away from the lights of the city by taking an evening boat tour out to the beaches of the Tapajós River. Ask the boat captain to turn off the boat generator and lights. Enjoy being part of the universe.

The Southern Cross is by far the most popular constellation of travelers coming to this part of the world. Unfortunately for those coming between November and February, it is too low on the horizon to be seen even from this latitude. Pyrotechnic displays on distant thunderclouds will make up the difference.

The Brazilian Flag

On riverboat trips we have the pleasure of seeing the Brazilian national flag flying in the wind. Visitors regularly ask about the design and symbolism of the flag. Like many other national flags throughout the world, stars represent states. In the case of Brazil, the states are Acre, Alagoas, Amapá, Amazonas, Bahia, Ceará, Distrito Federal (Brasília), Espirito Santo, Goiás, Maranhão, Mato Grosso, Mato Grosso do Sul, Minas Gerais, Pará, Paraíba, Paraná, Pernambuco, Piauí, Rio de Janeiro, Rio Grande do Norte, Rio Grande do Sul, Santa Catarina, Rondônia, Roraima, São Paulo, Sergipe and Tocantins.

On the founding of the Republic of Brazil on November 15, 1889, there were only twenty states, plus the federal district of that time, Rio de Janeiro. Configurations of the stars symbolize the night sky on that occasion. Included are a compilation of Sires, Procycon, Canopus, Spicus, stars of the Southern Cross, Scorpius and other constellations. The theme *Ordem e Progresso* (Order and Progress) was adapted from the motto of a political association of the era. The colors were taken from the previous flag used during the reign of Dom Pedro II, 1822-1889. It is said that green symbolizes the forest, yellow is for gold and blue for the sky. States forming *Amazônia Legal* (the official Amazon Region of Brazil) are Acre, Amapá, Amazonas, Pará, Rondônia and Roraima.

A final note: all tour and travel agencies are required by law to register and comply with regulations established by EMBRATUR, the federal tourism and travel regulatory agency; PARATUR, the administrating agency for the State of Pará; and SEMTUR, the Office of Tourism for Municipality of Santarém.

"WE WANT TO SEE THE RAINFOREST" – CONSERVATION

In November of 1994, I found myself stranded in Iquitos, Peru, because commercial flights to Tabatinga had been suspended. Not looking forward to another ten-to-twelve hours ride in a noisy cramped speedboat, I asked Amazon Tours and Cruises to check out other options. One day later I was in the co-pilot seat of a floatplane that had been hired to transport some misplaced luggage to its owners on the *M/V Rio Amazonas*, which had arrived in Leticia that day. My 100 kilos (220 pounds), plus the sixteen pieces of luggage, must have been a bit too much for the lift-off because the pilot raced up river at least half an hour before he was able to get up in the air. Slowly, but surely, we gained altitude then made our way downriver past Iquitos and then on to Leticia, two and a half hours away. I got stiff from supporting a large Samsonite bag on the back of my neck, but the flight was spectacular. For the most part we followed the Amazon River basin with occasional shortcuts across forest. We flew low enough to easily see farmers harvesting their golden fields of rice yet high enough to view the endless forest which started within a few kilometers of the main river banks. The next day I continued to fly eastward on a two-hour VARIG flight between Tabatinga and Manaus at approximately 10,000 meters (32,000 feet) and again the view was that of a flat river basin surrounded by boundless forest. Only in the immediate area of Tefé, and a larger area around Manaus, did we ever see a break in the sea of green.

The point is that the Amazon forest is by far the largest tropical forest on the planet and most of it is still primary forest. Compare this to what is left of old-tree growth in the United States and other First World countries. Those forests are no more than a few pinpoints on the map. But what will the Amazon look like a hundred years from now? Will Brazil and its neighboring countries allow their forests to be totally devastated as the rest of the world has? Will the finest forest of the planet be reduced to a few national parks and a symbolic representation of its biological diversity? "Do the Brazilians really care?" is a question that visitors often ask. "Are there conservation groups working for the preservation of the Amazon?" In response to these questions, and in no way forgetting the efforts of several powerful national and international non-governmental organizations (NGOs), I like to refer to SOPREN (Sociedade de Preservação dos Recursos Naturais e Culturais da Amazônia) as an example of Brazilians in action.

SOPREN was founded in 1968 under the leadership of Camilo Vianna, professor of medicine and vice-president of the Federal University of Pará in Belém. Camilo Vianna is the Johnny Appleseed of the Amazon, but his mission is much more than that of planting trees. It is to combat hunger. "There is no need in talking about preservation of the Amazon if the population is hungry. Hunger does not listen to reasoning. It creates violence, to both mankind and the environment," proclaims Vianna in his great number of lectures and speeches made throughout Brazil and abroad. "We can't stop to cry over what we've done wrong in the past," he continues. "We have to jump in right now to battle hunger. Hunger is the key issue to the question of saving the environment." While SOPREN has been active on many fronts, Vianna takes special pleasure in planting trees. Through a network of nurseries and organizational affiliates, SOPREN has distributed an untold number of seedlings, and in the process, has tucked in an environmental-education program that is changing the mentality of school children and adults alike. Camilo Vianna practices what he preaches. He does not miss an opportunity to spread his gospel, the propagation of *trees*. When people see Camilo Vianna, they think of *trees*. They may remember him also as an outstanding professor of medicine, but they think *trees*.

We had the pleasure of receiving Camilo Vianna out at Bosque Santa Lúcia some years ago. He did not have a lot of time because I had kidnapped him from a medical conference at the Tropical Hotel (now Amazon Park Hotel), but we did walk the main trail of the Bosque. I will never forget his comment as we ended the visit. "Tem muitas preciosidades," he said. I took it to mean that the Bosque has a lot of precious trees. On another occasion, Áurea and I invited him out to dinner and he talked about... hunger and *trees*. As I opened my billfold to pay the waiter, a gentleman from a neighboring table (José Fernando dos Santos, a retired auditor from the Receita Federal, now deceased) quickly jumped up, grabbed the bill from my hand and made a short, but eloquent speech honoring the ecological attributes of Dr. Vianna. In the middle of this unexpected event, our honored guest got up from the table and disappeared. He was back a few minutes later with two big plastic bags of *pitombas* (*Toulicia* spp.), a wild fruit from this region. During the course of the speech in his honor he had seen the vendor passing by the restaurant and he left to get the fruit. Later he told me that he had an excellent germination rate from the seeds, which he planted at one of SOPREN's nurseries outside of Belém.

Speaking of environmental education, I also like to tell the story about a Brazilian friend who came from the southern part of the country a few years ago to set up a lumber mill operation in Santarém. Coming from a traditional family of lumbermen, he did quite well in the business. His children studied at the same school as mine, so I was quite surprised to hear him confess that his children were picked on occasionally by their colleagues because of their father's involvement in "cutting the forest." It just goes to show you that there is much more local concern for the environment than one would ever suspect. I told this story to Camilo Vianna one day. He did not say anything in reply, but I noticed a quick and subtle smile on his face before he moved on to another conversation.

Visitors are quick to jump to the conclusion that the Amazon forests have been destroyed completely, since they see a lot of devastation, but little forest. "Steve, why didn't they conserve at least one creek in its natural setting?" protested Jeff, a passenger on the modern cruise ship, *Silver Wind,* when it came through in December of 1995. "Why didn't they save at least one piece of original forest, just to show people what it used to be like?" he continued. "Do you know what they sold us as an excursion? Eighty of us on the ship signed up for a tour that cost $30 each. We were put in three boats, two of which got stuck in the mud within twenty minutes after leaving the ship. People living along the banks had to get into the creek to help push us out. Then they put us in canoes and rowed us at the most 50 meters to a ranch where they showed us a buffalo and two caimans in a bucket. And that was it. It was the worst tour I've ever taken in my life."

Why Santarém has not conserved a few accessible areas of its former environment is not easy to explain. The naked truth is that there is not one piece of easy-to-get-to primary forest left near the city. The Amazon floodplain has been deforested almost completely for ranching and what remains is going fast—as can be seen in the Maicá area. The city is more than 300 years old, but does not have a public arboretum, a botanical garden, or a zoo. Only in recent times has it organized a museum. For sure, part of the answer lies in the fact that Santarém is located geographically in the heart of the Brazilian Amazon, and the principal struggle for livelihood has always been that of agriculture, ranching and timber. Thus, economic development has been that of extraction—an endless battle with the jungle.

The quest for land, even today, is based on the hypothesis that a standing forest is land not being used. "He's not using his land," is a comment I hear sometimes from some of my neighbors at Bosque Santa Lúcia. Even though they see ecological tours being conducted on the property, and know very well that our objective is that of maintaining a small stand of forest for the purpose of nature walks, they still consider it immoral that 270 acres be left in trees. "He's not using the land and he won't let anyone else use it," is yet another statement made, suggesting that the least we could do would be to let others work the land. Shifting agriculture requires that new areas of forest be cut and burned every year in order to replenish and strengthen the poor tropical soils. This system works out fine for farmers with a minimum of 240 acres (the size of standard homestead) because, as they open up new fields, the old ones are returning to forest. Within nine to ten years, there is enough biomass in the new forest that it can be cut and burned again. In other words, it is a rotation system that takes advantage of nutrients locked up in vegetation as opposed to the soil. Therefore, the greater the biomass burned, the greater the fertility of the soil. Farmers who own smaller pieces of land are always at a disadvantage because they run out of land on which to rotate. They simply cannot wait the required number of years it takes for the forest to grow back. It is, therefore, no coincidence that local farmers identify an attractive chunk of forest as good farmland. I try to explain that our objective is utilization of the area in the form of a forest. "You earn your living cutting the forest and I am trying to earn mine by keeping it," I jokingly remark. Deep down inside I know that they are not satisfied with my rationale.

Once I made the mistake of giving permission to a former caretaker's father to open up a patch of woods for planting his corn and rice. I had understood that it was to be an area around the house where his parents were living. When I returned two weeks later I was horrified to see that they had cut down an enormous area, around 15 acres or so. At that point there was nothing I could do about it. The whole family worked long hours, six days a week in that enormous cornfield and succeeded in making enough money to buy some personal belongs, including new dentures and wristwatches. They were also able to pay the cost of moving the whole family to another part of the state. I was left with one bag of rice and a smaller forest.

Other folks are more uncompromising about the issue of "unproductive land." One community leader at Poço Branco asked me, in writing, to sell part of our reserve by dividing it into small lots, thereby increasing the local population so that the community could justify the request for electricity and city bus service. In her mind, Bosque Santa Lúcia is getting in the way of progress. I can appreciate the reasoning. It is no fun walking over kilometers of muddy or dusty road every day to get to school or haul produce to market. We all know that electric lights sure beat the heck out of a dingy kerosene flame, and who does not enjoy watching the national news and a soap opera on television? I guess those are some of the reasons why most of us live in the city. Regardless, I firmly believe that accessible green areas are very important to Santarém, and, in such pursuit, I requested IBAMA (The Brazilian Institute for Environment and Renewable Natural Resources) for reclassification of Bosque Santa Lúcia to that of a Private Reserve (Reserva Particular do Patrimônio Natural), as permitted by a federal law. In 2005, after eight years of battling governmental bureaucracy, I gave up on the application. In that time span I saw the whole region go from traditional slash-and-burn farming to one of mechanized agriculture for soybeans and rice. Large numbers of farmers from southern Brazil migrated to this part of the Amazon to buy up most of the small farms and ranches of the area. They had one thing in mind—plant as much soy and rice as possible to compensate for bank loans and a lot of expensive heavy equipment, including bulldozers, tractors and harvesters. Ecological, social and legal implications seemed to be of little or no importance as these hardworking families saddled up on their machines twenty-four hours to down anything that might get in the way of a soybean plant or blade of rice, including Brazil nut trees. Local farmers have always respected a law that forbids the cutting of these gigantic trees; after all, they are a fantastic source of food and especially rich in protein. I am told that ONE soybean farmer down the road from the Bosque bulldozed 70 Brazil nut trees and then burned them to destroy the evidence. I cannot verify the scandal but when I look at my land, which is really quite extensive, I do not see any Brazil nut trees. On the community side of things, local dwellers are about as rare as Brazil nut trees. As an example, the local grade school was closed down by the municipality because the community could not come up with fifteen students! The few kids left are now going to school out on the highway at Cipoal, some four kilometers away.

"Where *is* the forest?" is a question that I often hear from travelers. I have to explain that there really is a gigantic forest out there, but it is a question of *access*. Wherever there is easy access, whether it is by water or by land, you can be sure that the forest has been cut. Maybe the intrusion was for rosewood, jacaranda, mahogany, cedar or virola. Perhaps it was for ranching or agriculture. Short of some special arrangements like using a helicopter or floatplane, it is unlikely that the average tourist will ever experience virgin Amazon forest. The flow of visitor traffic is always via easy access and entrée means deforestation. Luckily for the forest, a great chunk of the Amazon is inaccessible, explaining why it continues to be the largest tropical forest in the world.

The Amazon Package — Wrapped Up in Plastic
Conversations with visitors during the course of a tour now and then touch on sensitive issues, one being the conspicuous amount of trash and garbage on the streets and beaches of Santarém. "It's shocking to see what's happening with plastic. The country is absolutely littered with it," a lady traveler stated. "Steve, was all this plastic around when you first came to the Amazon?" asked another. "Doesn't Santarém have garbage collection?" questioned someone else as we drove past an unsightly number of plastic sacks, bottles and strewn paper on the eastern side of the airport road. "People live right here and, just a few feet away, all this trash and they don't even seem to care." "My God!" groaned another, shaking her head, as she looked out on a patchwork of plastic, dead fish and other pieces of litter on the beaches of city waterfront. The owner of a prominent local hotel, once herself a globetrotter, told me in many more words than I dare quote, "We Brazilians are the trashiest people in the world. In all my travels I've never seen worse, anywhere!" A charming person who spent two weeks in Santarém in 1998 writes me saying, "Can I tell you what a wonderful, wonderful time I had there? Every bit of it, including the pot holes, vultures and smell of burning trash, has settled into one of the most interesting times of my life." I do not mean to belabor the issue. Let it stand that tourists do comment on the lack of environmental education in Santarém. Brazilian visitors are normally much more candid in their remarks about the negative aspects of the local scene, as well as the quality of services rendered to them. Foreign tourists, on the other hand, tend to be much more reserved in making any comments that might be considered

inappropriate coming from an outsider. But even so, garbage is one of the issues that loosens tongues.

Living in Santarém all these years has dulled my visual acuity for noticing things that catch the eyes of people from elsewhere, but it is difficult to totally overlook the custom of littering and careless garbage disposal practiced by many residents. The local government has improved garbage collection tremendously over the last few years and has invested heavily in infrastructure, including trucks with compacting units. I remember a time when trash was collected in open-bed trucks and never made it to the garbage dump. Then, too, I remember a time in the past when we could not count on our garbage being collected on a regular basis. Needless to say, a city of 200,000 has to have a system for dealing with garbage and Santarém does a reasonably good job in that regard. Most of my comments are directed to the careless practice of littering and improper garbage disposal. Without public support, the best sanitation department in the world will never keep a city clean. I am reluctant to use the word "littering" when referring to the practice of throwing things on the ground or into the water because to me littering implies that the culprits know better. In the case of Santarém, and I think I can include most of the Amazon, it is a case of habit. Littering is practiced without any thought as to whether it is right or wrong. It is just the natural thing to do. It is a way of life. The response by government is to hire large numbers of street cleaners who diligently sweep the streets and dig litter out of the open gutter system. A great move for providing employment, but the litter almost always accumulates faster than the government can gather it up.

Leftover refuse from special events is staggering. A folklore festivity programmed every year at one of the best high schools in Santarém produces an unsightly amount of trash thrown onto the school grounds. Regional dances, music and foods highlight an affair that attracts hundreds of students, parents and public for several nights in a row. Sadly, very few paper cups, plates and napkins make their way into trash containers. The same occurs at public events taking place in the praças and streets of the city. An article appeared in one of the local newspapers in 1998 complaining about the lack of trash collection on the beach following the Independence Day parade on Avenida Tapajós. Three weeks had passed since the occasion and nothing had been done to clean up the litter! The article said nothing to denounce the litterbugs, or to even suggest the need for environmental education—only criticism of the local government for not doing its job. Believe me, there are times when the sanitation department succeeds in keeping most of Santarém clean, and the city really shines. On these occasions visitors comment on how beautiful the city is and how it is so much cleaner than some other cities in the Amazon.

Travelers inevitably declare that they have never seen so many vultures as in Santarém. Neither have I, and I attribute their presence to an unusual quantity of food in the region. Most of it comes from the aquatic environment, which is not lacking. Vultures also adapt themselves well to the urban scene and are not at all timid in scratching out a living in the streets of Santarém. Our high stepping, flatfooted friends can be seen on every street in the city long before the sun peeks over the horizon, and they are the last birds to head for the roost as total darkness settles in. Living up to their reputation as being sanitarians, vultures (*urubus*) are adept at consuming the remains of dead animals, as well as smelly, rotten, organic garbage left over from households. They are also the most awful litterbugs ever imaginable. In getting to their favorite morsels, they tear open plastic garbage bags, drag them from the sidewalks into the streets and scatter trash all over the place. Improvements in garbage containment must address construction of garbage bins that are vulture-proof. The best design I have seen is at the home of my friend, Wilson Calderaro, director of SENAI (Santarém's largest trade school). It is really quite simple, a rounded metal grill hinged over the elevated garbage bin.

Vacant lots in the city are favorite spots for people to throw trash. The wind also does its part in filling them with paper and plastic. Such is the case with an empty lot across the street from where we live. Without a doubt, Travessa Turiano Meira, where we live, is very privileged in terms of city garbage collection, but in spite of this, the aforementioned land gets filled with litter of every type. The absentee owner is forced to have someone clean it up every few months. It normally takes three or four days for the worker to cut brush and weeds and to rake up mountains of trash. Then the burning begins! This goes on for another three days or so, burning our eyes badly and leaving dust and ashes all over the place. All unoccupied urban properties likewise get filled with litter and as the dry season bears down on us, weeds and brush wither away, leaving an unsightly crop of paper and plastic. At some point, someone conveniently throws a lighted match into the mess, burning off parts of the field.

Driving home one afternoon I was momentarily taken aback when someone in a pickup truck in front of me threw an empty pop can out onto the street and then the wrappings left over from their street-bought snack. I wanted to blow the horn and call the people *sujão* (a stronger expression than litterbug) but I reminded myself that as an outsider, I would best keep my mouth shut. As I pondered the need for environmental education in Santarém, I abruptly remembered that there was a time in my life when I was just as unconcerned about the surroundings as the people in front of me. I grew up in a rural American setting where we habitually got rid of trash in the most convenient manner possible, sometimes right out the car window. This was back in the 1950s, when the word "environment" had less tread on it, and the metallic sound of empties bouncing off asphalt and gravel synchronized perfectly with the beat of Bill Haley, Fats Domino and Elvis. My first encounter with environmental education caught me by surprise when I was a freshman at Berea College in Kentucky. I do not remember the exact reason for being out with several colleagues and our sociology professor, but we were heading back to Berea, when to the amazement of everyone, I nonchalantly tossed my empty pop can out the window onto the roadside, as I had done on countless other occasions in my life. "Steven, *what* are you doing?" bellowed out someone. Call it environmental education, peer pressure, or whatever, but I never again threw trash out the window of a vehicle. Later in life I found myself hiking, cross-country skiing and kayaking in remote areas of Alaska in the company of ecologically-minded souls at the U.S. Public Health Service in Anchorage. Not only did I learn to carry out my own refuse, but also the infrequently found trash left by others who had preceded us.

When traveling by riverboat, I encourage people to throw organic matter into the river, since fish quickly consume it. Everything else goes into plastic bags, which are stored on the boat until we get back to the city. Just to reinforce the need of environmental education in Santarém, I tell the story about a crewman who had not been given proper orientation about garbage disposal prior to taking off on a riverboat tour. Over a period of five days, we collected several bags of trash with the intention of putting them in the city's garbage containers upon returning. After transferring our passengers to a hotel, I returned to the boat to unload equipment and supplies, and to remove the bags of refuse. After loading ice chests, pots and pans, linen and other supplies into the back of my pickup truck, I noticed that the trash was not included. "Where's the trash?" I asked my cook. His sheepish response was that José, the aforementioned crewman, had tossed all the bags in the river an hour before we arrived in Santarém. I guess José felt that was part of his job, since he had no guilt feeling at all in what he had done. It was a way of life on the river, so to speak.

We all have reasons for our environmental behavior. On reading a draft copy of this book, a friend wrote me the following note: "My stringent ecological ways were loosened up in Paraguay and after having worked at a couple of nuclear power plants. The logic behind my decision to not litter is based on the place of where I "litter" and the life of what I litter. Like you inferred, "litter" is what is unappealing to the eye. I don't think twice about throwing an apple core or a banana peel out the window when traveling a country road. When in lowlands wilderness, I toss my tin cans where others will not find them, as the steel in them has a life of one to ten years before fully degrading. Plastic, which has a life of about 900 years, is a definite no-no to litter anywhere."

To The Passerby

You who pass me by and raise your arm;
before doing me wrong, look at me well.
I am the heat of your home during the cold winter nights.
I am the kind shade that you find under the hot August sun.
I am the refreshing, delicious fruit, which quenches your thirst on the trail.
I am the friendly lock of your home, the board of your table,
the bed in which you rest and the log from which your
boat is made. I am the handle of your hoe, the door of your dwelling,
the wood of your cradle and of your coffin.
I am the bread of excellence and the flower of beauty.
You, who pass me by, look at me well—and don't do me wrong.

> The above message is posted in English and Portuguese on a beautiful shade tree located on a Tapajós River beach in Alter do Chão. My compliments to lawyers Rodolfo Geller and Miguel Borghezan for their effort in protecting a little piece of our nature.

Homebody

"You're as bad as a snail," said a friend I had not seen in quite a while.
"How's that?" I replied.
"You never leave home," he responded.

"THERE GOES A MORPHO BUTTERFLY" — COMMON FAUNA

Wildlife on the Amazon is the most diverse on the terrestrial planet, but for the fast-moving visitor, it is unfortunately difficult to see. High diversity normally means fewer individuals, highly scattered populations, and often nocturnal habits. It is understandable that many visitors come with high expectations of seeing a "Hollywood jungle" with large number of animals, and it only makes sense that such expectations leave visitors highly disappointed. Aside from the phenotypic considerations, one must realize that the accessible areas of the Amazon have been inhabited for a long time, making for an altered environment. The deleterious effects of ranching, agriculture, logging, intensive hunting and fishing have inevitably reduced animal populations.

Although the Amazon may not match Africa, or even the Pantanal, for seeing animals, you will certainly have the opportunity to make some significant sightings on any tour you take. The longer you are outdoors and the more diverse the environment you visit, the more you will see—guaranteed.

Fresh-Water Dolphins

Unlike some parts of the world where dolphins are slaughtered indiscriminately, the Brazilians have a lot of respect for these mammals, seldom harming them intentionally. You will see both the *boto* and *tucuxi* species on any riverboat tour you take around Santarém. The *botos* are the larger of the two and are distinguished by their pink color. The *tucuxis* are gray and are recognized for their acrobatic maneuvers. Dolphins have a formidable set of teeth for the task of cutting and crushing their principal food, fish. A few years ago I found the skeleton of a dolphin on a sandy beach of the Arapiuns River and, to this day, I keep the skull of the animal in the Bosque Santa Lúcia museum. At first glance most visitors mistakenly identify it as a caiman skull, so prominent are the long rows of teeth. After a closer look, however, they discover the blowhole at the top of the skull, and from there, identification becomes easier. If you hear some loud snorting around your boat during the night, do not expect to see horses; they are just curious dolphins coming up for a "breather." Also do not expect to get a good photo; all dolphins are, as described by my friend, Sharon McGladdery, masters of camera-elusion.

Squirrel Monkeys

The most commonly seen monkey in this region is the squirrel monkey (*Saimiri ustus*). Even though they weigh only 1 kilogram (2.2 pounds), squirrel monkeys are giants compared to marmosets and tamarins. You will notice the long black-tipped tails of squirrel monkeys are not prehensile. On the other hand (excuse the pun), they are still great trapeze artists, demonstrating the ability to jump from tree to tree at great heights. At Bosque Santa Lúcia, there were many squirrel monkey residents, all of who returned from their food-finding mission at the end of the day to huddle together for the night in a very tall *ipê* tree. They must be creatures of habit because my caretaker, Raimundo Teixeira, tells me that he has lived in Poço Branco for more than 40 years and that they seldom missed a day of returning to this spot. Unfortunately, the devastation of the forest areas around the Bosque for the planting of rice and soybeans has reduced the number of animals drastically so that today we cannot count on seeing any animals. Up on the Rio Negro, at Ariaú Jungle Tower, a number of squirrel monkeys have taken up residence at the hotel and they are known for their innate ability to grab personal objects from the guests and then head for the trees. I remember one incident of a lady who was changing film in her camera and had placed the new film canister on the chair next to her, only to have a squirrel monkey grab it and run up a tree limb out of her reach.

Ricardo, one of the regular guides at the Ariaú Jungle Tower, tells us that the Indians take advantage of monkey intelligence by using them in the jungle to find edible food. Finding none, the Indians eat the monkeys.

Silvery Marmosets
Another common monkey in this part of the Amazon is the silvery marmoset (*Callithrix argentata*). It is about half the size of the squirrel monkey and, except for a black tail, all silvery-white in color. These monkeys also come together as a family unit at the end of the day. There was a time when Bosque Santa Lúcia hosted about 50 of them, but now fewer are seen. A distinguishing feature of the marmosets is the forward slanting teeth they have for carving out holes in the trunk of select trees (*Tapirira guianensis*). The sap and the dried resin serve as food, especially during the dry season. These trees look like they have smallpox.

Howler Monkeys
If you think the sound of a rock concert is loud, you have not heard a howler monkey. A friend tells me that a past edition of *Guinness Book of Records* lists the howler monkey as the loudest animal on the planet. As one of my clients correctly observed, they do not howl— they roar. To me the sound is that of a cross between a jet plane taking off and a bunch of noisy hogs, a sound you can hear from miles away. The anatomical feature that allows the howler monkey to communicate so adeptly is a very large voice box (hyoid bone) present in both sexes. Males do most of the "talking" but females join in at times. You may have a chance to see excised hyoid bones at one of the market places, either here in Santarém or in Belém. The most popular use of the voice box is as a vessel from which medicines are taken, especially for laryngitis and other loss of voice conditions. It is said to get the voiceless up and yelling in no time at all. I do not predict a demise of the howler monkey population due to this miracle treatment. Mortality rates reflect rural predilection for monkey stew. I only need to look at one of the monkey skulls in my office to remember this detail. It has a large gaping hole on top of the cranium, from where a family living on the Mamori River in the State of Amazonas removed the cooked brains of the poor animal.

Pet Monkeys

Among mammals of the Amazon, monkeys seem to be the favorite target for the pet world. Although it is strictly forbidden by law to commercialize any type of wild animal in Brazil, large numbers can be found in the hands of private individuals. Regrettably, traders also keep coming up with unique ways of smuggling them out of the country, for instance in the engine rooms of ships. Seldom does one take a trip on the Amazon without seeing some pet monkeys. The "cutest" monkey and the one favored by women, is the pygmy marmoset (*Cebuella pygmaea*), a tiny little thing no more than six inches in height. Once on a trip aboard the *M/V Rio Amazonas*—a tour ship that runs between the Brazilian border and Iquitos, Peru—a young girl about ten years old made herself quite conspicuous by her exaggerated upright posture and her careful manner of walking around the craft. On the second day of the cruise she revealed the reason for her behavior. She was carrying a pygmy marmoset under her floppy hat. The little creature was firmly attached to the girl's hair and was frightened to death whenever the hat was removed. It reminded me of a miniature lion. By coincidence, a few days later, as I was coming back to Brazil from Caballococha, Peru, by speedboat, a very attractive young woman sitting next to me kept peering incessantly into her blouse. From time to time she wiggled and sniggered as though something was tickling her. You guessed it, another pygmy marmoset. It would be difficult to declare animal abuse in a case like this.

Fish

Even if you are not interested in getting a fishing line tangled up, you will still be impressed with the great variety of fish species in the waterways of the Amazon. There are more than fifteen hundred species to be exact. Biologists attribute the great number to the variety of waters and niches found throughout the northern part of the continent.

Though an astounding number of fish species exist in the Amazon Basin, only fifteen or so of these are regularly consumed. An analogy can be drawn between trees and fish. Availability is so great, consumers can be choosy. Given the ever-increasing world population and the demand for fish, one can predict that eventually the less desirable species will become marketable, perhaps to the salvation of the now favored species.

When you look at restaurant menus all over the Amazon, you will always find at least three species of fishes common to them all— *tucunaré, pirarucú* and *tambaquí*.

Tucunaré (*Cichla ocellaris*) is one of the most expensive fish on the market and also a favorite for sportsmen. Santarém, by the way, is host for an international *tucunaré* fishing contest almost every year. One of the most popular ways of eating *tucunaré* is *frito na manteiga* (fried in butter). When touring the local fish markets, observe the tail of the fish and you will understand why it is called "peacock bass."

Pirarucú (*Arapaima gigas*) is the largest scaled fish in the world and it is often referred to as the "codfish of the Amazon" because when sun-dried it looks and tastes like codfish from Norway. But the best way of eating *pirarucú* is fresh, be it grilled, fried, baked or made into soups. Whenever I think of *pirarucú,* I always remember a trip to Marajó Island, where at Fazendas Bomjardim, Eduardo and Eunice Ribeiro sent a couple of their cowboys out to one of the many lakes on the ranch to catch one of the giant fish. Timing was perfect. Just as we gathered for some early morning birding on the marvelous porch overlooking the pasture lands, we saw two distant figures coming towards the house, obviously carrying something heavy suspended from a pole on their shoulders. By this time everybody forgot the birds completely. All binoculars were focused in on the cowboys bringing in their catch, nothing less than a *pirarucú* nearly two meters long. Dona Eunice's kitchen staff prepared a piece of the fish for lunch and I can testify that it was scrumptious. Local fishermen tell me that there was a time when it was common to see *pirarucú* weighing 150 kilograms (330 pounds) or more. Over fishing of the creature has reduced catches of this size considerably.

An exceptional place, by the way, to see live *pirarucú* is at the *Museu de Ciências Naturais* (Museum of Natural Sciences), a museum owned and operated by the Japanese community in Manaus. The aquarium is the size of a swimming pool and is equipped with viewing windows, which allow for "nose to nose" contact with the huge fish. You will notice that every few minutes they will go up to the surface; they are air breathers (part of their oxygen is removed from water and part from air). It is this physiological feature that makes them very vulnerable to their primary predator, man. The *Museu de Ciências Naturais*, by the way, is also a good place to see insects you may not want to encounter in nature.

Tambaquí (*Colossoma macropomum*) is a scaled fish and noted as being one of the most delicious in the Amazon. Its main diet is that of fruit and seeds, placing it low on the food chain, in terms of accumulation of heavy metals. If you want to play the role of a dentist, examine the teeth of a *tambaquí* in the market place. You will see that their teeth look very much like our own, having upper and lower molars designed for crushing and mashing seeds and fruits. The best time to eat tambaquí is during the flood season when the fishes are fat from the abundance of feeding areas. Most people agree that the best way of preparing the tambaquí is to grill it. Grilled *tambaquí* ribs are my favorite.

Turtles
The turtle population of the Amazon has been reduced to the point that IBAMA (Instituto Brasileiro do Meio Ambiente e dos Recursos Naturais Renováveis) sees fit to protect the few nesting areas with 24-hours-a-day guards, some armed with machine guns. Consumption of turtle meat in this region is a tradition which I can compare only to the Eskimo fancy for eating whale. It is part of the culture. They have to have it, at least on occasion. Unlike whale, there is no hunting season for turtles. By law, it is expressly forbidden to be in the possession of turtles at any time for any reason. Therefore, it is not surprising that the commercialization of this once-so-abundant animal is one of cloak-and- dagger intrigue. When I answered the doorbell

one day, a middle-aged man wearing a leather pouch over his shoulder cautiously opened up conversation with me by saying, "I don't know if you eat this kind of thing or not, but I'm offering it at a good price." Unbuckling the top of the pouch, he exposed a turtle, perhaps ten inches in diameter. The price was the equivalent of about twenty dollars. On another occasion, at one of the better restaurants in Belém, a waiter referred to a "special" regional dish not to be found on the menu. The special was nothing less than one of a very small turtle species called muçuã (*Cinosternum scorpioides*). Aside from any legal or moral issues, I learned long ago that eating turtle is not for me and I learned the hard way. Jocôndio Gonçalves had invited me to a birthday party at his home where his mother had painstakingly prepared a dozen different kinds of turtle dishes for her guests. Having a good appetite, as well as having a track record for tolerating any kind of food concoction in the world, I thought nothing of trying everything on the table, including half a dozen turtle eggs. A few hours later I relinquished all titles. I was so sick that I thought I was going to die. Was it revenge of the river turtle? Maybe, but it really had more to do with the fact that turtle meat and eggs are super rich in fats and I had made a pig of myself.

The more commonly recognized species of turtles include *tartaruga,* which is the giant river turtle (*Podocnemis expansa*); *tracajá,* yellow-spotted Amazon turtle (*Podocnemis unifilis*), a medium-sized turtle getting up to about 50 centimeters; *pitiú* (*Podocnemis sextuberculata*), a small turtle about the size of a person's hand; and *matamatá* (*Chelus fimbriatus*), an archaic-looking turtle with a flattened out carapace and triangular head. *Jabuti* is the name for the yellow-footed tortoise (*Geochelone denticulata*).

Iguanas
Iguanas (*Iguana iguana*) can be seen in most environments, including the city. Seldom do we make a tour without seeing these harmless reptiles. The best viewing is from the top of a boat during high water season, when we can get at eye-level with them as they sunbathe in the branches of trees. Without much effort one can prod them to drop

into the water from the tops of very high trees. Iguanas can grow up to two meters (six feet) long and are considered good eating on the part of many rural people. They are primarily vegetarians. On the floodplain I have observed them feeding on mimosa blossoms. If you really want to see large numbers of iguanas, ask your tour guide to take you for a tour up the Jari River, a small stream passing the village of Arapixuna. When I conduct tours there, I normally begin at the mouth, on the Tapajós River, and then move north past Arapixuna into the Amazon River. During the low-water season this exit may be difficult, thereby requiring a return to Santarém via the Jari. You will not be sorry for having to repeat this routing. Aside from seeing many iguanas, bird watching is excellent.

Termites

It is impossible to find an area in the Amazon not infested with termites. Rapid decomposition of vegetable matter is one of the secrets of the closed eco-system and termites play a very important role in this process. Many different species of termites exist, some constructing their nests up in the trees, others living underground. My favorite termite nest was one located just a few meters off the main trail at Bosque Santa Lúcia. It must have been at least three meters tall and was the result of an invasion of termites on a tree that had been broken in half by the wind. As the nest grew to gigantic proportions, it became the host to a number of critters, including bees, wasps, spiders, snakes and other *bichinhos*. The termite nest was the most photographed object on the property. But it took only a couple of years for the termites to get down to the "heart" of the matter and the whole nest fell over on the ground. Many termite nests exist around the Bosque, but I have fond memories of that one.

I would rather forget other termite encounters. When I first arrived in Santarém, I rented a neat little house on Avenida Rui Barbosa, where, in my second year of residency, a termite colony moved in with me. One day my landlord showed up and nearly had a heart attack when she discovered termite tunnels leading up from the backyard to the rafters of her house. So from that time on I have been more cautious about such intrusions, especially after building our own house here on Travessa Turiano Meira. But termites are the epitome of persistence and, besides, they are devious little creatures. Only a few months ago I was rummaging through a cabinet here in my office to find that they had secretly devoured my collection of childhood books, many of which dated back to the early 1940s. On first observation it appeared that the volumes were intact because the hardback covers were in near perfect condition. One after another, I opened the first-edition copies of *The Lone Ranger, Hardy Boys* and other series to discover that the termites were eating up the last bits of paper. Literally, there was nothing left except for the covers. It is no wonder archeologists find so little left of earlier indigenous civilizations in the Amazon.

One of my favorite guides in Manaus, a young man affectionately called Mocinho (Little Boy), reminds us that termites also have some very immediate benefits for man. For instance, it is quite common for farmers to remove termite nests from trees for poultry fodder. The nesting material can, in turn, be burned in the early evening to smoke mosquitoes away from homes or simply be added to potted plants as a fertilizer.

Ants
Like termites, ants are everywhere in the Amazon. In my opinion, fire ants are the most difficult to deal with because they like to take up residence around humans. They are tiny, but make up the difference in numbers and aggressiveness. I have read of entire villages having to move to get away from them. Army ants are the most interesting because of their carnivorous and nomadic ways. One of my most exciting finds at Bosque Santa Lúcia was a colony of army ants bivouacking under the roof of our roundhouse. It is normal for them to find temporary housing for the night, but this particular stop lasted for several days while the queen laid her eggs. Curious as to what was happening inside the ball of ants (they actually maintain the rigidity of the sphere by grasping on to one anther), I inserted a machete into it one day. To my surprise, eggs poured out of the live nest as though it were a container of milk. Within a few hours the

ants picked up all the displaced eggs and returned them to the nest. Just to end the story, I was back at the roundhouse a few days later to find the ants gone. The only sign of the rendezvous was a pile of what appeared to be empty rice hulls on the floor—the leftover eggshells.

Snakes

You will probably get through your entire journey in the Amazon without seeing a snake. That seems to be an average for most tours. I have known herpetologists to come to the Santarém in search of emerald tree boas (*Boa canina*), as though they could be plucked off trees in a single outing. Most leave empty-handed, unless they make prior arrangements with a local person to "keep your eyes open for such and such a snake. I'll be back next year." Given the essential ingredients of patience, persistence and reward, all is possible. But, coming back to that jungle hike you are planning; do not let your guard down. Many venomous snakes are around and you may encounter one when you least expect it. The most common one in the Amazon is a pit viper called fer-de-lance (*Bothrops asper*) or jararaca. You may hear the word "jararaca" quite often as you mix with Brazilians because it is a nickname to describe a person who is madder than a nest of hornets, a person who flies off the handle, a person who verbally or physically attacks others and so on. These are all personal attributes for a snake. More than sixty percent of venomous snakebites in Brazil are attributed to the jararaca.

Another venomous snake, considered to be the largest pit viper in the world, is the bushmaster (*Lachesis mutus*), or surucucu. It can grow up to four meters long and is the terror of forest—especially at night. Raimundo Teixeira, mentioned earlier as the caretaker at Bosque Santa Lúcia, still turns white when he tells the story of encountering a mature surucucu early one morning as he collected Brazil nut pods. He had just bent over to pick up one of the large, heavy pods when he found himself looking into the eyes of the snake only a few feet away. Teixeira back-stepped very slowly, rushed home to get his shotgun, but the snake was gone when he returned. The bushmaster is for the most part a nocturnal snake, feeding on small forest mammals, such as forest rats and paca. Many stories are told about how bushmasters stalk man at night and how they are attracted to fire or light. Teixeira tells of being attacked by a bushmaster one night while walking home from the main road. He threw his flashlight at the serpent and while running ahead, looked back to see the snake rolling in the road with the discarded torch. Bushmasters are also said to be attracted by campfires and have been observed attacking red-hot embers. Local hunters tell me that they carry two flashlights, one for the bushmasters and another for getting away from them as fast as possible.

There are also a number of coral snakes around, including false corals. In all my tromping around the woods of this area, I have seen only two coral snakes. The first sighting was but a mere glimpse as it crossed the trail in front of me. The second snake I discovered only a few feet from me on a trail at Bosque Santa Lúcia. It was coiled up ready for action. After calmly waiting for a few minutes, it moved into the forest. In fact, I have no idea whether these snakes were true or false corals, but the colors were impressive.

Taking the time to rummage through boxes of amulets at market places, you may encounter the rattlers from *Crotalus durissus*. William Magnusson, internationally distinguished reptilian researcher at INPA (National Institute for Amazonia Research) in Manaus, tells me that rattlesnakes are more common to the tropical savanna (cerrado), such as Alter do Chão, where he conducted studies back in 1979, the year I arrived in Santarém. When climbing Serra de Alter do Chão (more commonly referred to as Serra Piroca), the volcanic-looking hill on the outskirts of town, one would often encounter a slim young man (wearing not much more than an old pair of shorts) meandering through the bushes and looking into rock piles. That person was no other than our Australian friend, William Magnusson. He was not looking for the lost city of El Dorado. He was looking for snakes!

Among the many non-venomous snakes, the ones most frequently seen are the tree-climbing varieties, the ones that eat bird eggs and chicks. Some are called *papa-ovo* (egg eaters). I use the term "tree climbing" lightly because in reality they are real trapeze artists. Once I saw three aracaris (toucan family) fighting off a *papa-ovo* snake high up in the tree and I was impressed with the agility of the nearly two-meter-long snake. It moved incredibly fast from branch to branch, at times standing on its tail to defend itself from the powerful beaks of the araçaris. Then, too, I remember seeing another *papa-ovo* pretending to be an *escada de jabuti* vine (a flattened-out, ribbon-looking vine of the genus *Bauinha)*. Someone in our group called it to the attention of our local guides. It was mimicry at its best and even the guides were a bit puzzled by the caricature of the *cobra.* I overheard one guide say to another, "I think this snake is sick." As he prodded it with a stick, the snake suddenly came back to his normal shape, quickly fell to the ground and nearly escaped before the guides caught it. On that same jungle hike (on Rio Negro) a person in front of me spotted a young fer-de-lance, in the middle of the trail. It was coiled up and ready for action. The remarkable part of the tale is that at least ten people had just walked over the same spot.

Spiders

It is remarkable the number of persons, especially women, who jump off their tuffets when they encounter spiders. Tarantulas, some almost the size of dinner plates, are the ones that really get people out of the hammock fast. I joke because this actually happened one night at the roundhouse at Bosque Santa Lúcia. "Slim," our resident tarantula, was up to his usual tricks of catching his dinner at the top of the conical ceiling and made the blunder of lunging out too far in an attempt to seize an insect. He was very lucky, indeed, to have landed in Sebastião's hammock, rather than on the cement floor. Sebastião was also fortunate to have had the sides of the hammock pulled over him.

Tarantulas are found throughout Central and South America and even in the southern part of North America. Among many species, some live up high, like Slim, and others make their homes underground. When walking on the trails, you will see camouflaged holes in the ground, appearing much like those of trap-door spiders. Looking ahead, it is easy to observe tarantulas ducking into these holes as they sense your intrusion. By waiting quietly, you can see them return topside to their hunting position. On one occasion I was taken aback by a spider that made overtures in returning to its hole, but did not. It looked at the opening, looked back at me, approached the hole again, but backed off. "Strange behavior," I thought to myself. Moments later I was surprised to see a small, thin snake come up out of the chamber. The serpent took one glance at me and quickly returned to the spider's home. The spider finally decided that the snake was the lesser of its problems and joined its new roommate.

Tarantulas, despite their frightening appearance, are not a great threat to mankind. Personally, I only know of one individual, Manoel Alfonso Jimnez Garay, a professional photographer, who had a close encounter with one of our eight-legged friends. I should remark that the rendezvous, which took place in January of 1996, was an accidental occurrence rather than an act of aggression. Alfonso simply rolled over on it in the bed. Self-defense on the part of the tarantula, but Alfonso ended up with a nasty bite and a lot of skin allergies which required the care of a physician over some weeks. Alfonso also ended up taking a lot of harassment by friends, who suggested that he be more careful with whom he sleeps. I was meaning to ask him if he danced the tarantella following the incident, but politely forgot.

Caiman

People frequently ask me, "What is the difference between crocodiles, alligators and caimans?" Big teeth are big teeth, so it is no surprise that biologists classify all three in the order Crocodilia. The major difference between the crocodile and the alligator is that the former has a narrower snout and its fourth tooth on each side of the lower jaw protrudes outside the mouth when closed. Crocodiles are also reported to be much more aggressive than alligators and caiman. But true crocodiles are not found in the Amazon. Although true alligators exist on the northern edge of South America, they, too, are not found in the Amazon. We do have several species of caiman (caimans and alligators together form the family Alligatoridae), all of which are referred to as *jacaré* in Brazil. As for the caiman, the aforementioned teeth of the lower jaw fit into cavities in the upper jaw when closed. This peculiarity is easily seen on the two caiman skulls (one being a black caiman and the other a spectacled caiman) in my collection at Bosque Santa Lúcia.

You will undoubtedly see caiman on your trip to the Amazon. "Caiman flashing" is a popular activity for night tours at most eco-lodges, especially around Manaus. Local guides get the *jacaré's* attention by shining a bright light into its eyes and then snatching it out of the water by the back of its neck. Clearly, "family-size" specimens are not invited to participate in the fun. In identifying the toothy catch, your local guide will probably refer to it as either a *tinga* or an *açu*. *Tinga* is the spectacled caiman and *açu* refers to the black caiman. The animals are always returned to the water unharmed after the guide's demonstration.

Jaguars
The jaguar (*Panthera onca*) is not an endangered species, but it is difficult to see in the wild. It is, nonetheless, prevalent throughout the forests of the Amazon and is the one animal that locals fear more than any other, since it is said to stalk and attack human beings. Downed pilots have been known to survive plane crashes in the jungle, only to be eaten by jaguars. My forester friends at IBAMA, Rionaldo Almeida and Sebastião Santos da Silva, recommend that people do not walk alone in the Tapajós National Forest because the jaguar is much more prone to attack an individual than two or more persons together. Contrary to what you might think, jaguars are not confined to the untouched portions of the Amazon. Bosque Santa Lúcia is practically on the edge of Santarém, a city of more than 260,000 people, but up until recently someone has killed a jaguar in the immediate area almost every year. It is sad to report that since the

soybean farmers deforested most of the region, jaguars are no longer seen. In 1997, a friend told me that he spotted a very large *onça* on the road to Alter do Chão. I have never seen a live one, only skins drying out around the houses of hunters. On a stop at San Pablo das Amazonas, Peru, a few years ago we witnessed two young boys hauling in a very rotten-smelling, skinned-out jaguar carcass. It had been killed, not for a head trophy and throw rug, but for something much more basic—food.

Sharks

I never stop in Leticia, Colombia, without taking my visitors to a souvenir shop just around the corner from the Anaconda Hotel. It is a small shop with a big name: Alfonso Galindo—Casa Brasil—Uirapuru. Although some fine items can be purchased there, my main reason for promoting the store is the back room, where the owners maintain a private museum of odds and ends pertaining to the fauna of the Amazon. The first time I looked at the collection, my eyes immediately focused on several very large jawbones filled with big shark-like teeth. "My God!" said someone. "Look at the size of the piranhas they grow around here." As it turned out, we had just discovered that sharks also take vacations up the Amazon River. A few months later, Captain William Wheeler, from Dunedin, Florida, sent me a newspaper clipping reporting that a local fisherman had caught a seven-foot bull shark (*Carcharhinus leucas*) 1,860 miles up the Amazon. It was noted as a rather rare event, but local fishermen in Santarém tell me that these catches are not infrequent. As a matter of fact, the March 16, 1994, issue of the local newspaper, *Gazeta,* featured a photo of a two-meter-long *tubarão* that had been caught that week.

Bats

Bats are present everywhere in the Amazon in large numbers and species. As the sun begins to drop below the horizon, they come out of every hole and crevice imaginable. From personal observation, most of the urban bats are insectivores. When out on the river, you will see fishing bats, *Noctilio leporinus*. These are large light-colored bats that detect fish via their built-in radar systems. According to Emmons in her *Neotropical Rainforest Mammals*, the fishes are "gaffed" by the clawed feet of the bat and then transferred to the mouth for eating. Wherever there is a niche, there is a bat specialized for it. The fringe-lipped bat, *Trachops cirrhosus*, feeds mostly on frogs. How do they distinguish between the poisonous and non-poisonous frogs? Scientists say by their call. I wonder if anyone has ever researched mimicry of frog calls. If butterflies can fool their predators, why cannot frogs do the same? Another group, the vampire bats, *Desmodus* spp., feeds on the blood of mammals, mostly cattle. One more vampire is the hairy-legged vampire bat, *Diphylla ecaudata*. It feeds mainly on the blood of birds.[15]

Then there are diurnal or "day" bats. These little bats flutter silently around dim swamp areas after being aroused from their poorly-concealed sleeping quarters. Many other species of bats inhabit the Amazon if you care to research them.

You would think that bats love people, given their delight in sharing homes with us. The truth is that they like the dark protection of our roofs and attics, with or without us. When we built our house on Travessa Turiano Meira in 1983, the bats moved in before we did and it was not easy to evict them. As a matter of fact, we tried poison, smoke and a series of other measures over a period of two years to no avail. The only remedy was to seal off every single opening to the roof area with cement. I was worried about the smell of dying bats, but within a few days they gnawed a hole through the wooden boards of the ceiling, thus escaping entombment. Roof leaks and bat entrances seem to have something in common. They provoke the wrath of the women folk and they are very difficult to find. Just outside my office door, under a pitomba tree, I find other evidence of bats feasts almost every day—seeds and remains of fruit, like black olive, goiaba, açaí, castanhola, mango, etc. I always know what fruit is in season by looking under the tree that serves as their snack bar.

Sloths

The *preguiça*, which means *lazy*, is another mammal that most people see on their trip to the Amazon. Occasionally we see them slowly making their way across roads, but most of the time they are found up in the trees, where they divide their time between munching on leaves and taking frequent naps. In times past, giant ground-dwelling sloths, the size of bears, roamed the Amazon, but they became extinct shortly after *Homo sapiens'* arrival in South America. Speculation has it that they were easy prey for hunters.

Butterflies

Depending on the season and many other circumstances, you may see a bountiful array of *borboletas* during your stay in the Amazon. Everybody's favorite is the morpho, the iridescent-blue butterfly that has made it around the world, under glass and plastic. These plates and trays were the most sought after souvenir from Brazil for many decades. The morpho is actually not a single species, but a family (*Morphidae*) made up of about 80 species of large, flashy butterflies, some of which are blue. At Bosque Santa Lúcia, we see them bobbing up and down along the trail almost every sunny day. They are greatly attracted to tatajuba (*Bagassa guianensis*) fruit, which begins to ferment soon after falling on the ground. Someone commented that morphos are "lush" butterflies, slang for someone who drinks a lot.

Moths differ from butterflies in that they are mostly nocturnal. Their bodies are stout and they present duller colors. Their wings are smaller proportionately to their body and their antennae can be feathery. It has been my experience that the best place to see a variety of moths is on the decks of the cruise ships. It is amazing to see the number of them brought in at night by the bright lights of a ship. For those of us who like to get a good nights sleep, no problem. There are still many "grounded" moths around early in the morning.

Birds Commonly Seen in Santarém

Travelers may leave the Amazon disgruntled for not having seen a jaguar, but they will never abandon these parts without seeing and hearing many birds. One traveler from Philadelphia, Pennsylvania, added 102 new species to his life list on a 15-day tour of the region in July of 1997. On the same trip, I saw a new one myself, the black-backed water tyrant.

The following inventory is a partial listing of the more commonly seen birds in this region. In addition to English and local/national names, I have also given the scientific names for the visitors who do not speak English or Portuguese. This gives them a chance to study the birds in their own language. Local names of birds can be rather confusing at times, since they vary so much. When in doubt I have used nomenclature provided by Helmut Sick in *Ornitologia Brasileira*. The translation of Sick's book, *Birds in Brazil* is a must, if you have space in your luggage. If I had to recommend only one publication for light traveling, it would be John Dunning's *South American Birds: A Photographic Aid to Identification*. The photographs, plus the range maps, facilitate identification. For more details, I use Schauensee & Phelps' *Birds of Venezuela* or Hilty & Brown's *Birds of Colombia*. *The Birds of South America* (volumes I and II) by Robert Ridgely and Guy Tudor are also rather voluminous, but represent the most complete and update publications on the subject.

While mentioning names of books, let me advise my readers that publications of this nature are not easily found in the Amazon. Many visitors come with the "misguided" belief that technical books on the Amazon can be bought locally. As a matter of fact, they are not easily found even in North America and Europe, except on a special-order basis. I thank my former clients and friends for remembering me in this regard. My first acquisition, as a beginning birder, was *Birds of Venezuela*, which was given to me by William Overal, zoologist at the E. Goeldi Museum in Belém. For a person who had not one reference book, it was a gift from heaven. In the following years I have been very fortunate to receive numerous technical books, many of which were brought down personally by Robert Stein and his wife, Alice, on their many sojourns to the Amazon.

It would be negligent on my part not to refer to the foremost ornithologists in the Amazon, David Oren at the E. Goeldi Museum in Belém and Renato Cintra at the Institute for Amazonian Research (INPA) in Manaus.

Likewise, I mention Gil Serique as our foremost birder among local guides here in Santarém and, I dare say, one of the best in the Amazon. His availability for conducting local tours has been curtailed greatly over few years because of his involvement in ornithological research in Brazil and Peru, via Bio-Brazil Foundation.

The following is a list of the more commonly seen birds of Santarém and the region. You do not have to be a birder to appreciate the best of wildlife in this part of the world. Have fun.

- ❏ **Black vulture**: You will not have to go very far to see black vultures, as they are everywhere in the city. Visitors from other parts of the world tell me they have never seen so many as in Santarém. Keen eyesight is the vultures' greatest asset in finding a great variety of foods, including our garbage. *"Urubu Comum"* (local name). *Coragyps atratus* (scientific name).

- ❏ **Turkey vulture**: Considerably fewer individuals than our friends above, but quite noticeable because of larger wingspan, red head and great ability to glide. Turkey vultures rely on their sense of smell more than eyesight. *"Urubu-de-cabeça-vermelho"* (*Cathartes aura*).

- ❏ **Yellow-headed caracara**: Very common on the city waterfront. Kite-shaped with white wing-bars, which are especially conspicuous when in flight. A "jack-of-all trades" in terms of diet. *"Carrapateiro* or *caracará* or *caracaraí"* (*Milvago Chimachima*).

123

- *Neotropical cormorant*: Looks a lot like a loon. The bird takes a while to get airborne and flies low. *"Biguá* or *Mergulhão"* (*Phalacrocorax olivaceu*).

- *Large-billed tern*: Appearance of a small gull, but in flight, has long pointed wings. Rather raucous, especially when they are in large numbers. *"Gaivota"* (*Phaetusa simplex*).

- *Yellow-billed tern*: A smaller version of the above with a distinctive yellow beak. *"Trinta-réis"* or *"anão"* or *"gaivota"* (*Sterna superciliaris*).

- *Great egret*: Unmistakable. Large, all elegantly white stork-like bird that flies with its neck curved. Some urbanites leave the city in the early morning and return late afternoon in loose-knit flocks. See their rookery just two blocks west of Banco do Brasil on Rui Barbosa Avenue. *"Garça branca"* (*Casmerodius abbus*).

- *Black skimmer*: These are best seen at nightfall under the lights of the Mascotinho Restaurant. Normally in pairs or in small numbers. Fantastic ability to fly at water-level with lower bill skimming the surface. *"Corta-água"* or *"Talha-mar"* (*Rynchops niger*).

- *Roadside hawk*: Not too common in the city, but may be seen from time to time on the road to the airport. They normally alight on an open branch, from which they soar off to catch a lizard or other prey. *"Gavião-indaié"* or *"Gavião pega pinto"* (*Buteo magnirostris*).

- *Smooth-billed ani*: Large black birds with a long tail and high-ridged beak. Often half a dozen or more aggregate together. *"Anú-preto"* or *"Anú-pequena"* (*Crotopphaga ani*).

- *Great kiskadee*: The best-known member of the flycatcher family. Yellow breast with a white band around a black head. Its call, "Kiss-Ka-Dee," is unmistakable. *"Bem-te-vi"* (*Pitangus sulphuratus*).

❑ ***Tropical kingbird***: Also a member of the flycatcher family. Many local people refer to it as a kiskadee. It has a yellow breast with a gray head, rather than the black and white of a kiskadee. *"Siriri"* (*Tyrannus melancholicus*).

❑ ***Fork-tailed flycatcher***: This long-tailed beauty can best be seen at the end of the day. Often in large numbers, they always provide spectacular aerial shows, as they dine on dragonflies and other high-flying insects. *"Tesoura"* (*Muscivora tyrannus*).

❑ ***Spotted tody flycatcher***: Very common in the city, but do not expect to see it without some effort. Very small in size, but it compensates with a call that resembles machine gun fire. *"Ferreirinho-estriado"* (*Todirostrum maculatum*).

❑ ***Blue-gray tanager***: The most common tanager in town. If you thought you saw a streak of blue zipping between trees, you just saw a blue-gray tanager. Some people call them "violinists," referring to the "see-saw" calls. *"Sanhaço-da-Amazônia"* or *"Pipira azul"* (*Thraupis episcopus*).

❑ ***Burnished-buff tanager***: Not easy to see, but keep an eye open around goiaba and papaya trees when in fruit. Multi-colored black, blue and golden with a distinctly rufous crown. *"Saíra-amarela"* (*Tangara cayana*).

❑ ***Palm tanager***: The same size as the blue-gray tanager, but pale-green in color. As the name implies, they are often found on palm leaves. *"Sanhaço-do-coqueiro"* (*Thraupis palmarum*).

❑ ***Silver-beaked tanager***: As with other tanagers, look for them around fruit trees. The mature male is reddish-black (from a distance, he appears to be all black) with a very flashy silvery-white lower beak. Listen for the distinguishable "click, click" sounds as they make 90-degree turns in the vegetation. *"Pipira-vermelho/Bico-de-prata"* (*Ramphocelus carbo*).

❑ *Bananaquit*: Some folks refer to them as "baby kiskadees," which, of course, they are not. Common around fruit-producing trees. *"Saí"* or *"Tem-tem-coronado"* (*Coereba flaveola*).

❑ *House wren*: A small bird with an up-turned tail. Likes to hang out and nest around our homes. Melodic songs all day long. *"Garricha"* (*Trolodytes aedon*).

❑ *Common ground dove*: Common throughout the city. More often than not, seen on the ground. *"Rolinha-taruéi"* (*Columbina passerina*).

❑ *Ruddy-ground dove*: Reddish in color, except for the gray head. *"Rolinha-caldo-de-feijão"* (*Columbina talpacoti*).

❑ *Canary-winged parakeet*: You cannot miss them when mangos ripen. A very large parakeet with a distinct patch of yellow on the wings. Very noisy. *"Maracanã"* (*Brotogeris versicolurus*).

❑ *Rough-winged swallow*: Very large swallow with a cinnamon-colored throat. Look for them on the electrical lines. *"Androrinha-asa-de-serra"* (*Stelgidopteryx ruficollis*).

❑ *Black-throated mango*: A metallic-green hummingbird often seen feeding from yard flowers, especially the red ones. *"Beija-flor-preto"* (*Anthracothorax nigricollis*).

❑ *Barn owl*: A large, whitish-owl that can be seen and heard at night throughout the city. Locals call it "rip the cloth," referring to the strange sound it produces. *"Rasga pano"* (*Tyto alba*).

I am sure you would never imagine finding an egret rookery in the busiest and nosiest part of downtown Santarém, but it exists. At approximately 5 PM, the trees around 1331 Avenida Rui Barbosa fill up with hundreds of egrets and herons. Early in the morning, you can see them flying out to their feeding grounds on the Amazon floodplain. This oddity came about when Sr. Armando Corrêa, a retired Banco do Brasil employee, and his wife adopted a pair of egrets some years ago. This first pair came to reproduce and to bring friends home from the Amazon River. A few days ago, I was passing in front of the city in a riverboat and noted, even from that distance, that Armando's trees were chock-full of egrets in early afternoon. Sabá, our cook, reminded me that we were looking at young birds still dependent on their parents and Mr. Armando for food.

In the meantime, back on the floodplains, relatives of our city-slicker friends gather for the night at rookeries, *pousadas das garças*. On tours to Maicá we observe thousands of egrets gathering for the night. Waves of white come in from all directions. Rookeries can be quite distant, but with binoculars we can see the birds roosting on trees at the edge of gigantic lakes formed by rising waters. Once on a tour, we were getting ready to return to Santarém when a large flock of golden-winged parakeets flew over us, veered off to one side and came in for a landing in the very jauari palm to which our boat was tied. The reflection of the setting sun on the underside of their wings left no doubt as to why they are called "golden-winged."

Other Birds Commonly Seen Along the Amazon River

❑ *Yellow-rumped cacique*: Black with yellow wing patches and a yellow rump. One of the more common birds throughout the Amazon. They build a colony of woven nests, often hanging around wasp nests or in a village setting, helping to reduce snake predation. "*Japim*" or "*Xexéu*" (*Cacicus cela*)

- *White-necked heron*: The largest of the herons (much larger than the great egret). Resembles the great blue heron (which does not inhabit the Amazon). The farther you get away from the city, the better your chances of seeing it. *"Socó-grande"* (*Ardea cocoi*)

- *Rufescent tiger heron*: Feathers of the immature give the appearance of a spotted leopard skin. Mature tiger herons are chestnut color with a white stripe down the breast. *"Socó-boi"* (*Tigrisoma lineatus*).

- *Little blue heron*: Small, slim and, as the name implies, slate blue. *"Garça-azul"* (*Egretta caerulea*).

- *Capped heron*: Sightings of this heron are not too common near Santarém. It is rare to see more than one at a time. Facial skin and bill blue. *"Garça-real"* (*Pilherodius pileatus*)

- *Horned screamer*: Most visible when they perch up in the very top of trees. They look like large Christmas tree decorations. Large rounded body with a horn-like quill on top of head. Hooting sounds. *"Cametaú"* (*Anhima cornuta*).

- *Snowy egret*: About the size of a cattle egret with a black bill and yellow feet. *"Graça-branca-pequena"* (*Egretta thula*).

- *Green ibis*: Long, curved bill. Shiny metallic-blue when in the sun. *"Corocoró"* (*Mesembrinibis cayennensis*).

- *Limpkin*: Looks a bit like the green ibis, but has a straight bill. *"Carão"* or *"Caricaca"* (*Aramus guarauna*).

- *Sun bittern*: Medium-sized, black head and white eyebrow with radiating circle pattern on the open wings. *"Pavãozinho-do-Pará"* (*Eurypga helias*).

- **Purple gallinule**: Metallic-green on the back with blue underneath the belly. Red beak with a yellow tip. *"Frango-d'àgua-azul" (Porphyrula martinica)*.

- **Wattled jacana**: You will see plenty of these long-legged, long-toed, noisy water birds. They are light enough to land on a floating blade of grass. *"Piaçoca"* or *"jaçanã"* (*Jacana jacana*).

- **Southern lapwing**: These birds are gray-black with reddish eyes and make a resounding call that sounds like "tell, tell." Often form very noisy flocks. *"Quero-quero"* or *"Téu-téu"* (*Vanellus chilensis*).

- **Gray-necked wood-rail**: Difficult to see, but easily heard, especially in the early morning and at dusk. Very blaring calls resembling "three pots, three pots" in a long sequence. *"Três-potes"* or *"saracura"* (*Aramides cajanea*).

- **Spotted sandpiper**: Diagnostic teeter-totter movements of a small, long-beaked, shore bird. *"Maçarico-pintado"* (*Actitis macularia*).

- **Anhinga**: Tall, buff-gray bird with long, pointed bill. Referred to as "snake bird" because of similarity when head, bill and neck are undulating out of water. *"Carará"* (*Anhinga anhinga*).

- **Muscovy**: Largest of all the ducks. Black with large, white wing patches. Domestic and wild. *"Pato-do-mato"* or *"Pato bravo"* (*Cairina moschata*).

- **Black-bellied whistling duck**: Pink bill, gray neck and white band on the wings. A black rump and belly. Often seen in large numbers. *"Asa-branca"* or *"marreca cabocla"* (*Dendrocygna auumnalis*).

❑ **Brazilian duck**: Also seen in large numbers. Brown with a pink bill. Black on the rump and tail. A white speculum. *"Ananaí"* (*Amazonetta brasiliensis*).

❑ **Snail kite**: Characterized by a highly hooked bill, plus a white rump and base of tail. Specialized diet of apple snails. *"Caramujeiro"* (*Rostrhamus sociablis*).

❑ **Great black-hawk**: Large bird with a yellow bill. Yellow legs and feet. The short tail is tipped white. *"Gavião-preto"* (*Buteogallus urubitinga*).

❑ **Black-collared hawk**: Striking bird seen frequently throughout the Amazon. Whitish head. Rusty-red above and below with a black streak across upper breast. *"Gavião-belo"* (*Busarellus nigricollis*).

❑ **Crested caracara**: Larger than the yellow-headed caracara with more color. Black crown. Red face. White rump. Ruffled crest and white wing tips. *"Caracará"* (*Polyborus plancus*).

❑ **Black caracara**: Black bird with bright orange facial skin. *"Gavião-de-anta"* (*Daptrius ater*).

❑ **Bat falcon**: Small bird with a very distinct white collar on a black background. *"Cauré"* or *"coleirinha"* (*Falco rufigularis*).

❑ **Pale-vented pigeon**: Large pigeon. Purplish brown. *"Pomba-galega"* (*Columba cayennensis*).

❑ **Chestnut-fronted macaw**: A small macaw with dingy red on underside of wings. Often seen in large numbers. *"Maracanã-guaçu"* (*Ara severa*).

❑ **Canary-winged parakeet**: The most common parakeet. It is large and green except for a yellow patch on wing coverts. These noisy birds often aggregate in large numbers. *"Periquito-de-asa-branca"* (*Brotogeris versicolurus*).

- **Mealy parrot**: The largest of all the parrots. Green with large eye-rings. *"Papagaio-moleiro"* or *"ajurú açu"* (*Amazona farinosa*).

- **Festive parrot**: Beautiful green parrot with a dark red forehead and distinct red rump. *"Papagaio-cacau"* (*Amazona festiva*).

- **Orange-winged parrot**: Green parrot with yellow cheeks and crown. Red speculum. *"Curica"* (*Amazona amazonica*).

- **Blue-winged parrotlet**: Only 11 cm long. All green except for blue rump and wing coverts. *"Periquito-santo"* (*Forpus conspicillatus*).

- **Greater ani**: Much larger than the smooth-billed ani. Metallic blue-black with white iris. Normally seen in flocks of a dozen or so. *"Anu-coroca"* (*Crotophaga major*).

- **Squirrel cuckoo**: The same size as the greater ani with black tail, but with white spots. Rufous back. Much more secretive than greater ani. *"Alma-de-gato"* (*Piaya cayana*).

- **White-winged swallow**: Frequent sightings over the waterways. Large white patch on each wing. White underside. *"Andorinho-do-rio"* (*Tachycineta albiventer*).

- **Ringed kingfisher**: Largest of the kingfishers. White collar. Breast and belly are chestnut. *"Martin-pescador-grande"* or *"ariramba"* (*Ceryle torquata*).

- **Amazon kingfisher**: Green back. White collar. Rufous breast. Female without chestnut breast. White breast and belly. *"Ariramba-verde"* (*Chloroceryle amazona*).

131

- *Green kingfisher*: Only 18 cm long. Green above with white spots on the wings. Breast chestnut in male. White belly. Female has two green bands across breast. *"Martim-pescador-pequeno"* or *"ariramba pequena"* (*Chloroceryle americana*).

- *Channel-billed toucan*: Black bill with red band across yellow throat. Red rump. *"Tucano-de-bico-preto"* or *"tucano de peito amarelo"* (*Ramphastos vitellinus*).

- *Crimson-crested woodpecker*: One of the large redheaded woodpeckers. White stripes join on back. *"Pica-pau-de-topete-vermelho"* (*Campephilus melanoleucos*).

- *Lineated woodpecker*: Large. White stripes do not join on back. *"Pica-pau-de-banda-branca"* (*Dryocopus lineatus*).

- *Wood creepers*: Many species inhabit the region and most are difficult to identify. Brown. As the name implies, they "creep" up the sides of trees looking for insects. They pry into the bark and crevices, as opposed to drilling like woodpeckers. *"Arapaçu."*

- *Pale-legged hornero*: Look for mud nests. Brown with conspicuous over-eye white stripe and rufous head. Melodic calls. *"João-de-barro"* or *"pedreiro"* (*Furnarius leucopus*).

- *Streaked flycatcher*: 20 cm long with tricolor streaked dark-brown on white. Heavy brown streak from bill through eye area. *"Bem-te-vi-rajado"* (*Myiodynastes maculatus*).

- *White-headed marsh-tyrant*: All black except for a white head and upper throat area. Strikingly beautiful. *"Lavadeira-de-cabeça-branca"* (*Arundinicola leucocephala*).

- *Black-capped mocking-thrush*: Black above. Yellow belly. Yellow eyes. Melodic calls. "*Casaca-de-couro*" (*Donacobius atricapillus*).

- *Crested oropendola*: Black with an ivory bill and yellow tail feathers. Look for long sock-like hanging nests much longer than the yellow-rumped cacique nest. "*Japu*" (*Psarocolius decumanus*).

- *Red-breasted blackbird*: Black with red throat and breast. Females are drab brown. Often seen in large flocks. "*Polícia-inglesa*" or "*rouxinol do campo*" (*Leistes militaris*).

- *Oriole blackbird*: Black back and wings. Black around eyes. Remainder a flashy yellow/orange. "*Irataúa-grande*" or "*tordo maicero*" (*Gymnomystax mexicanus*).

- *Red-capped cardinal*: Red head. Black wings tail and back. White breast and belly. "*Tangará*" (*Paroaria gularis*).

- *Saffron yellow finch*: Small. Yellow with some orange on crown. Normally several together. "*Canário-da-terra*" (*Sicalis flaveola*).

- *Variable seedeater*: Black crown and back. White throat and belly with black band across breast. Found around grassy areas. "*Coleira-do-norte*" (*Sporophila americana*).

- *Lined seedeater*: Black above with white line on crown. White below. Large malar stripes, thus the name *bigodinho*, which means "Little Mustache." "*Bigodinho*" (*Sporophila-lineola*).

Vultures

Travelers remark that the animal they see most often in the Amazon is the vulture. There must be several thousand of them in Santarém alone, surely indicative of an abundance of food. The black vulture, the most common species, is the smallest of the four in this region. Turkey vultures are noted for their red heads and longer wingspans.

Both are common in the city, as well as in the rural areas. The yellow-headed vulture is found mostly in the forest while the king vulture is rare and normally limited to uninhabited regions. *Urubu*, the Tupi-Guarani word for vulture, means "the bird with a big appetite." We can safely say that vultures were as common in the pre-Colombian era as they are now, since they are well represented on *Tapajônica* ceramics.

João Alberto, our local veterinarian, tells the indigenous legend of the vulture and the tortoise. It goes something like this: "Our Lady in Heaven resolved to throw a big party up in the sky and invited representatives from the animal kingdom, including the vulture and the tortoise. Knowing that it would take him forever to get to heaven on his own, the tortoise asked the vulture for a ride. 'Of course,' said the vulture and off they went. The tortoise should have known better because the vulture was well known as a malicious character. As they approached the gates of heaven, the vulture said, 'So long, sucker,' and let his friend fall back to earth, where he broke into many pieces. Little did the vulture know that Our Lady in Heaven saw this act of violence. She immediately descended to earth, where she carefully put the tortoise back together. You may see the results of her benevolent deed when you look at the carapace of a tortoise today. As for the vulture, she punished him by taking away his voice and making him as despicable as possible."

By the way, if you ever decide to eat vulture, here is a recipe, as given to me by Luiz Manoel Pedroso. "Put the slaughtered bird in a pressure cooker and cook the heck out of it for at least two hours. Open the pressure cooker; add onions, salt, pepper, tomatoes and a number-ten nail. Put the pressure cooker back on the fire. When the nail is soft, the meat is ready."

Tales of the River — Legend of the Boto
The most popular legend of the Amazon, without doubt, is the one of the *boto*, or river dolphin. In a personalized version, it goes something like this: The boto loves a party, and there is always one

going on among the numerous communities scattered along the river ways. As the festival gets warmed up, with the usual loud music and heavy shuffling of feet, the *boto* comes out of the water and transforms himself into a charming man in a white shirt, white pants and white shoes and even a white hat to cover his blowhole. He is very fast on the dance floor and also gifted for winning over the young ladies during the course of the night. Just before the sun comes up, the *boto* returns to his everyday life as a dolphin, and the young maiden returns home. Nine months later, the girl's parents want to know who the father of the newborn is, and more often than not the reply is, "It's the *boto*."

The sexual attributes of dolphins are widely admired by people of the Amazon and it is, therefore, not surprising that organs of the animal are used as amulets. Looking at a person you would like to befriend through the dried eyeball of a dolphin is but one of many beliefs associated with this friendly mammal. Penis bones and vaginas of dolphins are also to be found among the many amulets being sold at market places around the Amazon.

The Legendary Muiraquitã
"Steven, you should include something about *muiraquitãs* in your book," suggested S. Thanarajasingam, Malaysian ambassador to Brazil. It was June of 1999, and we were on a riverboat traveling upstream to Alter do Chão on the Tapajós River. The trip was part of an official two-day itinerary for the ambassador and his wife, Sara, on their first visit to Santarém. Alexandre Wanghon, Acting Mayor, and Hélcio Amaral, Secretary of Culture, were representing the local government and I had been invited along to help with translation. I may have inadvertently broken bureaucratic protocol the day before by giving the ambassador a draft copy of *Santarém—Riverboat Town*, but I thought he would enjoy reading something in English. That turned out to be the case because he had read the entire book before we began the boat trip—and to my astonishment, remembered details of the content.

135

Ambassador Thanarajasingam had good reason to mention the famed amulets of the Amazon because he had seen them on our visit to the Museu João Fona in the city and Hélcio had shown-off his own private collection on this trip. There may or may not be an authoritative version of the *muiraquitã* legend. I have certainly heard many variations over the years. The most common is associated with the Amazonas, the women warriors described by Francisco Orellana on his historic trip down the Amazon River in 1542. The story goes that they maintained a nation far removed from men folk but came together now and then for procreation. It was on these occasions that the women dived into a mountain lake to bring up *muiraquitãs*, a stone usually carved in the image of a frog. These were presented to the men, who wore them around their necks or foreheads in the form of a medallion. As Hélcio pointed out to the ambassador, frogs rightfully symbolize fertility since they are prolific egg-layers.

The most prized *muiraquitãs*, worth small fortunes nowadays, are those made of jade, a stone not naturally found in the Amazon. A number of other minerals were also utilized for crafting the amulets, and motifs were not limited to the renowned frog. Both zoomorphic and anthropomorphic motifs are found in public and private collections. One of the amulets owned by Hélcio is in the form of an embryo, which is a very rare find. He purchased it more than 30 years ago in a village along the Nhamundá River—in the same general area where Orellana reported seeing one-breasted women warriors, to whom he gave the name "Amazonas." Hélcio tells me that when he purchased the *muiraquitã*, it was already distinguished as a rare motif since the price he paid was equivalent to several heads of cattle. Along with some ceramics from the Museu João Fona, this piece went on national display in 2000, as part of Brazil's five-hundredth anniversary.

Legend of the Owl

Soon after my first son, Steven David, was born in 1981, I began to hear remarks from people referring to me as *pai corujo*, or "father owl." In 1984, Arthur Daniel was born and again I heard the same references. In the rush of life, I kept forgetting to ask Áurea what these comments meant. I was beginning to think it had something to do with my age, since I was getting off to a late start in raising a family. One day while talking about a spectacled owl I had seen on a Napo River island in Peru, Áurea told me the legend of the "*corujo.*" It goes something like this: Mother owl was greatly concerned over the safety of her newly born chicks because of a certain Mr. Hawk, who had the reputation of raiding nests to devour young birds. She decided to plead with the hawk personally, asking him not to eat her brood. "But how am I to know which chicks are yours?" asked Mr. Hawk. "Well, that's very easy," replied Mother Owl, "Mine are the most beautiful in the world." One day she returned to the nest to find that her offspring had been inadvertently eaten by the hawk, which never suspected that they belonged to the owl. The moral of the story is that parents are always convinced that their children are the greatest. I have never seen young owls, but I am told they are quite ugly. The hawk must have thought so, too. As for myself, I guess I lucked out because my two boys are indeed the finest.

Fly-Fishing Heron
Keeping a perfectly straight face, one of our guides in Peru told us that the striated heron (*Butorides striatus*) is considered to be a very intelligent bird for having learned to catch mosquitoes. "But why mosquitoes?" someone shouted out. "Don't herons eat fish, snakes, lizards and things like that?" "Exactly," responded the guide with a smile. "But this heron catches a mosquito and very carefully places it on top of the water. When the fish comes up to eat the mosquito, the bird nabs it."

Animal Intelligence
Speaking of intelligence, a couple, representing the Rotary Club International at Fundação Esperança, in January 1997, asked me a very difficult question one day as we bounced over the road to Belterra. "What's the most intelligent animal in the world?" asked Susan. Upholding the honor of all guides in the past, present and future, I fired back a reply based on local superstition involving the yellow-rumped cacique, originally told to me by my veterinarian

137

friend, João Alberto. As all birders know, the yellow-rumped cacique is considered to be one sharp "cookie," avoiding predators by building its woven nest next to a wasp nest or next to someone's home. They are also known for their ability to imitate human voices. Because of an anomaly of the tongue, they are not capable of pronouncing specific words like their distant cousin, the parrot, but they can mimic sounds in general. João tells me that when he was a kid growing up in the rural area of Juriti, a village west of Santarém, he hunted this bird, not for the meat, but for the brain. The transfer of intelligence was directly from the bird to the hunter. I suspect that João was spinning a tale for my benefit, but I would like to believe the story, since he is one of the brightest persons I have ever known. "Well, at least, I've come up with an interesting story in response to Susan's question," I said to myself. "Wrong," replied the inquisitor to my very long-winded, complicated answer. "It's not a bird, it's a frog." "Holy smoke," I thought, "it's a frog?" "I consider the frog the most intelligent of the animal kingdom," she went on to say, "because the last time I visited the Library of Congress in Washington, D.C., I discovered, by chance, that a frog that had taken up residence there. To my surprise, every time I pulled a volume from the bookshelf the frog croaked, 'I read it, I read it, I read it, I read it.' That's how I came to the conclusion that the frog is the most intelligent of all."

Botanists and other scientists agree that the Amazon contains the most diverse vegetation on the planet, so diverse, complex and immense that many species are yet to be discovered. In this myriad of green, it is rare that one encounters a person knowledgeable enough to identify even a fraction of the existing trees and plants. To illustrate the extent of biodiversity, nearly 200 different species of trees have been initially identified and perhaps that number will double when the survey is complete at Bosque Santa Lúcia, an area of only 270 acres.

Luiz Manoel Pedroso, retired forestry engineer at the Superintendência do Desenvolvimento da Amazônia (SUDAM), tells me that within this diverse environment making up the Amazon region more than 5,000 species of trees have been identified. Each possesses its own set of characteristics, such as:

Building Materials
Species called *Madeira de lei* (tree species originally set aside for the Portuguese throne because of its exceptional qualities for boat building, furniture making and construction). Some examples are cedar (*Cedrela odorata*), mahogany (*Swietenia macrophylla*) and *maçaranduba* (*Manilkara huberi*).

Latex-bearing
Rubber trees (*Hevea brasiliensis*), sorva (*Couma macrocarpa*) and *balata* (*Manilkara bidentada*).

Oil-bearing
Babaçu (*Orbignya martiana*), *patauá*, *bacaba*, *bacainha* (*Oenocarpus, sp*), *buriti* (*Mauritia flexuosa*), *mirriti* (*Bactriy*), *ucuuba* (*Virola*) and *andiroba* (*Carapa guianensis*).

Aromatic
Rose wood (*Aniba canelilla*), *camuru grande* (*Dipteryx odorata*) and *pau cravo* (*Dicypellium*).

Medicinal
Guaraná (*Paullinia cupana*), copaíba (*Copaifera, sp*), andiroba (*Carapa guianensis*) and *pedra-ume-caá* (*Myrcia sphaerocarpa*).

Travelers regularly encounter logging trucks on the road and rightfully ask which trees are cut for lumber. Out of the more than 5,000 species, only a few are used commercially. Some of the more common are:

- Angelim pedra (*Dinizia excelsa*)
- Angelim Vermelho (*Dinizia excelsa*)
- Cedar (*Cedrela odorata*)
- Cumuru (*Dipterix odorata*)
- Freijó (*Cordia goeldiana*)
- Itaúba (*Mezilaurus itauba*)
- Jatobá (*Hymenaea courbaril*)
- Maçaranduba (*Manilkara huberi*)
- Mahogany (*Swietenia macrophylla*)
- Muiracatiara (*Astronium lecointei*)
- Pau Amerela (*Euxylophora paraensis*)
- Pau d'arco or Ipê (*Tabebuia serratifolia*)
- Quaruba (*Vochysia spp.*)
- Tauari (*Couratari spp.*)
- Virola (*Virola spp.*)

Why are so few varieties used commercially? Surely, out of more than 5,000 species, there must be many more trees suitable for lumber. Obviously so, but the aforementioned ones have been used traditionally and are, thus, the most sought-after type of lumber. Furthermore, there is still a vast quantity of these trees in the Amazon forests. I hear sawmill owners predict that timber such as mahogany and cedar will become quite rare within the next five years. But then

I hear other people say that this "end of the world" story has been around for the last few decades. Nevertheless, everyone agrees that, at some point, there will be a dwindling supply of premium woods in the world. Then, for sure, we will see commercial use of many currently unused species. An English buyer recently told me that some ship builders in Europe are now replacing Asian teak (*Tectona grandis*) with *tatajuba* (*Bagassa guianensis*), a very common tree in the Amazon. Likewise *Ceiba pentandra* of the Bombacaceae family is now in demand. A giant among the trees of South and Central America, it was never considered to be of commercial value until a few decades ago, when it was found to be excellent for chipboard and plywood. It is now common to see barges equipped with derricks and heavy-duty logging equipment traveling on all the waterways of the Amazon, especially Peru, in pursuit of the huge trees considered to be sacred by the Incas. The next time we buy a sheet of Peruvian-produced plywood, we should make note of the hundreds and thousands of plants, insects and birds, including the Harpy Eagle, associated with this tree. Once the "sacred tree" of the Maya civilization, then renamed the "telephone tree" by the tourist industry because of the reverberating sounds produced by beating on the massive buttress roots, it is now referred to as the "plywood tree." I guess everything and everybody has to be reduced to some common denominator for reference sake.

Stand in the Shade — Common Trees in Santarém

If you are a typical visitor from the temperate zone of the world, you will be interested in getting to know some common tree species found in the Amazon. Santarém is a good place to begin your observations. From the list below, see how many you can identify. You may recognize a few right away, since some are originally from other parts of the world.

Acacia trees are by far the most common trees planted along the streets of Santarém. Their trunks are twisted and gnarled, much like trees that struggle for survival along windy oceanfront of Monterey, California. The reason for their physical peculiarity is that they are pruned radically at least once a year in orders to keep the limbs out of electrical and telephone lines. The first time I witnessed the cutting I predicted the worst for the trees. To my surprise, they bounced right back and continue to grow, cutting after cutting. I was beginning to think that only I get worried over such trivialities, when to my surprise an article appeared in the *A Província do Pará* (February 3, 2000, issue of the newspaper) denouncing the most recent pruning of *acácias* on Avenida Barão Branco. The article, along with a photograph of a stark-naked acacia, was correctly placed under the heading of "Environmental Crime."

Mango trees can be found all over town. There was a time when most of the major streets were lined with them, much like Belém today. A few decades ago some authority saw fit to clean house, and the big old mango trees got the axe. Fortunately, the ecology movement is bringing them back. Every year students and other groups carry out tree-planting campaigns and the mango is one of their favorite species. In addition to the beauty of the tree and its tasty fruits, it provides lots of needed shade. People avoid walking under the trees during harvest time, when children throw sticks, rocks and other objects up into the branches to knock off the fruit. Between parakeets, children and the commercial gatherers, few fruits are left over for the casual visitor. To the surprise of many people, the mango is an exotic to South America. It originally came from Asia, where it has been cultivated for more than 4,000 years. According to an article in *O Liberal*, March 2, 1997, the first mango trees brought to Brazil came from Africa via Portuguese explorers and, thereafter, spread to other parts of South America. More than 200 species exist, the most-prized being those with little fiber. Eduardo Ribeiro tells me that a neighbor rancher on Marajó Island has more than 70 species in his collection.

If you happen to be in Santarém during mango season, you will not have any problem identifying the trees, for they will be full of noisy canary-winged parakeets. It is remarkable to see a hundred or so parakeets disappear into a single tree. Their incessant screeching can be heard for blocks away, but it takes good eyesight to find even a few of them.

"She talks more than a parakeet in a mango tree" is a local saying to describe a person who cannot stop talking. The first person I remember using this adage was "Pacu," who was our nearby auto mechanic. One day I mentioned a person whose name I will not reveal. As I was describing her, Pacu suddenly said, "I know who you're talking about. She talks more than a parakeet in a mango tree." There was no doubt.

Castanhola trees (*Terminalia catappa*) looks like a big multi-tiered umbrella, and for that characteristic it makes a great shade tree. The leaves are quite large and turn to beautiful shades of red, yellow and orange during the dry season. Some refer to it as the "Brazilian almond" tree because of its seeds, which evidently taste like almond. Imported from Asia (Indian almond), the castanhola tree is appreciated throughout the Amazon. Wherever people reside, you will find the inviting shade of this tree.

Jambeiro trees (*Eugenia malaccensis*) have a Christmas-tree shape and, like castanhola trees, are appreciated for the fine shade they produce. I have friends who say that the trees are air-conditioned because the temperature under them is so much cooler than the environment. Notwithstanding, many people refuse to have jambeiro trees in their yards because there is never a minute of peace as long as they are in fruit. Children will challenge vicious dogs, broken-glass-studded walls, electric fences and any other obstacle to get to the fruit. Then too, some local dwellers regret having planted the tree because of the "mess" it makes during the blooming season. Everything below the tree gets covered with a carpet of purple tassels. They are truly beautiful, but keep the owners busy cleaning up. *Jambeiro* is another exotic tree, originally coming from Asia.

Ipê or *pau d'arco trees* (*Tabebuia serratifolia*) were planted a few years ago along Avenida Mendonça Furtado and Avenida Presidente

Getúlio Vargas. Many varieties of *ipê* grow in Brazil, but these are the yellow-blooming types. During the early part of the dry season they lose their foliage almost entirely and burst into an explosion of yellow. *Ipê* is one of the *Madeira de Lei* species, set aside for the Portuguese crown in the early days of colonialism.

When seeing *ipê* in bloom in the forest, we can also expect to see howler monkeys. As witnessed many times at Bosque Santa Lúcia, they like to snack on the freshly-opened blooms and buds. Also note the very large bumblebees going in and out of the huge trumpet-like blossoms.

Flamboyant trees (*Poinciana regia*) are easy to recognize because of the delicate lace-like leaf structure and the beautiful red flowers, which are more prominent during the summer months. The tree is originally from Madagascar.

Muruci trees (*Byrsonima crassifolia*) are native to this region and are easily recognized during the dry season, when they are loaded with marble-sized, yellow fruit. This is a relatively small tree and it is appreciated more for its fruit than for shade. *Muruci* fruit can be eaten fresh off the tree, but is more commonly used for making fruit juices and ice cream.

Cashew trees (*Anacardium occidentale*) are also native to the tropical savanna region of Santarém. They can get quite large, as evidenced by the ones growing around the Municipal Hospital. Most foreign visitors associate this tree with the cashew nut, but they are not familiar with the large colored fruit it bears. People here eat the fruit or make juice from it, and more often than not throw the nut away. Occasionally though, they will throw them on the coals of the barbecue pit for toasting, which also eliminates the poisonous resins found in the fleshy part of the nut.

Açaí palms (*Euterpe oleracea*) are the most famous of the native palms of this region. They are very slim, tall, and normally contain several individuals in a clump. Fortunately for the persons who climb up the trunks, they are without thorns. *Açaí* palms produce a maidenhair-type inflorescence and the marble-sized fruits are purple. A purple-colored juice, extracted from the pulp of the fruit, is a favorite food item for people from Pará. Belém is the largest producer and consumer of *açaí* in Brazil. Occasionally this palm becomes the center of international attention because a large number of them are being cut for extraction of hearts of palm.

Coconut palms (*Cocos nucifera*) are quite plentiful around the city as well as the rural areas. Most sidewalk snack bars sell iced coconut water. Vendors will cut off the end of the coconut, or punch a hole into it and provide a straw for ultra-fresh coconut water.

Papaya trees (*Carica papaya* L.) are also very common in Santarém. The *mamão* is a welcome sight on any table. The papaya is native of the Americas, probably Central America. It is considered a blessing for those travelers with constipation problems.

Banana (*Musa* sp) is not exactly a tree, but we always refer to it as a "banana tree" anyway. You will surely find them in most backyards in Santarém. Are bananas native of the Amazon? No. Bananas come originally from Asia and were transplanted to the Americas by Portuguese and Spanish explorers. If you are having the opposite problem of constipation, bananas in your diet will help.

Common House Plants in Santarém
Identification of even a fraction of all the plants found in town is obviously beyond the scope and purpose of this guide, but here are a few you will encounter:

Comigo ninguém pode (*Dieffenbachia picta*) is a potted plant that you will undoubtedly find in every home and every store in Santarém. I do not know the history behind the unanimous popularity of the plant, but it has something to do with warding off bad spirits and negative energies. If ingested, it will paralyze the throat muscles.

Hibiscus (*Hibiscus rosa*) will catch your eye very quickly after arriving in town. The flowers are large and come in a variety of colors ranging from white to brilliant red.

Allamanda (*Allamanda cathartica*) is a vine that produces large yellow bell-shaped flowers year around. Sometimes they catch a ride from a neighboring tree and climb right to the top. One of the most beautiful plant combinations I have seen was an *allamanda* vine in a jambeiro tree. It looked like a gigantic Christmas tree decorated with yellow glass bulbs. It is native to Brazil.

Bougainvillea (*Nyctaginaceae* family) is another commonly-planted shrub in this region. It can get very large and, if not radically pruned, requires support of fences or other props. Sometimes they climb trees and make for some interesting combinations. Bougainvilleas come in a variety of colors and are at their best during the hot dry season. Bougainvillea took on a French name but it is native of South America.

Flamboyantzinho (*Caesalpinia sp*) is a shrub often planted around walls. It is constantly full of small, red and yellow flowers with very long stamens.

Flame of the Woods (*Ixora coccinea*) is a common yard plant growing to medium height. Clusters of small star-shaped red flowers contrast with the dark-green background of this shrub.

Caladium (called *tajá* locally): The most beautiful are the variegated red and white varieties (*Caladium bicolor*). Entire fields of them can be seen in Belterra during the rainy season.

Crotons (*Codiaeum variegatum*) decorate most homes in Santarém. Originally from Malaysia, they come in a number of varieties, each with its own leaf pattern and colors. Santarenos like crotons, not just for the attractiveness of the shrub, but also because they require less watering during the dry season. It is truly a sun lover. The more sun

146

the waxy leaves get, the greater the effervescence of red, orange, yellow and purple.

Ficus benjamina (fig family) is another decorative plant you will see quite often in Santarém. More and more of them are being planted along streets, where they will grow into trees of considerable size. Some older samples may be seen in front of the cathedral, Nossa Senhora de Conceição. They are referred to as "Benjaminas."

Ficus elastica, the famous rubber tree plant, is the distinguished cousin of *Ficus benjamina*. This big thick-leafed plant is not to be confused with the rubber tree.

Wax Mallow (*Malvaviscus arboreus*) is another favorite yard shrub that produces a profusion of red flowers, all of which remain in rolled- up formations, looking like they would like to open up to the light of day. They are shy.

Red Flag Bush (*Mussaenda erythrophylla)* and the lavender-colored variety of *Mussaenda* are prominent in many front yards of Santarém. The red one is often confused with poinsettia.

Some Notable Flora on the Amazon River and Its Floodplain
I include the following checklist for people to take back home, a reminder of what they saw and a point of departure for additional reading.

Water hyacinth (*Eichornia crassipes*) can be observed year-round in the water of the Amazon River, as well as in the backwaters and lakes of the floodplain. Look for clumps of plants with swollen stems and beautiful purple flowers. They are often mixed with other aquatic plants. Several species are to be seen in the Amazon.

Water-lettuce (*Pistia stratiotes*) is yet another one of those aquatic plants we see daily, especially after a good rain flushes them out of smaller tributaries and lakes. On these occasions, one has the impression that the boat is floating in the middle of a vegetable garden. Sorry, no plucking of water lettuce for the luncheon salad. Nobody seems to have acquired a taste for this well-known plant. While being prepared as an Amazon salad, what did the water lettuce say to the water hyacinth? "Lettuce alone."

Salvínia (*Salvinia auriculata*), also a free-floating aquatic plant, is made up of very small rounded leaves bundled up in groups of a dozen or so. It is more common around backwaters.

Amazon Water-lilies (*Victoria régis/amazonica*) are on everyone's priority list to see, but they are not easy to find because they tend to be located in inaccessible areas, like isolated, shallow ponds and lakes. If you are traveling by ship or two-deck riverboats, where you can see over the embankments, you will surely spot these plants. *Victória régia* are the largest of all water lilies, some getting up to two meters (80 inches) in diameter. They produce large white flowers, which emerge to the side of its plate-shaped leaf. After one night of "presentation," the flower turns dark pink color.

The best place to see *Victória régia* near Santarém used to be off the eastern banks of Igarapé Açu, a waterway that can be entered from the northern banks of the Tapajós River, right across from the city. Last year, I did not see one plant. I am told that grazing buffalo had something to do with that. During the high flood season, lilies are often washed out of their favorite habitat and can be seen in more accessible areas, though in terrible condition. Can they support the weight of a child? I have seen foreign-produced pictures of children, and even adults, on top of these water lilies but I am not sure whether they were staged or not. I do know that when asking local fishermen about the probability of such an occurrence, they indicate that birds would certainly have no problems. Looking at the big, long thorns on the underside of the leaf, I am convinced that neither of us would benefit from an encounter.

Nymphaea water-lilies are also to be found in large numbers on the quieter waters of the floodplain. Most are about 25 centimeters (about ten inches) in diameter and have heart-shaped leaves and single flowers in yellow, white, pink and purple, depending on the species.

Canarana (*Panicum* sp.) is one of the predominant grasses of the Amazon floodplain. The word *canarana*, I am told, means false sugarcane, probably a distant cousin of the latter. The thick stems are full of large air cells, which gives it the buoyancy to form very large floating meadows, some so huge you think you are looking at hundreds of acres of pasture land. You can only appreciate the density of this vegetable matter when your riverboat is literally torn away from its anchoring position by a "floating island." It is common for boats to anchor out in the middle of small tributaries at night to get away from mosquitoes, and on one such occasion I remember vividly awakening in the middle of the night to find our vessel being dragged down the river while thousands of ants and insects crawled on board. When water levels drop, the canarana transforms the floodplain into gigantic, lush grasslands on which thousands of ranchers depend for the fattening of their cattle and buffalo.

Willows (*Salix ambuldiana*) and (*Salix martiana*) are immigrants from North America, having found their way to the Amazon only after the joining of Central and South America. Plotkin reminds us that North American Indians used ingredients from the willow tree for making a very effective painkiller, today produced artificially as aspirin.

Cannonball trees (*Couroupita guianensis*) are common along the banks of the Amazon, especially around ranch houses. These are large trees and quite easy to identify when in fruit. As the name implies, the pod looks exactly like a cannonball, and seems to be about the same density. Inside you will find a very neat package of large seeds covered with dense pulp. People do not eat this fruit, but it does serve as a backup diet for domestic swine. The cannonball is an excellent shade tree.

Aninga (*Montrichardia arborescens*) is most likely a plant you never heard of, but if you travel the Amazon, it will become part of your everyday vocabulary. Belonging to the araceae family, the same one boasting *Dieffenbachia, Monstera* and *Philodendron,* this water-loving plant reaches to heights of around three meters (approximately ten feet), has a long slim trunk with upside-down heart-shaped leaves at the top. It presents a large white inflorescence and the fruit resembles a small pineapple. Normally found in isolated groups or "islands," aninga is not a floater. It is well-rooted and often referred to as a "soil stabilizer," much like the mangrove. When you are around one of these areas keep your eyes open for the hoatzin, a chicken-sized bird that feeds on the leaf and fruit of the plant. Often referred to as the "stink bird," the hoatzin's claim to fame is to having the stomach of a cow, i.e., fermenting pouches to help digest the *aninga* leaves, as well as other vegetation. Therefore, you may wish to stay "upwind."

Cecropia trees are so abundant people often ask if they are planted commercially. Called *embaiuba* locally and "trumpet tree" in English, they are easily recognized because they remind people of a birch tree, at least from a distance. They are tall, thin, white-barked trees with high crowns, adorned with a "hand-spread" of large leaves. More than one hundred species exist in the tropics, but I find the ones on the floodplain unique in that the undersides of the leaves shine silver-white when hit by sunlight. Many an overturned cecropia leaf has been mistaken from afar for a "white bird." Cecropia are pioneer trees, which means they are among the first to sprout after an area has met the right soil and sunlight conditions. In the case of high forest, the change might have come about due to the falling of a large tree, lightning burns, or logging. On the floodplain, whole islands of cecropia are formed after fast-moving currents raze other vegetation. I always tell clients that trees are like people. Some people are more famous than others and such is the case with our friend, the cecropia.

Aside from being a pioneer, it is also classified as an "ant-plant," meaning that it harbors untold numbers of tiny, but vicious, *Azteca* ants in its hollow trunks and stems. All you need to do is to bump into the tree to bring them out in defense of their home. You will seldom, if ever, find a liana making its way up into the crown of the cecropia tree. The ants keep them pruned back. Birds enjoy cecropia seeds (long finger-like fruit, called catkins) and the sloth has a way of ignoring the ants as he munches away at the tender leaves.

Mata-pasto (*Cassia alata*) can be found on *terra firme*, but is more prominent on the floodplain. In Portuguese, *mato-pasto* means literally "kill the pasture." Look for large shrubs with beautiful bright-yellow "candlesticks."

Calabash gourds have been important utensils for the indigenous population of the Amazon for thousands of years, so we need not be surprised to find a few *cuieiras* (*Crescentia cajute*) around every household on the Amazon. Look for small trees with long, dangling branches with big, green fruit the size of a soccer ball. When mature, the fruit is picked, dried and cut in half for a variety of purposes, such as bowls, containers and dippers. In the arts and crafts stores you can buy decorated gourds with replicas of the designs used by Indians in prehistoric times. By the way, do not get your appetite up while looking at this shiny-green gourd. There is absolutely nothing inside except for some seeds.

Jauari (*Astrocaryum jauary*) is the most common palm on the Amazon River and, I believe, on the tributaries. Look for tall palms, high crowns and a very thorny trunk. The fruit, a little smaller than a golf ball, is an important food for many fruit and seed-eating fish, especially during the high-water season when they are reproducing. The fish, in turn, help with seed dispersal.

Munguba (*Pseudobombax munguba*) trees are most beautiful when in fruit, just prior to the dispersal of the very small seeds, which are neatly tucked away among cotton-like filaments. In the Santarém region an average tree may have a hundred or so rose-colored pods hanging from its almost leafless branches come May. The pods, which remind me of heavy, oversized rose mangos, begin to open up in June, allowing the winds to carry the "cotton" near and far. I have noticed that in the western portion of the Amazon, fruit development occurs a month behind that of the Santarém area.

Kapok (*Ceiba pentandra*) is generally considered to be *the* kapok tree. This is the giant referred to earlier in my text as the "plywood tree"— appropriately describing the regretful destination of one of the most beautiful trees in the Amazon. Carol Gracie, botanist at the New York Botanical Gardens, tells me that it was once the source of fibers used to stuff life vests and cushions before the advent of synthetics. The fibers are much superior to those of the aforementioned munguba tree.

Brazil nut trees (*Bertholetia excelsa*) are *not* water-tolerant, so you will not see them on the Amazon floodplain. You will see them on *terra firme* environment along some segments of the Amazon. These are the areas where the highlands come down right to the banks of the river, making for an interesting situation of floodplain on one side of the river and *terra firme* on the other. Wherever you see the latter, you will certainly see Brazil nut trees. They are easy to identify because they are tall, have big thick-barked trunks, are well-endowed with large leaves forming high rounded crowns, and are adorned with dark brown softball-sized pods. Brazil nut trees are deciduous, losing most of their leaves during the height of the dry season. In this part of the Amazon, most pods fall during the months of January and February.

"Where's the Drugstore?" – *Medicinal Plants of the Amazon*
As a foreign visitor, you may be unduly subject to a number of cloak-and-dagger operations, including contraband of tropical plants from which many modern-day miracle drugs are derived. You may think this ludicrous, but everyone knows that many of the pharmaceutical concoctions sold behind the counters of our drugstores and

pharmacies around the world have plant origins. According to Mark J. Plotkin, botanist and author of the celebrated book, *Tales of a Shaman's Apprentice*, fully 25 percent of all prescription drugs sold in the United States have plant chemicals as active ingredients and about half of these come from tropical species. He goes on to say that consumers spend about $6 billion a year on just this segment of the market.[16] It is very unlikely that any of my clients or other tourists traveling to the Amazon come in pursuit of the "miracle drug of the twentieth century." Should it be so easy? Nevertheless, we know that the vast majority of tropical plants, totaling more than 100,000 species, have never been analyzed for their chemical composition and that, indeed, vast numbers of medicines are possibly yet to be discovered.

"They're after our gold. They're here to take our oil, our diamonds and our plants," my guides hear occasionally from villagers who see tourists tromping off into the jungle on ecological tours. "They're up to no good" is the flavor of behind the doors conversations. "Did you see that *máquina*?" says an observer. "They say it's a camera, but it's really a machine for finding gold," he goes on. "I wonder how many kilograms of gold they brought out with them?" was a comment I heard from an educated city person who watched several young American natural science students getting off a riverboat in front of the city after finishing up a nine-day tour of the region. "They're taking our gold out in those cruise ships" was another remark I heard from an individual who works for a federal agency. Take it from me, there's no need in coming to blows over such accusations. People will believe what they want and nothing is going to change their minds. A local guide in Fordlândia showed us the remains of an underground "vault" where, he says, the Americans kept their loot. Others declare that Ford's purpose in being in the Amazon had nothing to do with rubber. His interest was in smuggling gold and other valuables out of the country, in hollowed-out logs. "Such and such missionary school" is really a front for the CIA. The stories go on and on, and you can be sure that many of them become legendary. Why all this mistrust of outsiders?

Obviously it has a lot to do with the educational level of the population and their conception of the outside world and history. Ever hear of Francisco Pizarro? Francisco Orellana? Charles Ledger? Richard Spruce? Henry Wickham? Explorers and exploitation seemed to have had a lot in common and that is part of the history and culture. My only satisfaction in responding to "the Amazon is crawling with foreigners" story is to remind everyone that more Brazilians go through Miami in a single day than there are foreigners coming to the Amazon in a whole year. True, Wickham took the rubber tree seeds from the Amazon, but how did coffee seeds get to Brazil? And what about those delicious bananas? Are they native, by chance? How about mango trees? Breadfruit? Jackfruit? Acerola? Jute? Jambeiro? Castanhola trees? Black pepper? Sugar cane? The "crops and robbers" game is an old one and impossible to contain. To my knowledge, not one country in the world has ever been able to impede the human transfer of flora to other parts of the earth. The controversy comes when that original plant *comes back* into Brazil, in this case, as a pharmaceutical medicine with patent royalties attached to the production and sale. Brazilians get emotional whenever they talk about the subject, and sometimes the consequences echo right down to the soul of how we would like to conduct tourism. I have been told by reliable sources that maritime protocol now requires very stringent planning of ship stops along the Amazon River, in protest to the royalty issue. All stops, even to conduct ecological tours, must be programmed ahead of time and submitted to authorities for approval. What might be a question of big business and political exploitation comes to rest on the shoulder of the "little old lady in tennis shoes."

The backyard drugstore fascinates visitors and all guides enjoy talking about the plants or just acting as an interpreter between tourists and local residents. Likewise, the homeopathic-medicine department, often mixed up with an array of strange amulets, is always a favorite stopping point in the market places. If you have ever visited the Ver o Peso market in Belém, you surely saw one of the largest assortments of homeopathic remedies in the world. It is no wonder; the native populations have been in charge of the "Amazon Pharmacy" for several thousand years.

It has been my experience that just about all plants and trees in the Amazon have some medicinal use for someone, somewhere. So as not to list too many, here are a few of the more common ones you are apt to see or hear of during a stay here:

Óleo de copaiba (*copaifera officinalis*) is one of my favorites because we have a fine old copaiba tree growing at Bosque Santa Lúcia. Instead of latex, like the rubber tree, the sap is fragrant-smelling oil that is removed much like tapping a maple tree. The oil can be bought in any modern-day drug store in Santarém, in arts and crafts stores, and outdoor markets. It has a lot of different medicinal applications, but the most popular is for application to cuts and wounds, given its special cauterizing attributes. I understand that most *copaiba* oil is actually exported to France, where it is used as a fixer for some of the finest perfumes on the market. I also read somewhere that diesel engines run perfectly on copaiba oil, giving rise to the theory that the forest could provide a substitute to petroleum-based products, if there were sufficient numbers of copaiba trees. Scientists have been able to synthesize natural medicines, why not *copaiba* oil? Here is a challenge.

Óleo de andiroba (*Carapa guianensis*) is another vegetable oil to be found in any drugstore or places where homeopathic medicines are being marketed. Unlike *copaiba* oil, which is taken directly from the tree in the form of sap, this oil comes from the seeds of the *andiroba* tree, which are subjected to a boiling process. It is not the best-tasting stuff in the world, but I use it when I have a bad cold, to clear my throat and lungs of phlegm. Just a drop on the end of an inserted finger is sufficient. If you gag easily, please close the bathroom door. Some years ago I discovered that *andiroba* oil is a great repellent for all types of insect bites, especially chiggers, our most noted tormentors. On longer trips upriver I always take along a small bottle of this oil and apply it directly to my ankles and legs whenever I think we will enter the forest, or even a grassy, weedy yard. Amazingly, when I am careful in following this procedure, I never get a bite the whole trip. During the rainy season, I even use *andiroba* oil when working in my office to repel those invisible pesky little gnats that bite me around the ankles. I would not worry about such minor disturbances, but they create the need to scratch, which in turn draws blood and opens the skin, providing access for bacterial infections, like phlebitis and general infections of the lymphatic circulatory systems. Thank goodness for *andiroba* oil because if I had to depend on commercial repellents containing DEET, I am sure I would be a lot less careful in protecting myself. By the end of a tour visitors are also disgusted with the smell of commercial repellants and tired of losing the paint on their cameras and binoculars. They are willing to trust my more ecological solution, so I share my *andiroba* oil with them.

Boldo (*Pneumus boldus*) is one of the best remedies for gallbladder pains as well as liver ailments. Occasionally my own gallbladder lets me know that I have gone beyond my allowable quota of fats and spices, and nothing calms the biliary tract faster than boldo tea. Boldo may have come originally from Chile, not the Amazon. Regardless, it is used extensively here.

Mangarataia (*Zingiber* spp.) was another prescription given to me for gallbladder problems. "Make a very strong tea from the root and apply it as a compress over the area of the gallbladder and liver," I was told. The downtime lost in the process made me lose interest in this particular treatment, but it did help. On another occasion I was so desperate I sought out the advice of a homeopathic healer at the market place for the same problem. Expecting great revelations, or at least a hard sell for some exotic medicine from deep within the jungle, the lady looked me in the eye and said, "You should talk with Dr. Edson Mesquita. Sounds like you need surgery." As a matter of fact, I had an ultrasound with the good doctor to discover that the problem did not require surgery, only boldo tea and a drugstore medicine I take from time to time when I feel acute pain.

Capim Santo (*Andropogon nardus*), lemon or citronella grass, comes originally from the tropics of Africa and Asia. The distilled oil from this grass is used in some parts of the world for cosmetics and insect repellents. Here in the Amazon a very fine tea is brewed from the leaves and used as a diuretic. It is also said to improve digestion. Very seldom will you find a rural home without several big clumps of this tall-growing grass. The very distinctive smell of a broken or crushed leaf will leave no doubt in your mind as to what it is. The translation of *capim santo*, by the way, means "Saint's grass."

Canela (*Cinnamonum* sp.), cinnamon, is another popular medicine in the Amazon, as well as the rest of Brazil. Francisco Orellana was actually in search of a South American species of cinnamon when he accidentally discovered the Amazon River. He and Gonzalo Pizarro, brother to the famed conquistador, Francisco Pizarro, found cinnamon trees, but they turned out to be of lesser quality than those of the East Indies.[22] Cinnamon is used in Santarém for confectionery purposes and the dried leaves for brewing medicinal teas. Our kitchen dispensary is more often than not host to a big sack of dried-cinnamon leaves from which our maid supplies the teapot.

Pião (*Jatropha curcas*) is found in every backyard, almost without fail. Two varieties grow in this region, one called *pião roxo* (red) and another *pião branco* (white). Both provide thick latex used for healing cuts and wounds. In Rodrigues' book, *A Flora da Amazônia*, he notes that the seed, toasted, ground and added to coffee or water, is a very strong purgative and can be overly toxic if not used properly.[18]

Quebra Pedra, which translates into "break the stone," is commonly used for the treatment of kidney and gallstones. It grows everywhere. Here at home it can be found in every flowerpot or any little piece of ground not cemented over. Planted? Hardly, they just pop up everywhere on their own accord and everyone is quick to let you know what it is. It is that well-known. I am not sure how it is prepared traditionally, but I have experimented boiling the green leaves into a tea. It has sort of an indifferent taste, which surprised me.

Maracujá (*Passiflora* spp.), or passion fruit, is one of the favorite juices in the Amazon and everyone is aware of its sedative properties. Are you nervous about something? Drink a glass of passion fruit juice. It will help calm you down. It is said to have analgesic, diuretic, anti-depressant and anti-convulsant attributes as well. Brazilians drink a lot of juices, and I dare say that maracujá is one of their favorites. Many people along the Amazon River plant passion fruit commercially, so it is easily found in market places, as well as in any supermarket. When mature, the fruit is about the size of a baseball and green to bright yellow in color. Preparation of the juice is very simple: cut the fruit in half, scoop out the seeds and semi-liquid pulp around them, and put them in a blender for a few seconds. Add water and sugar to your own taste. You may also buy prepared concentrates at supermarkets.

Pata de Vaca (*Bauhinia sp.*), a plant with hypoglycemic and diuretic properties, has local fame as one of the best medicines for the treatment of diabetes. The name in English means "cow's foot" because of the resemblance of the leaf to that of a cow's hoof. Some people also refer to it as *pata de boi,* or "bull's foot." It is a very common plant at our Bosque Santa Lúcia and I always point it out on my ecological tour. At least three species are found there: one with very large leaves, another with miniature leaves and an odd one that turns into a gigantic, leafless vine called *escada de jabuti* (tortoise's ladder). It is my impression that the latter is a species that presents long pointed leaves before transforming itself into a contorted twisted ribbon-like vine. Someone living in the city recently asked me to bring some *pata de boi* from the Bosque for a diabetic friend. I was in doubt as to which variety was best indicated as a remedy, but ended up collecting the large-leaved species, hoping it was *Bauhinia fortificata*, which I understand is the best.

Coati's milk to treat a back problem? Our beloved maid, Dona Joana, brought this strange prescription to my attention one day by insisting that I listen to an announcement coming over her small incessant portable radio. The heart throbbing plea, "For the love of God," was for coati's milk and was being made by the son of the patient. According to his testimony he had taken his father to Manaus to consult with a well-known *curandeiro*, who had prescribed this bizarre remedy. The radio announcement had been repeated several times during the course of the day and I guess it must have caught Dona Joana's attention as being of interest to me. I often wonder if the poor fellow ever found a source for the milk. I sort of doubt it, because coatis, South American raccoons, are not commonly kept as household pets. They are, in fact, beautiful animals with high-flying tails and fluffy thick fur. Several of them hang out at the Ariaú Jungle Tower Lodge near Manaus and I can testify that their disposition does not match their appearance as an animal you would like to cuddle. Tourists at Ariaú try snuggling up next to them, but they are normally met with indifference and occasional bites from razor-sharp teeth. Can you imagine trying to milk one?

"YOU DIDN'T TELL US ABOUT THE CHIGGERS!" — HEALTH AND SAFETY TIPS

Most people take a vacation to improve their mental and physical health, and that is exactly what happens when they come to Santarém. In fact, some people get to feel so much better that they keep coming back. Others decide to stay. Henry Bates, the famed British naturalist of the last century, eulogized Santarém in his book, *The Naturalist on the River Amazons,* by describing the merits of fine climate, the lack of nasty insects and other ills often associated with living in the tropics.[15] He stayed almost three years. Chances are good that you, too, will leave Santarém and the Amazon just as healthy as you came, if not better. Here are a few tips to help you achieve that goal.

Dehydration

Keep yourself well hydrated. The loss of body liquids occurs frequently in tropical climates, especially on sunny, windy days. If you are walking or hiking or doing some other strenuous activity, you will be surprised how much you sweat and how quickly your body liquids disappear. One reason for the lack of long-distance trekking tours in the region is that it is nearly impossible to carry enough drinking water. Most people do not get into an extreme activity like trekking but it is, nevertheless, important to pay attention to your intake of liquids. If you find that you are urinating less than normal, it could be a clue that your body needs more liquids. Leg cramps are a sign that you have lost body salts and electrolytes, in which case you should consider oral re-hydration therapy. Drugstores sell oral re-hydration powders, which can be mixed with water and taken orally in small doses. It is called *soro oral*.

When I think of liquid intake vs. liquid loss, I remember a visiting plastic surgeon, who noted that he was urinating much less than at home. To test his theory of loss of liquids via perspiration, he invited a group of friends over for a Saturday night party and asked each person to keep tabs on how many times they urinated. Cold beer was the drink of choice and there was an abundance of it. The party started around 8:30 PM and there was plenty of physical activity in the form of breath-taking dances. It was almost midnight before the first person meandered off to the bathroom. It may have been me! In Alaska, we ran to the bathroom every five minutes under similar circumstances. Likewise we could wear the same clothes for days at a time without body odor. Here in the Amazon, just a walk around the block calls for another shower and a clean set of clothes, as well as another heavy application of deodorant. Even though we have one of the few washing machines around, I still feel sorry for our maid, who spends an average of four hours per day just washing and ironing clothes. I insist on wearing my clothes for a full day or more, thus lessening the maid's drudgery. In compensation, I take a lot of harassment from the rest of the family. As the years pass, the chiding has actually diminished. More and more, Áurea takes the attitude, "If he wants to be that way, what can I do?"

Sunburn

"When in the tropics, walk in the shade," is a trite saying, but one to respect. If you think all those ladies carry umbrellas for rain, you are mistaken—it is for shade. When people do not have an umbrella or a hat, they use a banana leaf, a tree branch or anything to keep the sun off. Do you think local people take that long lunch break because they are sleepy? Hardly! This is the hottest interval of the day, a good time to get out of the sun. Visitors from the more temperate climates often get skin burns much faster than they ever thought possible. A morning of walking downtown, an hour on the beach, or even half an hour of resting an arm on the car window can cause noticeable sunburn. This is in part due to the fact that Santarém is located just two degrees south of the equator, and at that latitude the sunlight comes down at a 90-degree angle, as opposed to the longer, slanted rays of the more temperate latitudes. When you cannot find shade, protect your skin by using sunscreen lotions, light-colored clothes, long-sleeve shirts, long pants and hats. This is not to imply that you should avoid the sun altogether; just be prepared. Francimary Silva, our local dermatologist and director of the Municipality Hospital, reports seeing many cases of skin cancer among her patients, especially the "white-skinned" ones. She recommends that we try to avoid exposure to the sun between 10:00 AM and 3:00 PM. Sunglasses with ultraviolet filters are also highly recommended in order to reduce the glare of the sun off the water, especially when taking riverboat tours.

Sanitation

While traveling in the Amazon, enjoy the wonderful variety of foods, including fruits, meats, fish and even salads. Just be discreet in terms of selecting restaurants with proper sanitary conditions. Most hotel restaurants are careful in this regard and it is seldom that one gets sick from the food. The rule of thumb for safe drinking is to stick with bottled liquids. Avoid juices being sold on the streets, since you have no idea where they were prepared. Of course, there is nothing better than a coconut, tapped right in front of you. Generally speaking, the juices offered by the better hotels are okay to drink. Another safety precaution is that of eating foods which have been well-cooked. Oftentimes we see vendors barbecuing fish and meat in front of the city and just the smell makes us hungry. But after looking at the unsanitary condition of the area we decide not to eat. Actually, the barbecue is quite safe because it has been well-cooked. It is the rest that gets you in trouble, like the contaminated glasses, silverware, and even other foods that might come with the fish.

Fish Bones

When you eat fish in the Amazon, you must remember that you are eating real fish, not a fast-food concoction between two pieces of bread. Many species of local fish have invisible needle-sharp bones and they can get stuck in your gullet. You may think that the local Brazilians are immune to such misfortune. Not so; it happens all the time. I have a neighbor, an agronomist, who suffered terribly for two weeks with a bone stuck in his throat. He tried all kinds of home remedies without success and finally traveled to Belém for specialized care. ENT (ear/nose/throat) doctors are called upon daily to remove fish bones from the throats of their patients. I was such a patient at least twice. My older boy, David, experienced a traumatic experience with a fishbone stuck in his throat when he was only five years old and, to this day, will not eat fish. All this advice is not to scare anyone away from eating fresh fish. It is one of the finest choices you can make while in the Amazon. If in doubt about the skeletal attributes of a fish on your plate, play the role of those thin, finicky eaters, who meticulously consume their meals in very small bites. Wolfing food down will increase the chances of your meeting up with an ENT specialist. By the way, I am delighted to report that one of our ENT doctors, Jocivan Pedroso, is a passionate orchid collector.

Intestinal Parasites

Some of the more common water and food-borne diseases in the Amazon are ascaris (roundworm), amoebae and giardia. It is not uncommon for visitors to become the host to these little organisms, especially those travelers who are making the most out of their budget. Eating in the better restaurants is certainly no guarantee against intestinal parasites, but it does reduce the risk. If you think you might have some unwanted guests in your alimentary tract, have a stool exam done. With laboratory results, you know what you have and how to treat it. Put a small dab of feces (laboratory technicians do not appreciate kilogram samples) in a film canister and take it to either Laboratório de Analises Clinicas Celso Matos, Travessa dos Mártires, 226—or to Laboratório Santarém de Dr. Hoiama Miranda for examination. If you leave the sample in the morning, results will be ready by early afternoon. Should the result prove positive for intestinal parasites, you may want to check with a medical doctor for proper treatment. Another route is to go to a drugstore, where someone will know what medicine you need. Check with your tour operator or hotel manager for recommendations. If you go to the doctor, remember that an office visit is cheaper than a house call at the hotel.

Other Guests

Another condition that will have you running to the bathroom is bacterial infections caused by eating contaminated foods. I remember once upriver most of our Nature Expeditions International group came down with explosive cases of diarrhea all about the same time and at a very prominent hotel in Manaus. Howard Searright—a physician from Munice, Indiana, and a member of our party—conducted an epidemiological investigation to discover that the one person who did not get sick was taking tetracycline during the course of the trip. This was the first and last time I experienced what may have been food poisoning.

The superlative of the word *diarrhea* is cholera. A major outbreak of this disease occurred on the western coast of Peru in the early 1990s and eventually reached the Amazon. Thanks to some very fine work on the part of Brazilian health authorities, it never reached pandemic proportions here. Being careful with what you eat and drink will keep you free of this disease. To my knowledge, there has never been a case of cholera among foreign travelers, but you may still be susceptible.

Very few travelers get diarrhea as a result of pernicious disease agents. Most of the time the cause is nothing more than a change of diet, different foods and seasonings, maybe a higher *E-coli* count than normal, perhaps stress from leaving home, the radical switch from a fast-paced work environment to total relaxation, etc. Brazilians encounter the same problems when they travel to other countries. I have known people to get diarrhea just from switching brands of beer or from drinking it in above-normal quantities. Sometimes we find ourselves spending too much time in the bathroom as a result of some seemingly inconsequential thing such as eating watermelon. Once an epidemiological investigation revealed that an outbreak of diarrhea among several of us on a riverboat tour was the result of our eating too much watermelon. I then remembered that every time I had diarrhea on earlier boat trips, I had eaten watermelon. It made sense. Walt Stein reminded me that the problem is not with the watermelon but with the excess water intake rate. Not to belabor the point, but it just goes to show you that a number of factors can put us in the most embarrassing of situations.

Look Before Jumping

Swimming in the clear water of the Tapajós River is great fun and most people find themselves jumping off the boat in a matter of minutes after beaching. That is part of the show and we encourage it. You should, however, observe a couple of safety rules. First of all, never dive from the boat without knowing the depth of the water. Our regional boats have flat bottoms, specifically for getting into very shallow water. Also keep an eye on the position of the boat. Often a wind will push the rear of the boat closer to shore, which could make a big difference in the depth of water. Broken necks are no fun, as David Richardson, founder of the Center for the Preservation of Indigenous Art in Alter do Chão (now closed), discovered. He was seriously injured a few years ago when diving off his riverboat, the *B/M Tucuxí*. Another danger you want to avoid is that of swimming around the propeller of the boat, especially if you have long hair. I have not heard of any specific cases of visitors getting involved in this type of an accident, but many local persons have lost their hair, along with their scalps, from having gotten too close to a spinning propeller. Alfred Falcone, itinerant plastic surgeon at Fundação Esperança, can provide more details.

Monster Fish

Another precaution when swimming in local waters is to pay attention to currents. They can be much stronger than you could ever imagine. When traveling on the Amazon River, we often anchor out in the mouth of a tributary, taking advantage of air currents in order to reduce mosquito infestation. On one of these occasions two of my passengers, Alan Simon and Jim Undercoffer, asked if it would be okay to take a swim. "Sure," I naively responded, thinking more in terms of their ability to climb back onto the boat. Alan, the first to dive in, immediately yelled back that the current was very strong and thereafter stayed very close to the side of the riverboat. Jim, the 13-

year-old, was about to "go for it" when the crew warned me that it was not wise to swim in open water, referring to not only the current, but also the very large fish famed for taking human beings underwater with them. One such fish is the *piraíba* (*Brachyplatystoma filamentosum*), the largest of the catfish species. They can get up to 110 kilograms (242 pounds). I am not sure an occurrence of this nature has been officially documented, but I have heard it mentioned from time to time when locals talk of the *piraíba*. My friend, Edney Farias, civil engineer from Parintins, tells me that this fish has an extraordinarily large head and mouth. He doubts whether it would actually swallow a human but believes it is capable of living up to its fame for pulling them into the muddy waters of the Amazon. Theodore Roosevelt in his classic, *Through the Brazilian Wilderness*, wrote of his men catching a very large catfish in which they discovered the whole body of a monkey. Roosevelt, a bit astounded over the event, was told by his Brazilian hosts about a monster fish in the Amazon River that makes prey of man himself. The name of this gigantic man-eating fish was reported as being the *piraíba*.[20]

Hands Down

Guides at Amazon Lodge (Nature Safaris) in Manaus alert guests not to walk around with their hands in their pockets. If you fall, keeping your hands free could protect you from plunging onto sticks and tree stumps, some of which are as sharp as a spears. A hand injury is obviously less traumatic than a face or torso "mishap." Bushwhackers have the habit of cutting vegetation about ten inches above the ground—and at an angle. You get the idea. Avoid falling on them.

Mosquitoes

The story of the mosquito landing at the airport and being filled up with aviation fuel before being identified is one reserved for Alaska. That is not to say that Santarém does not have mosquitoes but only to state that they are few and malaria is not endemic to the immediate area. Most malaria comes from the gold mining areas of the upper Tapajós River, where prospectors work in very isolated, uncontrolled environments. If you take overnight tours on the Amazon River, you will find (better to say that they will find you) many mosquitoes, especially around sunrise and sunset. Take insect repellent and make sure you have a mosquito net for your hammock. In case your tour operator does not provide nets, you can buy them at a number of stores along Lameira Bittencourt Street. You may also purchase a bed sheet to line the hammock, thus lessening the chance of mosquitoes jabbing your underside through the fabric.

Chiggers

If you spend any time at all in the forest or walk in grassy areas around riverbanks and villages, you will get chiggers, tiny insects belonging to the mite family. They are called *mucuim* locally. When they parasitize vertebrates, they are actually in the larval stage of development and they are so small that they can pass directly through your clothing, *even if* you put your pants legs inside your socks. What they lack in size is overcompensated in irritation, especially around areas of tight clothing—like socks, panties, shorts and brassieres. The itching is so intense, people literally scratch their skin off and then the wounds can get infected. I have noticed that the whiter the skin, the more severe the sensitivity of the individual. Maybe that is the reason the little critters like the skin that seldom sees the light of day. Insect repellent on the ankles and legs before getting into chigger country is the best preventative measure. Should you get infested, apply Foldan cream. It can be bought at most drugstores and normally two or three applications will reduce itching and the allergic reaction. A colleague in Manaus, Antônio Baptista, tells me that Deltacid Shampoo does the trick for him and his clients. This shampoo can also be purchased at local drugstores. I personally find that andiroba oil is the best insect repellent. *Óleo de andiroba* is available at any of the local arts and crafts stores in Santarém, as well as marketplaces.

Occasionally we see clients who react violently to chigger bites. I remember one person who developed blisters the size of golf balls around her ankles. Medical attention is recommended in such cases. Should medical help not be available, soak the infected areas in a potassium permanganate solution. Tablets or powders are available at most drugstores. Mix the potassium permanganate in sterile water in the proportions recommended in the pharmaceutical literature and soak the infected areas every few hours. This will help "dry up" the blisters. It is important to prevent broken blisters from becoming infected. If they do, use antibiotic salves, e.g., Neomycin or Bacitracina, on these wounds.

It is not uncommon to see older people with swollen ankles, a condition which is due to the poor circulation and maybe overuse of salt in their diet. Mosquitoes, gnats and other man-attacking insects target these areas and can cause some serious problems. Insect repellent, andiroba oil and long pants are the best preventive measures.

Perlipimpim
My physician friend, Paulo Sergio Pimentel, tongue in cheek, describes another insect much smaller than a chigger, the *perlipimpim.* He says that its favorite spot for feeding is on the testicles of the chigger. Now that is "mitey" small.

Chigoe Flea
Another "critter" that will have you scratching, normally under your toes, is the chigoe flea, called the *bicho de pé* (varmint of the foot). This condition is quite common throughout the Amazon and maybe all of Brazil. I have been victim of the pest several times because I like to wear sandals. The first sign is a delightful itch that can go on for days before you realize that somebody is having a party at your expense. Treatment is that of opening up the sore to remove the flea (it is actually an adult flea at this stage) and the pus from the infected area. The last time I went through this "minor surgery" even Áurea was surprised at the size of the crater left behind. Use antibiotic salves and keep the wound clean following the removal of your guest.

Ticks

Ticks can be a problem only on rare occasions. Insect repellent will help keep them off. If you do discover a tick attached to your body, do not pull it off because you may end up with its torso between your fingers and the head still implanted in your skin. This situation can lead to a very nasty infection and in some cases serious necrosis and other undesirable conditions. Try vinegar, salt, or insect repellent.

The Stingers

A potentially dangerous situation you want to consider when traveling throughout the region is that of bees and wasps. Some are quite noticeable, but others, especially those making their nests underground can catch you by surprise. The largest concentration of wasps I have ever seen was in an abandoned house on the Maicuru River, northwest of Monte Alegre. Captain Gonzaga of the *B/M Mucuxi* had edged up to a cannonball tree next to an old wooden house so that members of a photography club from the state of New York could take pictures. As we got closer, I noticed yellow-rumped cacique nests hanging from the branches. "Great. We can get a lot of fine pictures in one stop," I thought to myself. Everybody was excitedly setting up cameras on tripods when I, by chance, glanced inside the open house, only a few feet from where we had stopped the riverboat. I could not have been more startled had I seen a ghost. There must have been tens of thousands of wasps in the building, all large, social wasps of the Vespidae family. Two of our people had been stung earlier on the tour and I knew we were in for big trouble should these attack us. Although one photographer insisted in getting pictures "on the run," we managed to back the boat out into the mainstream without arousing the wasps. We speculated about what would happen if someone were to come by during the night looking for a place to hang his or her hammock. Friend and topographer, Pacifico Siqueira, tells me that the local name for these wasps is *caba de igreja*, or church wasp. Interestingly enough, he reports that they are not overly aggressive and, if one is careful in not disturbing them, that it is possible to walk through a large colony without being stung. I will leave that test up to him, but it does confirm what I tell people when they start swatting at wasps on riverboat trips. "You either swat to kill or you leave them alone." Most people get stung when they haphazardly swat at them.

On another excursion, we discovered a very large number of wasps on the ceilings of a cavern near Monte Alegre, where we had gone to see indigenous cave paintings dating back some 12,000 years. Nelsí Sadeck, leader of the tour, was quick to warn us of the danger and reported that one year there were so many wasps in this location it was impossible to enter the cavern. Yet I once entered the same cave without seeing a single wasp.

I hope you will not have an unfavorable encounter with our stinging residents, but should you be so unfortunate, apply a topical anesthetic to the stung area immediately. Xildase is one local brand name and one that I have used on several occasions with excellent results. Some patients call it the "miracle ointment" because they get instantaneous results. I also carry a tube of Colgate toothpaste containing baking soda, *bicarbonato de sódio*, in my daypack, which I am told is excellent for these painful moments in the jungle. Some day I am sure I will have the opportunity to give it a try, but in the meanwhile, I get such satisfying results from the Xildase, I prefer not to waste a second in providing first aid. If you are prone to allergic shock, seek medical assistance as soon as possible, or better yet, carry your own medications for quick treatment.

Caterpillars
You should always keep your distance from caterpillars because some exude chemical substances which produce very painful itches and rashes. The more you scratch, the more it spreads to other parts of your body. Washing the area with soap and water has no effect. A topical anesthetic is the best field solution, in my opinion. After applying it, do your best not to scratch the area. It normally takes a few minutes for the pain to subside. You do not actually have to touch the caterpillars. It is sufficient only to come into contact with chemical tracings left by the insects as they crawl from one place to

another. An incident I remember well was a very large migration of caterpillars coming from a sizable cassava plantation, which they had devoured completely, to the adjoining forest. Robert Stein, retired professor of biology at Buffalo State College in New York, was documenting the movement with a video camera and came down with an acute rash over both arms and shoulders. Not once did he come into direct contact with the caterpillars. The same had happened to me some years earlier right at home on Travessa Turiano Meira. At that time we still had a few old muruçi and cashew trees in our backyard, which seem to be favorites for *pararama* species of caterpillars. I accidentally came into contact with some of their leftover chemicals and, not knowing the cause of the itching on my back, made the situation worse by rubbing up against one of the cement block columns supporting our yard wall. The more I scratched, the more the rash spread—and the more miserable I became. Not knowing the proper treatment for the condition, I sought relief by washing with soap and water. Then I tried oils, salves and talcum powder, but nothing provided relief. After several hours of agony, the pain finally went away. Maybe I was lucky because in the southern part of Brazil, in 1998, there were actually several deaths attributed to secondary contacts with caterpillars.

Cashews

If you have eaten your share of cashew nuts in your life, you most likely know that cashew trees are native to the Amazon region (tropical savannah areas). You may even have drunk the wonderful juice made of the fruit, but chances are good that you do not know that the shell around the nut contains the same allergenic chemical substance found in American poison ivy and sumac. If you are allergic to either, be very careful when eating the raw fruit, especially if the nut is still attached. In the late 1980s I hosted a visitor from California who had indulged in the pleasures of cashew fruit somewhere in the northeastern part of Brazil, now the largest producer of cashew trees in the country. By the time he got to Santarém, he was suffering from swollen eyes, lips, and testicles. Upon returning home, our friend researched the subject and thereby discovered the cashew connection. He reported to me that mango skins also contain the same poisonous resin called urushiol. I have never known anyone to acquire an allergy from having come into contact with mango skins, but if you are very sensitive to poison ivy, poison oak and poison sumac, peel the fruit before eating it.

Stingrays

The probability of your being eaten to the bone by *piranhas* is very remote, but one danger you possibly never thought of encountering in the Amazon is being stung by a stingray. Riverside dwellers are well attuned to such hazards and, luckily for us, they are expeditious in warning us of the risk. Such was the case on a tour to Fordlândia in July of 1997, when we desperately looked for any patch of sandy beach where we could take a bath and give the boat crew a rest. The Tapajós River is very high this time of the year and we made several abortive landings, including one on a very attractive piece of land that turned out to be a cemetery. I suggested that we move on to find another spot so as not to cause indignation on the part of any approaching inhabitant. It was well after sunset when we settled for a less suitable location about a hundred meters in front of a mud-and-wattle house. Captain Domingos Lopes Pinto lowered the gangplank and immediately walked off to the house to let the suspicious family know what was happening. "All clear," he reported on his way back and instantly a couple of our people jumped into river with gleeful shouts of, "At last, a bath." As I changed into my swimming trunks, I overheard the high-pitched voice of a woman who excitedly tried to communicate with our non-Portuguese speaking swimmers that they were in jeopardy of being stung by stingrays. As it turned out, her own daughter had been victim of such an occurrence two years earlier, in this very same location. The lady's loud, detailed description of how her daughter suffered over several months was enough to convince us that we would settle for a quick shower in the tiny bathroom of the boat.

Stingrays (descendants of saltwater species) are quite abundant in local waters and can be a problem for beach enthusiasts. If you are the first to go out into the water, it is always good idea to probe the area in front of you with a stick or paddle to scare them off. Rolf Tambke, owner of Santarém Tur and an experienced, award-winning yachtsman, tells me, "Old sailors advise to shuffle feet when entering stingray territory. Don't wade or step." That counsel would have been in order for an Austrian filmmaker who told me the story of his losing a year of work after being stung by a stingray on the Rio Negro. The floppy creatures are not fond of attacking people, but they do not appreciate being stepped on. If you get stung, you will be the first to know about it. Victims report that the pain is unbearable. Treatment usually requires surgery to remove the venomous spine and to clean out the wound.

Sebastião Manoel dos Santos, more commonly referred to as "Sabá," once brought me a stinger that had been removed from a small-to-medium-sized stingray caught on a fishing trip. It does not take much imagination to understand why the sting of this animal hurts so much. This particular specimen is ten centimeters (four inches) long and as hard as steel. It has fine serrated teeth on both sides of the shaft, and the teeth that are arranged in such an angle that the shaft cannot be removed without ripping open the flesh. I should say "shafts" because there are actually two separate spearheads, one behind the other.

In 1997, Sabá was at the market buying fish for a tour, when the vendor asked him if he believed in the "*cobra grande*." He was just joking about the gigantic, legendary anaconda, but went on to tell Sabá that an immense stingray had been caught down river from Santarém and had been hauled in to a local packinghouse on Avenida Tapajós. It weighed 250 kilograms (550 pounds). Other persons who had seen it later confirmed this report. I would like to have seen the stinger on that one.

Piranhas
You will find *piranhas* all over the Amazon. Under normal circumstances you do not need to worry about taking a swim with our

toothy *peixinhos*. An exception would be oxbows, areas that have become isolated from the river channel after water levels drop. In this case, food sources become scarce, which means that the *piranhas* get hungry. But it is not likely that you would be in this kind of water anyway. As David Oren, senior ornithologist at the Museu Paraense Emílio Goeldi in Belém, says, "Man eats *piranha*. *Piranha* does not eat man."

Speaking of fish and survival instinct, I recall an incident that took place in Leticia, Colombia, in 1995. I had just finished a tour and, as usual, had to spend some time waiting for the VARIG flight from Tabatinga to Manaus. With some time to kill, I asked the folks at the Manígua Hotel to set up a small table out in the lobby so that I could do my trip report. From time to time I noticed the hotel employees tapping on the side of an aquarium and the response was always the same, a fierce attack from the ornamental fish inside. So violent was the charge, I could hear the thud of the small fish as they projected themselves onto the side of the glass plate. Asking about the unusual aggressiveness, the clerk replied that a brood had just hatched out and that the adults were simply protecting their young. Interestingly enough, that same week I saw a news report that piranha had attacked swimmers under a bridge in some small town in Mato Grosso, Brazil. A biologist determined that the piranhas were using the area under the bridge for raising their young. Again, it was a case of defending their kind. There was yet another TV report of a "killer dolphin" somewhere in central Brazil. In this case the dolphin had taken up residence in the waters of a highly-populated area and subsequently made many friends among local residents. One day it seriously injured a child and thus aroused the wrath of the local population. Getting down to details, the biologist discovered that kids were putting ice cream into the nostrils of the animal and bottles of soft drinks in its mouth and engaging in other acts of childish affection. The dolphin was merely reacting in a natural way to protect itself.

Most wild creatures of the Amazon are not aggressive to man, but when you enter their domain, even by accident, expect the worst. Try to be as non-intrusive as possible when you are walking around in the forest and do not touch anything until you have looked at it quite closely. The natural tendency is for people to put their hands on tree trunks, flowers, leaves and other objects. They forget that this is home-sweet-home for ants, scorpions, spiders, snakes and other residents. Do we roll out the red carpet for ants, spiders, cockroaches and other varmints? Please be vigilant.

MORE CULTURAL CONTRASTS

The Same to Your Mother

A great deal can be communicated by gestures and sign language, such as the universal thumbs up and thumbs down signals. Another one used here in Brazil, to indicate that you do not believe what the other person is saying, is to pull down the skin below your eyelid with your index finger, thus widening the view of your eyeball. While the thumb up gesture is quite common, another one to show pleasure or appreciation is to tug your earlobe very slightly. Some people exaggerate by reaching behind their head to do the same.

Vulgar signs seem to be universal, for example, the "finger" or *toco* and the "banana," referring to the whole forearm. The gesture we North Americans habitually use is the circle formed by the thumb and index finger, meaning, "perfect" or "right on." Although I see more and more Brazilians using this gesture nowadays, it normally has another meaning, referring to anal sex. Brazilian humorists continue to show the video scene of President Ronald Reagan making the sign many years ago at his hospital window, communicating to the public that all was well following a very serious surgery.

This scene of Reagan may be the classic example of a cultural difference, but the one I always remember, with chuckles, took place on the Amazon floodplain in 1996. We had made a stop next to a fisherman's canoe to see the fish he had caught. Looking at a very fine peacock bass, one of our guests gave him the above-mentioned gesture, to which the fisherman immediately responded with a violent shaking of a finger and a resounding, "No! No!" The funny part was that our guest recognized his blunder at once, turned red in the face, and tried unsuccessfully to explain in sign language that he was trying to say that it was a beautiful fish.

Take It Easy
The use of the word "gringo" by the Brazilians does not normally have the same derogatory meaning given to it in some other parts of the world. It refers to a person from the outside, a foreigner so to speak. People with lesser formal education do not always distinguish between nationalities and often refer to all foreigners as "Americanos" or gringos. It is spontaneity on their part, sort of "telling it the way it is," as seen via their perception of the world. Most of the time it is said without malicious intent, sometimes just to be funny or a way of joking with cohorts. The word is used so much, as a matter of fact, I have adopted it as everyday vocabulary in referring to foreigners. Then too, some persons address me intimately as *O Gringão*, the *Big Gringo*. I accept the nickname as an acknowledgement of friendship and never think otherwise. Without a doubt, though, the use of the word "*gringo*" can at other times carry tones of disgust and hate. If you pick up on this kind of rap, and you will, the best thing you can do is to ignore it.

What are They Saying about Me?
On occasion I find it very convenient not to understand Portuguese, or at least to pretend not to. Newcomers can get inquisitive about what is being said about them, for instance at public markets and other locations where large numbers of people gather. Contrary to what they think, most side-comments are not at all political or belligerent. My favorite spot for picking up on chitchat is at the Ver O Peso market in Belém. Venders there have character, and they are quite fearless in saying what they like. Some comments are hilarious. Just when I expect someone to say, "Go home, Yankee," "You fat imperialist pig," or "Suck my cock-a-doodle-do," some little old man looks up from his vegetable stand and politely asks, "Have you ever been a *corno?*" *What?* Have I ever been a *corno?* The word *corno* comes from the word "horn." The sexual connotation is what we might call "being horny" in English. To carry the meaning to its full extent, a *corno* is a man whose wife is cheating on him. He, therefore, grows horns (*chifres*). In the Latin culture, there is nothing more demeaning in life than to be a *corno*. Times are changing, but

177

the newspapers of the country continue to run stories and show photographs of the *corno's* wife and her lover together in the bed, the sheets splattered with blood and the bodies full of bullet holes. Legalities are also changing, but there was a time when the deceived husband was fully justified in murdering his beloved wife and mother of his children. Double standards being what they are, he may have several lovers and children outside the marriage—but he does not want to be a *corno*.

Turn Up the Sound

"Brazilians have an obsession for loud music," remarked a tourist coming through Santarém. I agree. People of the Amazon enjoy music to the *fullest* and also the *loudest.* Maybe it comes from wanting to share what is good in life with those around you that necessitates radios and sound systems be turned up full blast. Sometimes the desire to share the loud music starts very early in the morning or extends until the wee hours of night. There are rarely any complaints. Foreigners, on the other hand, often have a hard time dealing with these situations, so they can be an exception to the rule. Many travelers staying at the Amazon Park Hotel tell me that they register complaints with the management because of the Friday night live music presentations. Some, more desperate for sleep at any cost in their counteraction, get dressed and go down to the pool area to create a scandal that brings everything to a halt. Mind you, this normally takes place at 3 AM, after having called the desk several times to protest.

Outsiders are invariably thrilled when invited to carnival dances and other local parties, but they always comment on the deafening power of the speakers. It is so loud that you can hardly hear yourself think. A friend living in Rio de Janeiro reminded me that loud music is characteristic of Brazil as a whole not of just the Amazon.

Culture clashes work both ways. We "outsiders" do not appreciate loud dinner music, blasting stereo systems in cabs, broken loudspeakers hung up on the light poles next to our hotel rooms and so on. Likewise, many Brazilians have problems understanding our audacity in complaining over such issues. "I didn't come down here to listen to rock and roll music," complained a traveler on a riverboat tour. "This is the trip of my life. I want to hear sounds of the rain forest." We had just pulled into shore for some piranha fishing, and the captain did what was natural in this case: he turned on the sound system. People who work for tour agencies on a regular basis learn the ways of foreigners, and I can say, truthfully, that they go out of their way to please their customers. Others have difficulty in grasping the concept of how anyone could be so rude as to complain. After all, the intention is that of pleasure, not harassment.

The most humorous story I heard in this regard was that of an encounter that took place between a European scientist living just down the street from our home and his neighbor, who likes the volume of his music in the upper stratosphere. As you might guess, the shock of having his eustachian tubes blown out at any hour of the day or night was a bit too much for the newly-arrived scientist, and he did the unexpected— one day he *actually* asked his neighbor to turn down the volume. I am not sure what happened right there on the spot, but the neighbor's later comment to friends about the confrontation was classic: "What's-his-face ("*cara*") came all the way from Europe to tell me to turn down my music."

I can appreciate what the gentleman (now back home in "quiet" Europe) must have gone through because we also had to deal with a sound enthusiast in the neighborhood where we live. He enjoyed peaking volume on his pride-and-joy sound system. Frequent electrical failures in Santarém at that time had their compensations because it gave us a chance to listen to *nothing* for a change. Any overt irritation that I might have manifested in regard to this situation was mitigated by the fact that this neighbor is a very likable person and he, at least, warned us what was coming up in our lives. Meeting him at the corner *bodega* (bar) one night, he excitedly told me that he was getting a new *aparelho de som* (sound system) for Christmas and he hoped I enjoyed listening to music. "*Com certeza,*" (For sure) I responded, not knowing that he was planning an assault on every set of ears within the radius of a city block. Neighbors complained bitterly about not being able to listen to their televisions, talk over the telephone, or participate in any other activity requiring silence. But these intermittent protests were restricted to street chatter, proving that Brazilians place a very high value on individual liberty. We never hear the sound system anymore because he moved to another part of town. Otávio Gomes, friend and local dentist, put the situation in perspective when he said, "The fact that we tolerate exaggerated noise, doesn't mean we like it."

Putting up with loud *brega* music is not unbearable because it is at least popular Brazilian music. Suffering from the consequences of commercial and political bombardment from ambulatory sound systems is another matter. I am referring to the *barulho* (noise) coming from vehicles equipped with generators, over-powered amplifiers and loudspeakers— the combination of which will lower your cochlea hairs for a long time to come. Visitors often mistake this blaring sound for some important, pressing announcement being made by the government. They are amused to discover that they are merely listening to advertisements, departure times for boats, liquidation sales, upcoming *festas*, inauguration of new stores and so on. The concentration of these vehicles increases manifold during political campaigns, as does the decibel factor. *Políticos* who can afford it, and most can, equip large trucks with racks of loudspeakers—equal in number to the famed *trio elétrico* of carnival in Bahia, Rio de Janeiro and Recife. Counting on musicians, singers, pretty girls and an outlandish number of flashing lights on the truck, candidates come up with something that could pass for a spectacular Rolling Stones production. When one of these window-rattling shows passes by your home or office, you know you have a front-row seat.

During daylight hours, the favorite domain for parading ambulatory sound systems is the downtown area of Santarém, especially around the Praça de Pescador—where I maintained an office for two years. My tour agency was located on the second floor of a building overlooking Rua Senador Lameira Bittencourt and the Praça do Pescador. To the envy of all, my office had one of the best views of *Ponta Negra* in town—referring to the place where the Amazon and Tapajós Rivers meet. Very few tourists ever showed up at my office because there were few around, but it was a great place to get together with friends, and who could complain about having to look at the wedlock of two of the largest rivers in the world? The only "Catch-22" to this godsend address was something called "noise." It was just unbelievable. There were hours when it was impossible to hold a conversation or even hear what the other party was saying over the telephone. The amplified sound systems blasted my two open windows coming down Francisco Corrêa and then the other two on Senador Lameira Bittencourt, as they turned right. More often than not the vehicles doubled back on the other side of Praça do Pescador, just to annoy me from a different angle. The location of my office was perfect, the rent was certainly amenable, but the noise was insuperable.

At the end of the second year, I decided to return to my small backyard office on Travessa Turiano Meira. I forgot to mention that one of my reasons for transferring the office to the downtown location in the beginning was to escape the incessant barking of my neighbor's dog, which was usually chained to a very small area just a few meters from my office window. I am being kind when I say "barking" because it was more of an ongoing, obnoxious, mechanical yelp that got on my nerves over the years I operated out of my makeshift office. When I returned to the premises two years later, our canine friend was still barking and our neighbor was still completely oblivious to the fact that the noise could possibly inconvenience anyone. I should clarify that this person (now deceased) was very considerate in terms of respecting our privacy. I firmly believe that he simply did not consider the noise as an annoyance to anyone. In fact, I doubt that he ever heard it. To illustrate what I mean, one night we had several guests over for a birthday party and the dog barked so much, and so loudly, we could not carry on a conversation with our guests. I must have lost my "cool" because I finally decided it was time for a confrontation with our neighbor. Nothing outrageous, mind you, just a fast, emotional plea that he move the dog to the front yard, thereby putting some distance between the noise and us. Surprisingly enough, my neighbor accepted my petition in good spirits and the dog was re-chained in the front yard, where she continued to bark to no end—right in her master's ear. Our neighbor continued his conversation with his friend, not in the least disturbed by the incessant noise.

In the meanwhile, back downtown, the noise pollution is worse than ever. Most merchants nowadays hire street barkers equipped with microphones and potent amplifiers to attract potential customers. Given the number of stores participating in this abusive practice, the noise level is inconceivable. So as not to over generalize, I should add that not all merchants, nor customers, agree to such marketing techniques. Hélcio Amaral once owned a small hardware store right in the middle of this chaos and I remember his making every effort to convince his fellow merchants to put a stop to the noise. They would not listen! It seems to be an attribute of the trade, and it must have some commercial value, since most people cooperate to preserve the *status quo*. Hélcio finally took the attitude, "If you can't beat 'em, join 'em," but in a very retaliatory way. When the noise level outside his open door began to get on his nerves, he would turn on a ship siren that easily drowned out all competitors for two square blocks. His message was loud and clear. Hélcio eventually left the hardware business for the world of politics, first as a technical consultant to one of the past mayors and then as Secretary of Culture. I have been meaning to ask him if all that noise had anything to do with closing down his hardware store.

Hotels in the downtown section of Santarém are also subject to the harassment of unchecked noise pollution. A few years ago, Joaquim Costa da Pereira, one of the most successful entrepreneurs of Santarém, took me for a tour of his then vacant Hotel Modelo, located right in the heart of "Noiselândia," between Avenida Tapajós and Senador Lameira Bittencourt. Joaquim's intent was quite obvious—

he was trying to rent the old hotel building. It might have been an interesting proposal but for the noise coming from the street. One would have to be very tired, indeed, to get any rest under such circumstances. One of our leading guides in Santarém, Waldinor Mota (currently living in the United States), told me that he knew of several cases of tourists leaving downtown hotels accommodations for the more secluded Amazon Park Hotel because they could not get any rest.

Call a Cab

Taxis are always nearby, sometimes long lines of them. Except for the airport taxis, which charge a pre-fixed price of approximately US$ 20, all use meters. *Bandeira 1* rates are for commercial hours during weekdays and *Bandeira 2* for night, holiday and weekend "runs." For most of us foreigners, the most unpleasant experience associated with taxi service is that the drivers consider it their divine obligation to get you to your destination as fast as possible, which means traveling at high speeds. J. B. Heiss, professor of vertebrate natural history at Cornell University, summed up how many people feel when he told me, "When I have to take a cab, I just keep my eyes closed half the time. I really don't want to see what's happening." A humorous incident took place a few years ago when I found it necessary to hire an airport taxi to take two extra passengers and part of the group's luggage to the Amazon Park Hotel. The *motorista* of the taxi took off in front of us like a "bat out of hell," only to have a flat tire three or four miles down the road. When we caught up with them, our two uneasy riders demanded that they join the rest of the group in the VW van, even if they had to sit on top of others. I volunteered to stay behind with the tall, lanky cabby, now nicknamed Barney, to open up some space in the van and to keep an eye on the luggage. Off went the VW van leaving Barney to the task of changing the tire. He was just as fast with a tire wrench as he was behind the wheel of his car. In no time at all he got the taxi back on the road and passed the van like a rocket. He had the luggage unloaded at the hotel long before the rest of the group caught up with us.

Behind the Wheel

"Americans are educated drivers. We have rules and regulations to go by and we obey them," voiced the mother of a family visiting Santarém. She made these comments while narrating an experience that had taken place the evening before when she had hired a taxi from the Moscote Restaurant to her hotel. "He came this close to hitting two bicycles," she said, measuring half an inch between two fingers. "He was very rude to other drivers, cutting in and out of traffic and, besides, he drove too fast." Well, what could I say under the circumstances? I have to admit that drivers here function on a different wavelength than we foreigners do. I believe that local driving habits should not be judged as right or wrong. Let it stand that they are different and that they take some getting used to. As Professor Heiss remarked, sometimes it is better to just close your eyes and hope for the best.

I have come to accept the fact that, behind the steering wheel, many drivers can be aggressive, impatient, and often impolite—especially when even slightly inconvenienced. It is easy to get psyched into this same mentality, and I often find myself getting intolerant with rude drivers. My wife recognizes the foolishness of such behavior and is quick to bring me back to the realm of defensive driving. Understand that it is far better to play a submissive role in street conflicts than to get into life or property-threatening clashes. Most of the time the flare-up anger of a disagreeable encounter is forgotten quickly, and we get on with our life. As one person so discerningly stated, "I didn't come down here to get into a pissing contest." Getting to our destination and back home again, sound and safe, is surely a noble accomplishment.

Traffic Lights

Traffic signals are much more reliable in Santarém than some years ago. I remember when they functioned so badly that they were not to be trusted by anyone at any time. To put it bluntly, they were life threatening. On rare occasions, all units in the city were in full operation and, at other times, not one was functioning properly.

Sometimes a light worked in one direction, but not in the other, or a combination of other defects. When available, military police directed traffic at major intersections during peak hours to regulate the flow of traffic. Rightfully so, they never made decisions based on the color of the traffic light above them. They could not possibly see the lights anyway. The signal kept doing its thing, right or wrong, and the policeman did his. This situation required that drivers pay attention to what was going on at both levels, since the signal may be displaying green while the policeman is motioning for you to stop, or vice versa. When the work shift ended for the policemen, they simply took off their work vests, put their whistles and flashlights in their pockets and walked away, leaving us to the mercy of fate. With luck and a lot of patience, we avoided many accidents. Oscillation of electrical current, plus blackouts and electrical storms, played havoc with the innards of these ancient traffic lights, guaranteeing maintenance a nightmare for the traffic department.

While traffic lights work better these days in Santarém, there is a total lack of synchronization between units. Unless you want to practice Formula I tactics, it is necessary to stop at almost every traffic light. I consider it a true waste of time, gasoline and patience. When the latter becomes unusually thin, I space out to former years in Phoenix, Arizona, where I remember driving through miles and miles of traffic lights without ever having to stop once. Here, traffic maintenance teams have their hands full just trying to keep the lights working. Imagine trying to synchronize the operation of them.

A real engineering oddity and one that everyone discovers quickly is that most lights are installed up in the stars instead of being placed on the street corners at eye level. The consequence is that on a red light the driver must stop far back from the intersection in order to keep his signal in sight or stick his head out the window to look straight up. Tall people are definitely at a disadvantage in this situation—oh, my aching neck. Another irritating factor is that when a larger vehicle is in front of you, the signal is completely blocked from your view. The real inconvenience and challenge comes when one advances to make a left turn with heavy oncoming traffic. Once in the middle of the intersection the signal is actually out of sight and it is easy to go into a state of stage fright, as you discover that all drivers are looking at you from all four directions and you do not have the slightest idea whether you still have the green light or not. There are no cues, so to speak, since you cannot see the signal. When drivers from the side streets start "gunning" their motors, you pray that the oncoming traffic will stop so you can complete your left turn.

"Lucy in the Sky" traffic signals also present hazards to night driving because they are easily confused with the common streetlights. The signals are obviously not up that high, but when looking at them from a distance, they all blend in very well, especially the yellows.

Follow that Bus

The most vivid memory of my first visit to Brazil, in 1958, was that of waking up in my hotel room to an incessant roar of traffic that could only be compared to a downtown stockcar race. A quick look from my window disclosed the source. Streams of buses were coming from every direction, all chock-full of passengers making their way into the city. In a country where the vast majority of the population depends on public transportation, one should not expect anything less. Santarém, although a small city, is certainly no exception to the rule. Buses are literally bumper-to-bumper on the major streets of downtown and continue running in "packs," even on the outer edges of the city. While they render the task of transporting large numbers of passengers from point to point, the safe management and operation of them are of great concern to most other drivers and pedestrians. Looking back at my initial driving experience in Santarém, I remember all too well having to slam on the brakes of my car as a bus simply stopped in the middle of the lane to drop off a passenger. I impulsively blew my horn in protest, only to get a dirty look from the bus driver, and some passengers.

"Be here, now," and accept the fact that there are very few places, if any, where the buses can get out of the traffic lanes—even on major highways like BR 163. There are designated bus stops but few places for the buses to pull over to the side of the street or road. They stop where they can, which is normally in the middle of the road, and cars coming from behind have to stop or edge around them, often moving into oncoming traffic. *Motoristas* in that lane recognize the motive for such touch-and-go behavior and make an effort to squeeze over to the side to provide some extra room. If the oncoming vehicles cannot move over, then a stop behind the bus is unavoidable. As the buses stop without warning, they also move forward without any regard as to what is happening around them. The greatest danger in passing in this situation is that the driver will move ahead before you get completely around, thus giving you less time than you figured you had to get back into your own lane. Even more frustrating is having a parked car suddenly move into the lane that had been previously deemed free for passing.

Relax and put your best defensive-driving skills to work when dealing with larger vehicles. I learned this lesson one day when a bus driver decided that the side of my car needed a shave. The best I can figure out is that the driver was simply playing around to see how close he could pass me without actually bashing my car, since we were not in a congested traffic area. He neatly hit my side-view mirror in such a way that it flipped forward on its hinge without even damaging the mirror. Nevertheless, the noise was great enough that I anticipated much more damage, and I went after him. A "cops and robber" chase was on, but to no avail. I blew my horn and yelled for the impudent driver to stop, but he just kept going. I angrily took note of the license plate number, the company name and finally got ahead of the bus to meet him personally at a distant bus stop. "You hit my car," I cried out on entering the front of the bus. "You were parked in the middle of the street," he retorted. "I'm going to report you to the police," I responded. "Go ahead" were his final words. After cooling off, I finally resolved that the damage did not warrant the time and energy of reporting him to his company nor the police. Nothing would have come of it anyway, so why get stressed out over such a minor accident? I have learned that the best approach in dealing with aggressive bus drivers is to avoid them as much as possible. The vehicles are gigantic and the drivers more often than not tired and irritated from long, hectic days with very little pay to compensate for their occupation. Nevertheless, many passengers, with good reason, complain of careless behavior on the part of drivers, like abrupt stops and takeoffs, which send them flying in all directions. I am not sure if local statistics are available, but on a national basis many people are killed annually as the result of careless bus drivers. If I were a passenger, I would protest against the practice of high-speed turns, some of which could be compared to knee-scraping tactics practiced by motorcycle racers.

Two-Wheelers

At the other end of the spectrum are the bicycles. We would all be better off using this kind of transportation but, unfortunately, bicycle riding in Santarém requires lots of street savvy and old-time effrontery in order to get around. As an American visitor pointed out, "Bicycle riders in Santarém are gutsy." I bought bicycles for both of my kids, but they were hardly ever used—because we were justifiably concerned about the safety of our children. Bicycles and motorized vehicles sharing the same space at the same time cause frequent accidents and deaths. Likewise, *motociclistas* are at high risk. I rode a motorcycle the first two years in Santarém but finally changed over to a car after several very close calls with death. Like an ex-smoker, I still have a lingering urge to get onto another motorcycle, but I keep delaying the action, hoping that the craving will go away. While riders of bicycles and motorcycles are continually subject to life threatening risks, they are also, in part, responsible for many of the accidents involving their kind. Bicyclists are immune to *all* traffic laws. For example, they run stop signs and traffic lights. They pass on the right-hand side of your car when you are about to make a turn. They come at you on one-way streets, wanting half of your lane. Furthermore, they do not use running lights at night and in many cases not even a reflector. What amazes me is that these transgressions occur right in front of traffic police, and never is a word said to the violators. Drivers of motored vehicles, on the other

188

hand, are scrutinized to the nth degree because *multas* (traffic fines) represent a sizable income to public coffers and license plates are easily recorded, to say nothing about the value of a confiscated vehicle. The only time I ever remember any bicycle surveillance was a few years ago when the local government made an attempt to get bicycles off the walkways of the retainer wall that separates the Tapajós River from the city. It was a noble undertaking because this walkway is a major link between the eastern and western part of town and is also the premier recreational area for many Santarenos. Bicycle riders obviously like the walkway, too, because it is a smooth, flat surface away from the heavy traffic of Avenida Tapajós and its many potholes. Remembering the fine bicycle paths of Anchorage, Alaska, I can comprehend the pleasure of riding a bike away from chaotic traffic. On the other hand, I can also applaud the city government's interest in restricting this area to foot traffic only. It is annoying to have groups of fast-moving bicycle riders bearing down on you, especially in the dark of the evening when one cannot forget simple security precautions. In the finest tradition of maintaining *status quo*, the bicyclists were not intimidated by a municipality decree and just plain refused to obey the law—even after policemen were stationed on the sidewalk to confiscate the bikes of the offenders. After some weeks of voiced outrage and some turmoil with bicyclists, law enforcement and walkers, the government finally gave in. To this day bicycles come and go as they like.

The introduction of motorcycle taxis in 2002 changed the status of traffic in Santarém from risky to dangerous. Overnight the streets of the city were clogged with two-wheelers transporting straddled passengers from one place to another—for a fraction of the cost of a taxi. The outrage expressed by long-established taxi and bus businesses was no match for the army-sized motorcycle *taxista* crowd. They were not to be intimidated by anyone, not even the law. Their numbers may have reached 2,000 or more as the municipality looked for ways to appease them and the public, now very appreciative of an alternative public transportation system. After months of meetings with the different factions, the local government licensed approximately 200 motorcycle drivers, a drop in the bucket compared with the number already providing this service. Despite some very rigid police supervision, the non-licensed drivers are still very much in the majority and the streets of Santarém are filled with motorcycles coming and going in all directions.

Keep off the Sidewalk

Last week I was sharing over MSN Messenger a digital photograph I had taken from my upstairs window with Gene Whitmer, who lives in Goiania. My intent was to show a cruise ship coming upriver, which, in my mind, is an attractive sight. I guess Gene was impressed with the scenery, but he quickly typed the question, "No sidewalks in Santarém?" I laughed because I had not even noticed the foreground of the photograph, which showed our neighboring homes across the street, all without sidewalks—just like most of the city. One should never come to the conclusion that streets are the exclusive domain of vehicles; they are always shared with human beings, who rarely ever see a sidewalk. The commercial section of Santarém maintains the greatest number of *calçadas*, but even there, one must take to the street in order to get around congested spots on the narrow walkways or to dodge the vendors and merchandise overflowing from the many stores. The best walkway in Santarém, to the envy of all other cities in the Amazon, is the aforementioned *Cais de Arrimo* (retainer wall) along the Tapajós River. Not only is it wide, smooth and lengthy (3.5 kilometers), it is also elevated, so that one is constantly in view of the city on one side and the river system on the other. Sadly, most other streets in the city are adorned with only bits and pieces of sidewalks, confirming the practice of individual liberty in terms of whether or not one should be built, and how. Take a walk on any major street in town—Avenidas Mendonça Furtado, Rui Barbosa, São Sebastião, Travessa Turiano Meira or any other thoroughfare—and you will find yourself walking in the street most of the time. Anything that might resemble a sidewalk or path is forever obstructed by driveways, parked cars, construction material, trash, vendor stands, weeds, mud-holes, small ravines and every other obstacle you can imagine, including entire families who set up their chairs in front of their homes in the evening to socialize or to catch a cool breeze. Take it from me, it is much easier to walk in the street, and that is exactly what most people do. The old philosophy of "walk the path of least resistance" is certainly of necessity in this case. But be very careful because there is a constant flow of buses, cars, trucks, motorcycles and bicycles racing by you with very little margin of safety. It is not infrequent to hear about people being killed by hit-and-run drivers in this situation. I walk from our home on Turiano Meira late every afternoon to buy bread at our local bakery only a block away, and there is no way of getting around it—I have to walk in the street. After some close calls I have learned to watch every step I make. I only need to remember that the father of a friend was killed by a hit-and-run motorcycle driver on this same stroll less than a year ago. Áurea's medical office is only three blocks down the street from home but it is seldom that she will venture to walk it because of the inconvenience and hazard of walking in the street.

Street People

To complicate the traffic-flow problem a bit more, some people are not satisfied with walking on the edge of the street. They insist on walking in the middle of it. Furthermore, the greater the number of persons involved, the more audacious they become in the invasion of thoroughfares or access to them. This statement in no way refers to authorized demonstrations and public affairs taking place in the streets of Santarém. These frequently occurring events disrupt traffic to no end but are planned ahead of time and are very well coordinated by public authorities. I am speaking of impromptu obstruction of transit by individuals and groups who simply will not get out of the way unless intimidated by a ton of rolling metal bearing down on them. Students and soccer teams are likely to indulge in such behavior when they walk in groups. When we face this situation, our immediate reaction is to take the attitude that the vehicle has the right of way and that the "jaywalkers" are in violation. Do not take anything for granted when dealing with a different culture. Back home you may declare, "These are my rights, these are yours; this is your side of the road, this is mine"— but do not count on such assumptions here. The best approach to this situation is to drive slowly and carefully so as not to hit some teenager absorbed in peer relationships. If you need to use the horn, do so timidly, so as to say, "Here I am. I'd like to get through, please." A heavy hand on the horn or impulsive verbal attack will certainly announce your intention of wanting passage, but you will not get through any faster.

Asphalt Jungle

The lack of well-constructed streets is another factor that makes driving conditions in the city complex. One can point to a number of reasons why streets are not of better quality, but the primary obstacle seems to be the large expanse of sandy knolls, remnants of past shorelines on the Tapajós River. Sand, being of high density, makes for a solid street foundation, if it can be held in place. Most streets in Santarém are not paved at all because it is an expensive proposition, requiring an extraordinary amount of infrastructure before ever putting down a layer of asphalt. Politics and the lack of public funding have led to the practice of using a relatively thin layer of chert (a clay and rock mixture) over the sand before adding the asphalt. Often, the road follows the course of dips, hills, and other natural contours and lacks proper drainage and curbstones and other basics so fundamental to street construction, the consequence of which becomes visible only after the first rains. Perhaps this explains why most streets are overhauled and paved during the dry season. The result of cheap construction is very expensive maintenance. Thus, the never-ending hassle of filling in potholes. Since *buracos*, as they are called, develop much faster than the city government can patch them, it is nearly impossible to keep tires, tire rims and front-end alignments in good order. Vehicle owners also legitimately complain about having to pay very expensive vehicle registration fees on an annual basis to the state of Pará, plus a number of other taxes, for very little in return. We are reminded of this fact when passing vehicles splash us with muddy water from potholes.

Getting splashed, by the way, is not a humorous event, but Áurea and I still laugh when recollecting an episode from a trip to Serra do

Navio in the state of Amapá, where we had gone to research a new tour route that would include that beautiful mining town. The mayor put us up at the official guesthouse and showed us around for the two days. Needless to say, we felt privileged that the mayor himself could take time away from his busy schedule for this purpose, and that he had a nice pick-up truck in which to take us. Right away we perceived that this man was a much respected authority in the region, not just because of the office he held, but also because he is an accomplished political leader, a man who had risen from the ranks of the working class at the ICOMI manganese mine. We soon got used to the out-pouring of homage paid to him wherever we went, so we were quite astonished one day to hear a young boy walking along the side of the road call him a *filho da puta*. Inadvertently the mayor had driven through a mud hole and had splashed muddy water on the pants of the unlucky young man. It happens all the time, but we still find this particular incident amusing because of the kid's spontaneity towards the unintentional act, and to whom it was being directed. I should add that getting a bath of muddy water is not restricted to pedestrians. A vehicle hitting a pothole in a paved street can splatter the contents of the puddle right up into adjacent cars. A smart driver has to know when to roll up the windows—and fast.

Law-of-the-land

It is unpleasant to mention traffic casualties while traveling in a country as beautiful as Brazil, but the subject matter is of some concern to all. I am told that the chances of getting injured in a vehicle are much greater than coming down with some pernicious tropical disease. Misfortune can happen anywhere in the world, yet, statisticians point their fingers at Brazil as being one of the champions of vehicle-related death and injuries. The figures are so shocking that the Brazilian Congress saw fit to completely overhaul all laws and regulations governing transit in the country.

The outcome is Law Number 9503, dated September 9, 1997, better known as the *Código de Trânsito Brasileiro*. I doubt that anything has ever changed driving habits as quickly as this law, mainly because it employs the "big stick" approach to irregularities. A pamphlet distributed in the streets of Santarém by the *Polícia Militar do Pará* and the Mayor's office of *Coordenadoria Municipal de Transportes* reports that 90 percent of accidents are the result of human errors, 6 percent the result of the physical conditions of the thoroughfares, and 4 percent the result of mechanical problems. I am a bit surprised by these statistics but assume they might represent the country as a whole. Regardless, the emphasis of liability is clearly placed on the *motorista*, as opposed to the road and vehicle conditions. The conclusion may be politically correct, as revenue from millions of driver violations is surely of greater significance for the government than that of increasing expenditures for safer streets and road conditions. As someone from New York pointed out, "These are third world roads, but regulated by first world laws." The temperament of the law is reflected in the long list of infractions and fines set forth in the code. Many of the *multas* are accompanied by other regulatory measures, including retention of vehicle and driver license. Expensive driver education, you might say, but at least it is a step towards reducing the free-for-all situation on our streets and highways. The use of seatbelts was never taken seriously in Santarém until this new law went into effect. As a matter of fact, I never bothered to buckle up prior to enforcement of the law. I am not sure how I got out of the habit of using seatbelts because I had always used them prior to coming to the Amazon. It surely had something to do with the fact that nobody else did, plus they are very hot to use. Driving past dozens of scrutinizing traffic officers, and the threat of heavy fines, guarantees that we do now. When the coast is clear, however, most drivers revert to their old driving habits. Never assume that drivers will stop for you on pedestrian street crossings, if not policed. Likewise, red lights and stop signs can be totally ignored by many drivers under these circumstances, especially the motorcycle drivers.

It is only fair to report that some positive changes are coming about at the local government level. I see more streets getting paved, rural roads being overhauled, street signs posted, some well-planned drainage systems under construction, and *fewer* potholes around than usual. New traffic lights are miraculously appearing at some very deserving locations, one of them at the heavily congested market place on Avenida Tapajós. More revolutionary yet, and a first for the city, are a few pedestrian traffic lights—those which tell us when to walk and when not to, using the universal colors of red and green.

The most noteworthy of all public works, and one that brought electrical energy back to our homes and to the streets of Santarém, was the construction of the high-tension power lines from the Tucuruí Dam on the Rio Tocantins, more than a thousand kilometers to the east. Referred to by many anxious citizens as the "construction project of the century," the *Linhão de Tucuruí* (Big Power Line from Tucuruí) was completed in February of 1999. Along with a more reliable source of electrical energy, the *Linhão* also brought *some* stability to traffic signals.

Got Some Small Change?
It is not uncommon to find visitors a bit irritated because they were not given the proper change following payment for some service or purchase. For example, the waiters not giving you the correct change after you pay a dinner bill. Notwithstanding the fact that some people are short-changed deliberately, most of the time this situation is due to the lack of small change to give you. Like finding a stamp of the exact domination needed, change is often difficult to come by. It is quite common in supermarkets that customers be given matches, candies, bread and other odds and ends in lieu of change. Some customers just say, "Forget it" or "Keep the change." Unexpectedly, sometimes the customer gets more change back than due. This business of figuring out change was a lot worse prior to the establishment of a new monetary system in mid-1994.

Where's Your Shirt?
In a hot tropical climate like the Amazon it is easy to rationalize that the fewer the clothes the better. The consequences are evident when we see *turistas* walking around downtown during regular business

hours without shirts or other essential pieces of clothing. For many, this kind of behavior is considered to be in poor taste. Few, if any, locals will make a case of the issue, but you can be assured that they are all looking and thinking that you are rude. I am told that to be without a shirt in public is actually prohibited by law. It may or may not be true but take notice that nearly everyone is wearing a shirt, including stevedores and other workers, who need all the ventilation they can get. Sometimes you might see a person without a shirt, but the chances are good that it is thrown over his shoulder or tied around his neck so that he can be properly dressed in short order. A teacher from Colorado recently passed on some good advice to me. "Look around. If you don't see anyone else doing what you're about to do, forget it." His insight proved to be useful on a riverboat trip from Belém to Santarém, when, on the first day of the three-day journey, he peeled off his shirt to get some sun. He sensed something was not "cool" and looked around to discover that he was the only shirtless person.

I am reminded sometimes that United States informality clashes not only with local dress code but also with just plain respect for individuals and authorities. An American professor at the Federal University of Pará in Belém still shakes his head when he tells the story of taking a group of American students to meet the mayor of a certain city in the eastern part of the state. To his surprise, one of the male students showed up at the mayor's office in cut-off jeans and hiking boots. Okay, students will be students and all Brazilians recognize that foreigners can deviate from the norm to which they are accustomed. But what really embarrassed the professor came during the actual meeting with the mayor when the same student nonchalantly peeled off his t-shirt, right in front of the *prefeito* and other dignitaries!

Cutoffs
"Don't they respect our culture?" grumbled a Brazilian friend in describing a male tourist he had seen walking around downtown in short cut-off jeans. I found it difficult to sympathize with him over

such a minor detail because it brought to mind a personal incident that had happened to me some time back at the local federal police agency where I had made a fast, impromptu stop to check on an identity card that took forever to arrive from Brasília. I am so accustomed to dressing informally (by Brazilian and European standards, not by American standards), I just plain forgot that I was in a pair of cut-off jeans. A secretary pointed me to the office of the agent assigned to *estrangeiros*, and as soon as I entered the small-congested room, I felt the weight of all eyes fall on me as though I were the Black Death. "Wait outside," admonished the agent, almost pushing me out of the room. "You can't come in here in your underwear." As I apprehensively backed out the door, I noticed that the same agent was wearing a pair of faded blue jeans and was badly in need of a shave. The occasion was certainly a blunder on my part, but I nevertheless did not expect such rigidity on the part of the government authorities since the dress code in Brazil has loosened up considerably over the years. I remember a time in Recife, in 1958, when long pants and a coat were required of men going to the movies, and I also recall being asked to leave a movie theater in the middle of the film because I had taken my coat off!

Hats Off

Foreigners must expect to make cultural goofs from time to time and I dare say that more often than not host nationals will look the other way, recognizing that "gringos" can be different. But then there are other times when an inadvertent gaffe on our part clashes profoundly with local mores and traditions. On these occasions we can expect to get feedback, whether we want it or not. Such was the case of a *New York Times* reporter who told me of an embarrassing incident that happened to her on a riverboat trip from Manaus to Santarém in June of 1999. The conflict that took place between her and the boat crew involved a beautiful Australian-style jungle hat that had become an integral part of her tropical attire while in the Amazon. Much like a birder who becomes incognizant to a pair of binoculars hung around his/her neck, our reporter friend sat down at the community dinner table completely unaware that she was still wearing the headpiece—

and that this kind of conduct is not taken lightly by the Brazilians. Although fluent in Spanish, her knowledge of Portuguese was limited so that she did not understand what was happening when a crewmember suggested that she remove her hat. Another crewman was called to help explain and in a less than tactful way made it clear that hats were not permitted at the table. Áurea tells me that wearing a hat at the table is considered to be a serious offense by host nationals, since it shows "disrespect" of others. The hour or so I spent talking with the reporter certainly demonstrated to me that she was an experienced journalist with all the traits of a person well-versed in etiquette and social graces—not the type of person to be deliberately discourteous to anyone at any time. Even though a few days had passed since the occurrence, I sensed that her feelings were still hurt.

I talked with another traveler who had a similar experience while in Belém. She told me that after a long morning of walking around the city, she and her husband had stopped at a luncheonette for something to eat. Feeling fatigued from the heat and unaware of the consequences, she propped up her feet on a chair. As she described it, the owner of the establishment immediately came over to her table to denounce her act and then walked away in "disgust." "The most humiliating part of the episode," said my client "was that of not being able to discuss the issue with him."

Restroom Blues

There are moments when we cannot comprehend why certain local practices take priority over others that *we* consider to be *much* more important. Take for instance, the use and upkeep of public bathrooms. Travelers are often taken aback by what they experience in this regard and the subject can become a topic of conversation when describing accommodations of boat travel on the Amazon. The anecdote I remember best was told by a mechanical engineer from Canada, Loy Bonazza, who routinely visits Brazil every three to five years and always makes it a point to stop in Santarém. On his last call we had some cold beers at the Mascotinho out over the city waterfront and talked about his most recent adventures on the Amazon, including the riverboat trip from Manaus to Santarém. He reported that the journey had been especially enjoyable because of friendships made with two female travelers he had met on board. One of their favorite places for getting together for long hours of conversation was the bar area located topside. My friend, long since accustomed to traveling in less than five-star environments, is not at all uncomfortable in having to use a messy bathroom but it seems that the one on the upper deck of this boat was awful—so much so that the two women made a vow not to drink anything on the entire trip, thus reducing the number of restroom visits. Logically, we might have problems trying to figure out why all the commotion over taking a hat off at the dinner table when so little attention is given to what *we* consider to be much more substantial—a clean restroom.

Etiquette in the Restroom
It is customary in Santarém and most other places in Brazil that tissue paper not be flushed down the toilet bowl. The tip-off will be a basket or another container conveniently located next to the commode, into which one places the used tissue. Persons accustomed to doing away with all evidence of their biological acts may have some problems in accepting this practice but, I assure you, toilets flush much better without wads of paper clogging up pipelines and septic tanks. I dare say that the vast majority of travelers get through their entire trip without ever discovering what that container is doing next to the toilet. They may also never figure out why the toilet does not flush properly. Dealing with the issue in a positive manner, I rationalize that it is far easier to confront a container of used toilet paper than a commode full of you know what.

"Steve, could you translate this for me?" asked a traveler who had copied a message placed in his hotel bathroom advising guests that toilet paper was to be placed in the wastepaper basket, not the toilet bowl. This person had made several visits to Brazil over the years and was still completely oblivious to the rules of bathroom etiquette. "This just can't be true! I can't ask the maid to clean up after me," he uttered. Actually, if everyone cooperates, the cleanup job for the chambermaid is not all difficult, nor demeaning. The repository is usually lined with a plastic sack that can be tied off or sealed before removal. Cleanup problems normally occur when users get messy in placing paper in the container. Techniques in dealing with the dirty toilet paper vary from person to person. Some fold the used tissue into small, neatly closed packages while others use a whole roll of paper, leaving half of the dirty paper hanging out of the receptacle.

Where's "John"?

Any restroom, even a primitive one, is a welcome sight when really needed. I was reminded of this self-evident truth one day when I found myself in street clothes on one of the glorious sandy beaches of Alter do Chão. I do not ordinarily go to the beach in long pants, shirt and shoes, but I had left home early in the morning without knowing the complete itinerary of two English clients making the rounds of several lumber mills in Santarém. Just before noon one of our hosts suggested that we take the two businessmen to Alter do Chão for lunch and in less than an hour we were all hydrating ourselves with cold *cerveja* and eating barbecued fish on the island in front of the main village. Beer on top of a morning of *cafézinhos* served at sawmill offices put me in the position of looking for a restroom soon after arriving. A quick look around the premises of the *barracão* (a thatched hut) indicated no relief available, so I asked our waiter the whereabouts of the *banheiro*. "Over there in the village," he said as he puckered up his lips in the direction of the Lago Verde Restaurant far in the distance. My bladder could not believe it. There was not one restroom of any kind or shape on this famed beach, a recreational area that at times accommodates hundreds of beach-loving people. Biting my tongue and repressing every muscle possible, I eventually made it back to the village without having to go for a *swim* in my street clothes. This was back in 1998. I am not sure if things have changed for the better, but some weeks after the incident I was having lunch with a group of friends when the subject of sanitation came up. Taking advantage of the discussion, I asked a well-known DJ in Santarém the weighty question, "What do people do when they need to take a crap?" After all, a little bit of urine mixed in the mighty waters of Lago Verde (Green Lake) and the Tapajós River is one thing, but *merda* is another. Our radio announcer friend, who was already worked up over the subject, responded forcefully, "You know *what* they do? They hire a canoe to take them way up the beach where they can run into the woods." "Okay," I thought to myself, "Why didn't I think of that?"

Stoke up the Boiler

What! No hot water? Except for the ranks of four- and five-star hotels, the only hot water you will experience will be from the sun-heated water pipes under the roof. If you are a hot water fan, you have about six seconds to enjoy the shower. I have known men to go days without shaving because they are not accustomed to shaving with cold water. Another little cultural difference around the washbasin is that hotels do not provide washcloths, nor do they provide sink-stoppers for filling the sink. It is customary to let the water run freely from the faucet while washing. Brazilians prefer to take showers several times a day as opposed to just washing their faces. Tub baths, by the way, are to be found only in the finest hotels of Brazil.

Not all travelers get into the kitchen, but when they do, they are taken aback to see that most dishes are hand-washed in cold water. Mechanical dishwashers with sterilizing features are rare specimens in hotels and restaurants.

More Clothing than Necessary

It used to be if you saw a person in Santarém wearing coat and tie, you could bet he was a lawyer. Likewise, if you saw a man wearing only shirt and tie, the chances were good that he was a Protestant minister. In early 1999, the state of Pará passed an administrative regulation mandating that heads of all government offices wear coats and ties. Now it is more difficult to know who is behind all that unessential clothing. Coat-and-tie dress for the rest of us is reserved for very special occasions such as weddings, graduations and funerals (suits normally worn by the deceased only). The last suit I owned was made here in Santarém in 1980, coincidentally tailored by Robson Riker, grandson of Robert Riker, one of the original American Confederates who came to Santarém following the Civil War in the United States. Unfortunately, I outgrew the fine tailored suit within a few years and I have never bought another, just to show you how informal life is here in the Amazon.

Too Little Clothing

Cultural clashes work both ways, so it is comprehensible that travelers are at times taken aback by what they see in terms of local clothing, or the lack of it. A serious gaffe is that of making erroneous conclusions about other people based on their clothes. Early one evening I was walking back to the riverboat with two foreign clients when I overheard one make the remark that there were "sure a lot of call girls walking around." I nearly fell over backward hearing what she said. Obviously, her conclusions were made on the fact that she saw many mini-skirted girls and women socializing on the sidewalk in front of the Mascotinho Restaurant. With all due respect, this was most likely the case of an older, formal person verbalizing disapproval of the chic mode of dress so fashionable at the time throughout Brazil. But it proved to me that we are all vulnerable to drawing hasty conclusions about others based on cultural likes and dislikes.

Lesser Yet

"We'd better get out of here before we get beaten up!" was a comment I overheard one boat crewman saying to another, in response to one of our foreign guests taking a swim in his birthday suit. This took place right in front of a village on the Tapajós River near Fordlândia. Nudity has found a home in very small enclaves on select beaches in Rio de Janeiro and a few other places in Brazil, but it is *not* accepted behavior in the Amazon. In a tropical paradise of clear water and endless stretching beaches, the Tapajós River is certainly an ideal place for returning to the natural side of life, but nudists should be very discreet in where they disrobe. Some folks find it incongruous that in a country of beautiful bodies, mini-skirts, dental-floss swimwear, and a marked accent on sexiness, that the Brazilians do not go one step further and take it all off while taking a swim. Sorry, but that is the way it is here in God's country.

Footwear, a Real Giveaway

One muggy evening several years ago, I was socializing with interns from the Universidade Federal de Pará at Fundação Esperança when my good friend, Paulo Sérgio Pimentel, took advantage of the informal gathering to make fun of my flip-flop sandals. "Look at the size of those canoes," he wisecracked. To add fuel to the fire, he pulled off my newly acquired tropical footwear and smelled them with the pretension of having discovered American *chulé* (the smell of athlete's foot). Paulo's good sense of humor keeps us laughing on such occasions, so I would not even have remembered the episode were it not for the fact that he repeated the "canoe" performance on at least two other occasions. Recognizing that I am big, even by American standards, I was beginning to accept the fact that wherever I went I left tracks equal to those of the Abominable Snowman. But to be honest about it, I could never understand why all the fuss over my sandals and not my shoes, size 11 (43 in the metric system). Eventually I came to realize that Paulo's teasing had little to do with the size of my feet—only the size of my sandals. As strange as it may seem, most people here buy and wear their flip-flop sandals in a smaller size than their street shoes. We foreigners normally use the same size for both and, thus, deviate from what is normal in this culture. I have always observed that most Brazilians, at least here in the Amazon, allow their heels to hang out over the end of their sandals but I could never understand why. I have yet to completely satisfy my curiosity in this regard, but evidently the practice of using undersized sandals makes for less of a clacking sound as the heels of the sandals come down on the floor or sidewalk. A person from Belém once told me that the unrestrained smacking of sandals is associated with the walk of persons lacking in social graces.

Although there seems to be no social stigma associated with the wearing of socks and sandals together, Brazilians very seldom dress in this manner. Foreigners, on the other hand, are quite comfortable in wearing sandals with or without socks. I have to admit that I am so accustomed to the local tradition that I automatically suspect anyone wearing socks of being a traveler.

All Soles Day

Chances are good that I would never have discovered that an overturned sandal is considered to be a bad omen had it not been for my friend and nearby neighbor, Flávio Serique. Flávio (now deceased), who was director of Cultura Inglesa (a school of English informally associated with the British Council), was kind enough to invite me over to his home for birthday parties and any other occasion that calls for the gathering of friends. Given that he and his former wife, Geanne, had many *amigos*, invitations were very generous, as is their hospitality. Flávio's favorite area for socializing was the heavenly ventilated patio outside his second-floor bedroom, and it was there where we grouped on a Saturday afternoon in July of 1999 for *pato no tucupi* (duck in tucupi), cold beer, music and conversation. The subject of sandals came up when Flávio, who was sitting in his hammock, made a move to retrieve his own flip-flops and inadvertently let one of them flip over. One of the teachers at Cultura Inglesa was very quick to turn the sandal right side up but I reckoned the gesture as being that of someone wanting to help, since Flávio was recuperating from a physical disorder that had nearly taken his life two years earlier. "Steven, look at this," said our host, pointing to his sandals on the floor. "Do you know that an overturned sandal is a sign of bad luck?" Well, as a matter of fact, I had never heard of it. Flávio took a fast survey among others in our company and, without fail, everyone knew of the superstition and responded that they would feel obliged to upright a sandal under these circumstances.

After returning home that evening I noticed that Daniel had carelessly tossed his sandals to one side of the living room—leaving both of them soles up. Obviously he had never heard of the superstition either. Wanting to sleep well that night, I turned them over and went to bed.

KEEPING AFLOAT ON THE AMAZON —
MONEY EXCHANGE

Santarém must be one of the few cities in Brazil without an official exchange service and it creates many problems for travelers and other people needing to transfer money from outside Brazil. All transactions end up in Belém and there is some time-consuming bureaucracy in getting the transfer on to Santarém. Cash and travelers checks can be exchanged at Banco do Brasil, but expect some long, slow-moving lines. Most travelers prefer to exchange their money with private dealers in the city. The blessing of all blessings is being able to withdrawal money from the ATM machines which are now found at most banks.

An increasing number of stores and service establishments in Santarém are accepting international credit cards these days. Travelers prefer to use plastic whenever possible, since the exchange rate on final billing will be much better than what you can get for the dollar on the parallel market. But before urbanely slapping down your credit card on the counter of some small commercial business for a beer and two cokes, remember that some require a predetermined minimum. Then, too, you have to remember that credit card verifications are dependent on interstate telephone connections, which at times are hard to make in Brazil. This proved to be the case not long ago when I took my clients from the *Royal Princess* to a local supermarket to purchase some Brazilian wine, coffee and guaraná powder. Not being able to exchange money locally, they tried to pay the bill in American dollars, but with no success. "We can't accept dollars," said the manager, "but you can use your credit card." Which? You name it; the store had a machine for every piece of plastic ever invented. Since there were three couples with me, three bills were involved, as were three credit cards. After ten minutes of inserting the first card through the electronic billing machine, while all of us and several supermarket employees all looked on attentively, the clerk informed us that the card was not accepted because one of the grouping of numbers had only three digits, not the standard four. So it was on to the other cards, which had the right number of digits. Another ten minutes of passing two more credit cards through the machines, but to no avail. It was around five o'clock in the afternoon and phone lines were so congested that there was no way of connecting with southern Brazil. Conversation between our important visitors sadly turned to having to return their prized purchases to the shelves when I suggested that I sign for the bill. In ten minutes I had them back at the ship.

More about the Real

In July of 1994, the Brazilian government established a new monetary system that abolished the cruzeiro and brought in the present currency, the *real*. The pronunciation is *he-all* in this part of Brazil. The plural of real is reais, pronounced *he-ice*. On the first day of implementation, this currency was indexed to the America dollar, one real to one dollar. Over the succeeding days, the exchange rate dropped as low as 81 cents per real on the open market. Touting the strong real as a measure of controlling inflation, the federal government refused to let the currency float. When Fernando Henrique Cardoso took oath for the second term in January 1999, the exchange rate had edged up to only 1.20 per dollar. Many economists felt that the exchange rate was out of line with reality, maybe as much as 30-40%. "I'd planned on spending a lot of time in Brazil, but everything was so expensive I found myself running to the bank everyday to withdraw money. So I decided to go back to Peru, where I could travel for less than half of what it took in Brazil." This was a very common declaration we heard from tourists. The forewarning of devaluation of the real proved to be correct. By mid-January of 1999, billions of dollars were making a retreat from Brazil and it was a question of days before the real lost more than 40% of its value.

The most difficult logistical problem in adopting the real in the early 1990s was that of making change. In the latter days of the cruzeiro, the inflation rate was running around 48% per month, and because everything was priced in the thousands and millions, paper money was the order of the day. With the advent of a stabilized economy, metal coins became a practical form of making small change. The one, five, ten, twenty-five and fifty-centavo pieces, plus the one real coin, made for a welcome change, excuse the pun. In the early days of the real, making change continued to be a problem because too few coins had been produced to take care of national needs. In addition to the scarcity of coins, the government also made the mistake of making all the coin denominations look the same—all of them made of aluminum, all round and about the same size. Furthermore, the denomination of the coin appears on only one side, thereby requiring that one turn them over in order to see the value. It takes awhile to sort out the right change under these circumstances. To remedy the problems the federal government began to issue new coins of different sizes and colors in July of 1998.

Cultural Contrasts

Much of the local paper currency, especially of the lower denominations, is practically worn out, but continues to circulate. The exchange market, on the other hand, will reject foreign currency, if the bill has the slightest defect, like tears and graffito, or any sign of being worn or defaced. Keep this in mind when saving cash dollars for any upcoming trip to Brazil.

When requesting an extended-tourist visa from a federal police agency, you should be prepared to prove that you have sufficient funds to carry you over to the date of your departure. It can be in the form of currency or credit cards, which you might have to show to the attending officer. You will also need to present your plane ticket and pay a fee at the Banco do Brasil. It is wise to begin this process a few days in advance.

Post offices tend to be busy, crowded places, with long lines of customers and few attendants. The problem is that they provide a myriad of services that we outsiders fail to recognize as mail service.

Most of the people you see in the lines are there to buy lottery tickets, pay water and electric bills, and to collect governmental benefits of one kind or another. While idling time away, you will rarely ever see anyone mailing a letter. Post-office attendants work very hard to keep up with the task of filling out forms, rubberstamping and tearing of paper. To give credit where credit is due, the post office at Praça de Bandeira is totally renovated and a single-line system of attendance instituted with a numbered pass system and computers for attendants. Although the post office is quite crowded, the flow is much faster than it has ever been in the past and seating is now available. It is no fun waiting, but it is much easier to deal with when organized.

A few travelers consider lightening the load of their suitcases or backpacks by mailing things back home. The idea is certainly a good one, except it is very expensive. In recent times a couple from Colorado told me of their experience of meticulously preparing two shoebox-sized containers for the post office, only to discover that the cost was going to be the equivalent of about sixty dollars. The two packages became part of their carry on baggage.

To dismiss any fears of poor delivery service on the part of the post office, I am pleased to report that in the many years I have lived in Santarém I have never, to my knowledge, lost a letter due to dishonesty or carelessness on the part of the post office. To the contrary, I have received letters that should have been returned to the senders, such as letters with only name and the city. Some of them had no street address, no zip code, nor even the state! I wish I could attribute the surprising deliveries to my being rich and famous, but I can only credit the alert and diligent postal employees.

SHOPPING FOR ARTS AND CRAFTS

If you happen to be in Santarém during the stopover of one of the cruise ships, you will find the public squares filled with vendors selling everything from fish scales to t-shirts. Between cruise ship stops, however, tourists are as rare as "anteater teeth" and the street vendors retreat like bushmasters after a hearty meal of forest rat. But arts and crafts stores are, fortunately, open year around. I notice that Brazilian travelers are the biggest buyers, which probably means that they have a greater appreciation and/or identification with regional products.

Ceramics
Anthropologists and archeologists associated with the Emilio Goeldi Museum in Belém have concluded that the art of ceramics in the Amazon goes back at least 3,000 years and it might have been one of the most advanced in the Western Hemisphere. Replicas of some of the *Tapajônica* ceramics (the style produced in this immediate region) may be purchased at some of the local arts and crafts stores in Santarém. Some are small enough that some careful packing will get them back home in one piece. Replicas of *Marajoara* ceramics (the style produced on Marajó Island) may also be acquired in Santarém.

Most of the high-quality clay used for ceramic and brick making comes from the Amazon floodplain just east of Santarém. Visitors taking a tour into the Maicá area during low water season (see tours section of the guide) inevitably encounter riverboats being loaded with heavy chunks of clay. This material is destined for ceramic and brick production.

Tapajônica Style Clothing
If you are looking for something very special in the way of regional arts and crafts, I recommend that you pay a visit to Dona Dica Frazão at Rua Floriano Peixoto, 281. Her Tapajônica style dresses, tunics,

purses, fans, table clothes, towels, flowers and other fineries for women are all made of natural bark and root/vine fibers gathered by Indians on the upper Tapajós River. Every piece is individually designed and handmade by Dona Dica, whose magical fingers transform the natural colored fibers into beautiful fabrics. Time permitting; you may get a tour of her workshop to see samples of the raw materials from which she creates her original fashions. Do not be surprised if she takes the liberty of leading you through her private living quarters to show you a flock of ducks, geese and turkeys in the backyard. The point she wants to get across is that the plumage used in her clothing no longer contributes to the destruction of rare tropical birds. Dona Dica has been in this business since 1949, and I dare say that very little of her production is sold locally. Her fame is such that she stays busy filling orders for the finest boutiques of the country, special orders for heads of governments, royalty, and gifts for special occasions. Reproduction of some of Dona Dica's more distinguished creations may be seen at the small museum next to her workshop. This is cottage industry at its very best.

Hammocks

People of the Amazon sleep, sit, work, play, and live important moments of their lives in a *rede*, so it will come as no surprise to find many stores and street vendors selling them—in every size, color and design imaginable. You may be in the market for one yourself, especially if you plan on traveling by boat. Most visitors come with a negative attitude towards hammocks because of having slept in undersized ones back home and usually the ones made out of fish net material. They never forget that tormenting night of trying unsuccessfully to sleep and then getting up with an aching back looking like an old waffle. Some folks come to the Amazon without ever having swung in a hammock and they tend to make the same mistake, that of buying hammocks much too small and of inferior materials. An Australian couple traveling from Manaus to Santarém by riverboat described to me how foolish they felt lying half in and half out of their tiny hammocks for two days and nights, while the Brazilians onboard ostentatiously sprawled out in huge, comfortable ones, some so large that mothers and children could share. To make hammock sleeping a positive affair, buy the largest size possible and sleep in it diagonally. In this position, you can lie as flat as on your bed at home, and you can actually turn over. Also choose a hammock made from soft, cotton fibers and use a sheet to line it. Swing yourself (better yet, have someone else do it) in the hammock for a few minutes before dropping off to sleep. You will be surprised how fast it cools off your body on a hot and humid night. A word of warning to couples who choose to share a hammock: the story goes that when two people sleep in a hammock, three get out of it. The Australian couple never got a chance to test the theory.

Diógenes Leal, noted cinematographer from Belém, collaborated with Professor Jim Bogan from the University of Missouri (and member of the Missouri/Pará Partners of the Americas) on a documentary film entitled, *Hammock Variations*. The film sums up the significance of the hammock in the Amazon in the following poem:

"Everything happens in a hammock—from before we are born through the arc of our life, til our friends carry us to the bone yard—It all happens in a hammock."[21]

I should have copyrighted the saying, "A hammock in Amazonia is equivalent to a sleeping bag in Alaska," because I said it first. Those of us working tourism have fond memories of the Aparecida hammock factory that was located on Avenida Borges Leal, 2561, before closing down in 1996. Aparecida hammocks were hand-woven on giant wooden looms by craftsmen who worked with lightning speed over intense sounds of fast-moving shuttles. We all keep our fingers crossed that the factory, owned and operated by the Diocese of Santarém, will open its doors again in the near future.

When buying a hammock for boat travel, remember that you will probably need rope to extend the length of it to the hooks on the boat. This item can be bought from a number of small shops along the waterfront, already cut in pieces appropriate for hammock tying.

Natural fibers are recommended over nylon rope since the knot of the latter can slip out of place when you least expect it. The best natural fiber of the region is *curauá*, a hemp-looking fiber produced from a plant by the same name. It looks much like an overgrown pineapple plant.

Out on the streets, as well as in other gift shops, you will find a variety of local handicrafts items made of wood, bamboo, fish bones, seeds, seed pods, fish scales, piranha teeth and so on. Although they may look quite "indigenous," most of them are not authentic Indian art. Not to disclaim them by any means because many nicely crafted pieces are offered and the prices are reasonable enough that most travelers can afford several items to take back home as gifts.

Gold
On occasion, visitors ask where they can purchase gold nuggets, or gold jewelry. As a matter of fact, Santarém boasts several outstanding goldsmiths, but most of them work on a custom-made basis for their clients. Thus, it is not easy to find a shop with any great selection of pieces from which to purchase on the spot. The closest is *Joalheria João Sena*, located in downtown Santarém on Travessa 15 de Agosto. An item of special interest is a flat gold pendant representing the legendary *Muiraquitã*, a frog amulet. João Sena, one of the most skilled goldsmiths in Santarém, makes diverse gold-crafted pendants portraying both Tapajônica and Marajoara designs. *Ouro* is *ouro* and the Brazilian standard for jewelry is 18-karat, so do not be surprised if prices reflect these little details. It is noteworthy to mention that when the first lady of Brazil, Dona Ruth Cardosa, visited Santarém in 1997, the gift presented to her by Santarenos was none other than a gold *muiraquitã* pendant. She was thrilled, as she should have been, for she is an anthropologist.

The governor of the State of Pará, Almir Gabriel, was another celebrity receiving a gold *muiraquitã*, on the inauguration of Tramoeste, on February 27, 1999. The gift not only symbolized the arrival of electricity from the Tucuruí Hydroelectric Dam but also the amelioration of a lengthy political altercation between the governor and the mayor of Santarém at that time, Joaquim de Lira Maia.

CLOSING OUT

In concluding this personal account of travels in the Amazon, I am reminded of an expression that goes something like "Everything is changing and I'm not feeling the same anymore." It would be naïve to think that the Amazon could possibly remain as I found it on my arrival in 1979. Santarém was a city of about 95,000 people at that time with few vehicles and only a couple of paved streets. Today the population is approaching 300,000 with yet a swelling suburban community residing on what were once homesteading lands along the Santarém-Cuiabá Highway, BR-163. Not one inch of the highway was paved back in 1979. Today hundreds of people commute from Cipoal and more distant points to their jobs in Santarém in a matter of twenty to thirty minutes. Getting to Belterra today is not exactly a "piece of cake," but I remember when I started doing tours there in 1987, it was an all-day affair and I never took the risk of promising to get clients to the airport in time to catch a plane at the end of the day. My mode of transportation was an old C-10 Chevy pickup with a makeshift housing on the back. During the rainy season there were times when the roads of Belterra turned into lakes and rivers and I felt I was navigating a boat instead of a vehicle. During the dry season I had to limit the number of passengers to the cabin because even the young and adventurous travelers could not survive the clouds of dust coming up into the open area in the back. Today I can do the Belterra tour in less than three hours! Many times I do a combination of the ecological tour at Bosque Santa Lúcia and Belterra in an easy day. In 1979, there were still thousands of acres of rubber trees left over from the Ford days. Even though they were old and unproductive trees lost in brush and secondary forest growth, I could show clients what was once a legendary plantation established by the one and only, Henry Ford. Today there are only a few symbolic rubber trees left around the mayor's office and the old hospital, which, by the way, burned down in 2005. Fields of soybean and dry-land rice have now replaced rubber trees plantations and forest in Belterra, as well as other

214

highland areas of the region. Our small forest reserve, Bosque Santa Lúcia is surrounded by these farms and the road passing through the Bosque has been widened and graded for passage of both grain and logging trucks. Access is definitely better but I miss the days when the forest came out to meet the very edge of the narrow dirt road, creating blissful shade. Mud holes rarely dried out during the rainy season. I remember my first ecological tour at the Bosque with three Dutch women in 1987. The mud holes in the low areas of the road were so big and deep, it was impossible to get in by vehicle, so we left the car on the highway and walked to the Bosque, three kilometers away. I use the word "walk" lightly because sloshing through mud and water isn't an easy affair. Nevertheless, we got there and still had time to do two hours of touring at the Bosque and then walk back out to the highway. My guests were in high spirits as we arrived back in the city. As they expressed it, this was their best day in Brazil. This was what they had come to do!

When I arrived in Santarém, Alter do Chão was already regarded by locals as the icon of tourism for this part of the Amazon, but access was difficult. My first trip there was done in a VW "Bug" loaned to me by José Garcia, a tropical medicine specialist at the Fundação Esperança. The thirty-three kilometers between Santarém and the Alter do Chão was not much more than a one-lane track winding through tropical savanna sand. There were few, if any, hotels at that time. Everyone stayed in *malocas* (thatched roundhouses) built on the beaches of the Tapajós River. The local population was made up of approximately one thousand families, most of whom were fishermen and rubber tappers. Eventually the State of Pará paved the road into the village and put in electricity, which sparked a real-estate boom that continues to this day. Everybody with the means to buy a piece of land on which to build a dwelling has done so. Most locals now earn their living in construction and care-taking. Several large hotels have been built and it is quite common to find tour groups going directly from the airport to Alter do Chão, rather than coming into Santarém. The Sairé festivity, which I described earlier in the book, used to take place at the village square next to the waterfront and visitors hardly ever filled up the few makeshift bleachers constructed for the occasion. Today the festivity attracts thousands of fun-loving people and the "shows" are concentrated at a much larger square located uphill from the old village. The dates of Sairé were also changed from July to September in order to accommodate a larger number of people on the spectacular beaches separating Green Lake from the Tapajós River. Needless to say, the *Ilha do Amor* (Island of Love) is the most popular camping ground for most people. And "love" may be the real thing in this case. The Secretary of Health distributed 15,000 condoms to visitors coming for the 2006 Sairé festival.

Paradoxically, not much has changed in regard to volume of tourists coming to the Tapajós since I arrived in 1979. I attribute this inconsistency to difficult access and the expense of getting here. I do not have the facts and figures to prove it, but it seems to me that we had many more visitors in the late 1980s and the early 1990s than today. Access was much easier when I got started in the tourism business because there were daily flights from New York and Miami to Belém and Manaus. This service was closed down for several years making it necessary to go all the way to São Paulo for connections to the Amazon. A trip to Santarém suddenly turned into a two-day ordeal, which was not a attractive to potential customers, especially the older folks. More recently TAM has brought back more convenient routes, making it possible to fly into Fortaleza, Belém and Manaus on a daily basis. I predict that we will see an increase in the numbers of guests coming our way because of these connections. But it is unlikely that anyone will need to fight off crowds of travelers on their arrival to this part of the world. As I stated in the introduction of this book, visitors can still come to one of the most attractive places on earth without fighting mobs of people.

The true value of this book, as I see it, is to expand our horizons about different places and people. It is a personal account of my living and traveling in the Amazon; and it was not written to vie with many excellent guides, such as *The Lonely Planet*. One of the

Missouri/Pará Partners of the Americas members questioned some of the negativity of the book, such as the sections about noise, littering, and the lack of sidewalks. I was pleased to learn that others looked at it differently because they interpreted the subtitle as a big qualifier. They were absolutely correct in this assessment of what I wanted to portray in the book, which is an account of tourism as I personally experienced it over the years — as a guide and also long-term resident of Santarém. If I wrote something downbeat about Santarém, it was not necessarily meant to be a negative statement about the place I call home. Many times I was merely quoting sentiments passed on to me by others, especially Brazilians. Over the years I have observed that foreigners very rarely complain or comment about questionable issues like sanitation and infrastructure. Many local people, on the other hand, are quite vocal about what they consider to be inadequate setting for receiving tourists — from wherever. "We don't have good hotels; our streets and roads are full of holes; there is trash all over the place; we don't have proper transportation; and so on. I have lost track of the number of times I have discussed these issues with groups planning for tourism. I testify to these groups that visitors coming to Santarém and this region have very positive experiences here and that any lack of infrastructure is a reality that most outsiders recognize as "part of the show." If everything was the same as back home, why would anyone want to travel anyway? In all the years I have guided here in the Amazon, I only remember one case of a person commenting negatively about his experience. We had just finished a three day riverboat trip to Monte Alegre and I was saying my goodbyes and "come back to see us" at the Santarém airport. This gentleman, who had seldom ever lifted his eyes from a book he was reading over those days looked me squarely in the eye and said, "Well Steve, when Brazil is more like the United States, I'll come back." To be honest about it, I thought his comment was ludicrous at the time, but when I gave it more thought, I realized that this person was being honest with me and more important — he was a very atypical guest. To listen to local planning experts, you might think that all visitors have negative experiences here in what I call

"Paradise." It isn't true! Santarém is a place that most people come to like right away and many come back for another taste

Appendix A – Bird's Eye View of Santarém

Geographical Position
Santarém is located in the State of Pará at 2 degrees 24' 52" latitude south of the equator at 54 degrees 42' 36" West Greenwich. The city is found at the confluence of the Tapajós and Amazon Rivers, two of the largest in the world.

Physical Area
The Municipality of Santarém covers an area of 24,154 square kilometers (14,975 square miles).

Population
Approximately 262,000 people live in Santarém. The municipality population is around 450,000.

Principal Highways
BR-163 (Santarém-Cuiabá) connects the Middle Amazon to other parts of the country. In the State of Pará, only the first 100 kilometers (62 miles) leaving Santarém are paved. Another highway, PA-370, connects Santarém to the Curuá-Una Hydroelectric Dam, 80 kilometers (49 miles) away. The most frequently used road is PA 457 to Alter do Chão. The distance is 33 kilometers (20 miles) and it is paved all the way.

Temperatures
Maximum 36.6°C (98°F). Minimum 22° C (71°F). The average annual temperature varies between 25°-28° C (77 °F to 82°F). The average annual humidity is 86%.

Rainfall
Approximately 2,000mm (79 inches) per year, most of which falls between January and June.

Economy
Commerce, fishing, agriculture, ranching, lumber and mineral exploration.

Radio Stations
Radio FM Guarany—Radio FM Tapajós—Radio Rural and Radio Tropical.

Telephones
Line-connected and cellular phones. Public phone booths located on major arteries throughout the city. Public phones are now available in major rural communities.

Television Station
Rede Globo (TV Tapajós) — *Cadeia Nacional de Televisão* (CNT) — *Sistema Brasileira de Televisão* (SBT) — *Guarany* (Record) — and *Bandeirante*.

Service Clubs
Lions and Rotary Clubs.

Newspapers
Journal de Santarém—O Tapajós— O Impacto and O *Estado do Tapajó.*

Government
Elected Mayor (*Prefeito*) and Council of Representatives (*Vereadores*). They preside over the entire Municipality of Santarém. Each village has its own elected president.

Source of Energy
Tucuruí Dam, 148 kw in the eastern part of the State, as well as the Curuá-Una Hydroelectric Dam.

Source of Energy for Cooking
Mostly butane gas. Some wood charcoal.

Source of Water
The public water system is administered by the Companhia de Saneamento do Pará (COSANPA). Artesian wells are located in various points of the city. There are also many private wells serving the population.

Sewage Disposal
Private septic tanks and outhouses.

Police System
Civil, military and federal police.

Public Health
SESPA (State Department of Health & Environment) and SESMA (Municipality Department of Health & Environment).

Hospitals and Clinics
Hospital Municipal, the former Fundação Nacional de Saúde; Hospital e Maternidade Sagrada Família (private); Imaculada Conçeição (private); Hospital e Maternidade João XXIII (private); Hospital São Raimundo Nonato (private); Hospital e Maternidade Santa Terezinha (private); Fundação Esperança (a non-profit foundation providing out-patient care, specialized surgery and continuing education).

Education
State, municipal, federal and private schools. Institutions of higher education include Núcleo da Universidade Federal do Pará (UFPA); Instituto Lutherano de Ensino Superior de Santarém (ILESS); Faculdades Integrados do Tapajós (FIT) and Instituto Esperança de Ensino Superior (IESPES).

Museums
Centro Cultural João Fona (Historical Museum of Santarém). Museu Judiciário (Judiciary Museum of Santarém) located at the Forum, Avenida Mendonça Furtado.

Libraries

Biblioteca Municipal, located at Casa de Cultura, Avenida Borges Leal and Instituto Cultural Boanerges Sena (ICBS), at Travessa 15 de Agosto, 1254.

Appendix B - Glossary of Foreign Words Used in the Text

Açaí	A thick dark purple pulp extracted from the fruit of the açaí palm, *Euterpe oleracea.* Normally served cold with farinha de tapioca and lots of sugar. A favorite regional food.
Açú	Tupi-Guarani word for *big.*
Açúcar	Sugar
Água	Water
Aldeia	Village. That part of Santarém inhabited by Indians during the Portuguese colonization.
Amazônia Legal	Geographical area of Brazil designated as Amazonia
Aparelho de Som	Stereo
Assado	Baked
Associação Comercial	Chamber of Commerce
Bandeira	Flag. Also used to describe a taximeter, as in the expressions *Bandeira 1* and *Bandeira 2.*
Barão	Baron
Barulho	Noise
Bastão	Stick or stick form
Batida	An alcoholic drink made of cachaça and fruit juices.
Bem gelada	Ice-cold, as in *cerveja bem gelada*
Bicarbonato de sódio	Bicarbonate of Sodium
Bicho de pé	Chigoe flea
Blocos	Carnival groups
Bodega	Bar
Boi	Bull
Bolo	Cake

Bolo de Tapioca	Tapioca cake
Borboletas	Butterflies
Bosque	Arboretum, small forest reserve, normally in a city setting.
Boto	Pink dolphin, *Inia geoffrensis*
Brega	Popular music
Buracos	Holes
Caba de igreja	Wasp, *Polistes canadensis*
Cachaça	Sugarcane rum
Café	Breakfast, or coffee
Cafézinho	Diminutive for coffee. Coffee served in demitasses.
Caipirinha	A popular Brazilian drink made of cachaça, crushed lime and sugar.
Cais de Arrimo	Protective wall separating the Tapajós River from the city.
Caju	Cashew
Calçados	Sidewalks
Calor	Heat
Câmbio	Money exchange
Canarana	Canarana grass. Literal translation of *canarana* is "false cane," since it looks very much like sugarcane.
Canjica	Pudding made of cornmeal, coconut and spices.
Caprichoso	One of the contending Boi-Bumbá dance groups in Parintins.
Cara	Colloquial expression for "what's his face."
Carambola	Five-star fruit
Carnaúba	Carnaúba palm, *Copernecia cerifera*
Casa	House/home
Castanha do Pará	Brazil Nut
Catando	To pick-at or pick-out
Centavos	Cents

Cerâmica	Ceramic
Cerrado	Tropical savana
Cerveja	Beer
Cerveja em lata	Canned beer
Chifre	Horn
Churrasco	Barbecue
Cidade do Sol	Sun City
Cobra	Snake
Cobra Grande	Legendary Big Snake
Com certeza	"For sure"
Confederados	Confederates
Corno	Horn. Demeaning expression for a man whose wife is cheating on him.
Correio	Post office
Couve	Collard-greens
Cuia	Calabash gourd
Cuieira	Calabash gourd tree, *Crescentia cajute*
Cupuaçu	*Theobroma grandiflorum.* Pulp of fruit used for making juice, ice cream and candies.
Curandeiro	Medicine-man
Curauá	Fiber of the bromeliad, *Ananas sativa.* Used for making rope and upholstering material.
Dendê	Oil from the dendê palm, *Elaeis melancocca.* An ingredient of many Afro-Brazilian dishes, including vatapá.
Doido	Crazy
Embaiuba	Cecropia tree
Escabeche	Sauce
Escada de jabuti	Ribbon-like vine, *Bauhinia splendens.* Literal translation is "tortoise's ladder."
Estrangeiros	Foreigners

Falta de energia	Lack of electrical energy
Farinha	Byproduct of the mandioca root.
Farinha de Tapioca	Tapioca beads, as used in tapioca pudding.
Farofa	Farinha fried in butter with salt, garlic and other ingredients.
Feijoada	Black beans and pork
Festas	Parties/festivals
Festas juninas	June festival
Filho da puta	Son-of-a-bitch
Filote	Fish (*Brachyplatystoma* SP.)
Frente polar	Cold front
Frito na manteiga	Fried in butter
Furo	"Hole," e.g., a stream leaving the main river.
Garantido	Contending Boi-Bumbá dance group in Parintins.
Garimpeiros	Gold miners
Garrafa	Bottle
Gaúchos	People from the southern state of Rio Grande do Sul
Goiaba	Guava fruit
Goma	Tapioca starch
Gorgeta	A tip, for example, to a waiter
Graças a Deus	"Thank God"
Graviola	Fruit from the tree bearing the same name (*Annona muricata*). Used for making juice, creams and ice cream.
Gringão	"Big Gringo"
Gringo	A foreigner
Guaraná	Soft drink made from the fruit of the guaraná plant (*Paullinia cupana*).
Guardanapos	Napkins
Hora de verão	Daylight savings time
Igarapé	Creek or a small stream leaving the

	main river, as *furo*.
Ipê	Tree. Also called *Pau d'arco* (*Tabebuia serratifolia*)
Jabuti	Yellow-footed Tortoise, *Geochelone denticulata*
Jacaré	Generic term for caiman
Jaçanã	Wattled jacana
Jambu	A spinach-like plant with anesthetic properties.
Jararaca	Fer-de-lance snake (*Bothrops asper*)
Jenipapo	Tree, *Genipa americana*, from which the indigenous population removes resin for making of a dark blue dye used in body paints. Jenipapo fruit used locally also for making liqueur and other drinks
Latinos	People from Latin America
Limão	Lime, lemon.
Linhão de Tucuruí	Electrical power-line connecting Santarém with the Tucuruí Hydroelectric Dam
Louro	Slang for "beer." Literal translation means "blond."
Macaco	Monkey
Macaxeira	Sweet mandioca, *Manihot aypi*
Macho	He-man
Madeira de lei	Top quality lumber. Originally those tree species reserved strictly for the Portuguese court.
Mais uma caipirinha , favor.	One more caipirinha, please
Mamão	Papaya, *Carica papaya*
Mandioca	Manioc, *Manihot esculenta*
Maniçoba	Regional food made of finely ground

	mandioca leaves and pork.
Marajoara	Pertaining to Marajó island, as in *cerâmica marajoara*
Matamatá	Turtle, *Chelus fimbriatus,* with a flattened out carapace and triangular head
Mercadão 2000	Santarém's largest market place
Merda	Feces/shit
Mercado	Market
Mocinho	Little boy
Motociclistas	Motorcyclists
Motorista	Driver
Muchica	A thick porridge of roasted/shredded fish, spices and farinha
Muçuã	a very small specie of turtle, *Cinosternum scorpioides*
Mucuim	Chigger
Muiraquitã	Legendary ornamental frog crafted from jade, stone and shell. An offering by a nation of Amazonian women to occasional lovers who produced children for them.
Multas	Fines
Munguzá	Sweet hominy
Muruci	Fruit of the muruci tree (*Byrsonima crassifolia*). Used in juices and ice cream.
Na brasa	Barbecued
Novela	Soap opera
Ôba	Explanatory remark, e.g., alright!"
Obrigado (a)	Thank you
Óleo de Andiroba	Oil from the andiroba tree, *Carapa guianensis*
Onça	Jaguar
Onça preta	Black jaguar

Ordem e Progresso	"Order and progress." Motto inscribed on the Brazilian flag.
Ouro	Gold
Pai corujo	Proud father. Literal translation, "father owl."
Papo-ovo	Non-poisonous snake
Parabéns para Você	Happy birthday to you
Pararamas	Caterpillars that exude allergic/lethal chemicals
Pata de Boi	Medicinal plant, *Bauinha* SP.
Pato no Tucupi	Duck in tucupi. Regional food of the Amazon
Pé de moleque	Peanut brittle
Peixinhos	Diminutive of *peixe*, fish
Perigoso	Dangerous
Perlipimpim	Fantasy mite said to attach itself to the testicles of chiggers. To denote something very small.
Pimenta malagueta	Small red hot peppers. Capsicum pepper.
Pimenta	Black pepper, *Piper nigrum*
Pimenta de Cheiro	Small round hot peppers emitting a peculiar smell when opened. Thus "smell peppers."
Piraíba	Catfish (*Brachyplatystoma filamentosum*)
Pirão	A thick porridge made of farinha cooked in fish broth
Pirarucu	*Arapaima gigas*, the largest scaled fish in the world. Often referred to as the "codfish of the Amazon."
Pitomba	*Talisia esculenta,* referred to as "Brazilian cherry."
Pitiú	A small turtle specie, *Podocnemis sextuberculata*

Planalto	Plateau or highland
Polícia Militar do Pará	Military Police of Pará
Políticos	Politicians
Ponta Negra	Geographical location of "meeting of the waters," where the Amazon and Tapajós Rivers come together.
Pousada das garças	Egret rookery
Pousada	Small hotel
Praça	Square
Praça Mirante	Lookout Square. Overview of the Tapajós and Amazon Rivers.
Praias bonitas	Beautiful beaches
Prefeito	Mayor
Preguiça	Sloth
Primeira Dama	First lady
Que calor!	Wow, it's hot!
Reais	Plural of *real*
Real	Brazilian currency
Receita	Recipe
Receita Federal	Brazilian Revenue Service
Rede	Hammock
Sairé (Çairé)	Annual folklore festival in Alter do Chão
Sal	Salt
Santarenos	People from Santarém
Sem água	Without water
Sítio	Small farm or out-of-town refuge
Soro Oral	Oral hydration
Sorvete	Ice cream
Sujão	Litterbug
Surubim	Catfish
Surucucu	Bushmaster snake, *Lachesis mutus*
Tambaquí	Fish, *Colossoma macropomum.*
Tapajônica	Pertaining to the Tapajós, as in

	cerâmica Tapajônica.
Taperebá	Fruit from the taperebá tree, *Spondias lutea*
Taperinha	Archeological site/ranch on the Amazon River Floodplain east of Santarém
Tapioca	Starch of the mandioca root
Tarde demais	Too late
Tartaruga	The giant river turtle, *Podocnemis expansa*
Tinga	Tupi-Guarani word for *white*. When referring to caiman, *tinga* is the word for "spectacled caiman."
Toco	Stump or "the finger."
Tracajá	Yellow-spotted Amazon turtle, *Podocnemis unifilis*
Tubarão	Shark
Tucunaré	Peacock bass, *Cichla ocellaris*
Tucupi	The juice from the mandioca root. Used in a variety of regional foods.
Tucuxi	The small gray dolphin, *Sotalia fluviatilis*
Urubu	Generic term for "vulture"
Urucu	Plant, *Bixa orellana*. Pulp of seed used for red body paint, as well as food coloring
Vatapá	Popular Afro-Brazilian dish served throughout the country. Ingredients include shrimp, dendê oil and a thick sauce made of flour or bread
Verão	Summer/dry season
Victória régis	The gigantic Amazon water-lily, *Victoria amazonica*

Appendix C

HIGH NOON ON THE EQUATOR

equimatinal
day of
Equinoctical
night
noon
sight
straight
up
directly
over
my
head
90 degrees
that is
the Sun
blazing
round
absolutely
tops--
for the moment

James Bogan
Belém, 21 March, Equinox

Jungle Grammar — the Verb "To Be"

Slash, slash, slash!
Wack, wack, wack!
Cutting this jungle brush
is killing my back.

My machete worn down
to a kitchen knife,
from wack, wack, wack
on its metallic life.

Slash, slash, slash!
Working on this land, so fine
proves to me that everything
is, has been or will be a damned vine.

Steven W. Alexander
Bosque Santa Lúcia
Poço Branco - Pará
19 October, 1999

Appendix E – The Metric System and U.S. Equivalents

Kilometer - 0.62 mile
Mile - 1.609 kilometers

Meter - 39.37 inches
Yard - 0.9144 meter
Foot - 30.48 centimeters

Centimeter - 0.39 inch
Millimeter - 0.039 inch
Inch - 2.54 centimeters

Hectare - 2.47 acres
Acre - 0.405 hectare

Liter - 1.057 quarts (liquid)
Gallon - 3.785 liters
Quart - 1.101 liters
Pint - 0.551 liter

Kilogram - 2.2046 pounds
Pound - 0.454 kilogram
Ounce - 28.350 grams

To convert Celsius to Fahrenheit: Multiply by 9 and divide the result by 5. Add 32.

To convert Fahrenheit to Celsius: Subtract 32 from the Fahrenheit temperature, and multiply the result by 5. Divide this number by 9.

Normal body temperature in 36.7°C

Maximum air temperature in Santarém is said to be 36.6°C (98°F). Remember that this figure refers to the temperature in the shade. Since it is obviously hotter out in the sun, one must be extra careful to avoid contact with heat-absorbing objects, for example, zinc roofing on boats or sandy beaches. On a sunny afternoon such exposed surfaces can reach 120°-130°F (50°C) and provide a wicked burn in short order.

Cultural Contrasts: For those of us set in our ways, even a simple thing like reading a date can be confusing in Brazil. For example, how would you interpret 03.02.2004? If you are coming from North America, you will surely say it means March 2, 2004. In Brazil it means February 3, 2004. The day always comes first and then the month and year.

When reading hand-written numbers, for instance on a restaurant bill, be careful with the ones and sevens. The Brazilians write their "one," close to how we write a "seven." The seven is much easier to distinguish because they cross the shaft of the number. Another difference in writing numbers is that Brazilians use commas where we use periods. For instance, the figure eight thousand is written 8.000 instead of 8,000. Fifty reais and thirty centavos is written R$50,30. Even dates can be written differently than that to which we are accustomed. As a case in point, it is quite common to see the year 2006 written as 2.006.

Furthermore, reading the time can be confusing for those not used to dealing with military-time. It is quite common to use the simple number system in many cases, such as when saying, "I'll see you at eight," when it is mutually understood that one is referring to either the morning or evening. Otherwise, the 24-hour system is used: for example, you may see a sign specifying the departure of a riverboat at 18:00 hrs. This means 6:00 PM. Noon is written as 12:00 hrs. and midnight, 24:00 hrs. Half past midnight is written 00:30 hrs. and so on.

Time Zone
Brazilians are not at all fanatical in reporting blow-by-blow details of time, so it is understandable that travelers arriving in Santarém from

Belém are often taken by surprise, sometimes the next day, to discover that they have changed time zones. Santarém is one hour earlier than Belém. The next change traveling up the Amazon is at the border with Peru, and then again in Iquitos. Travelers addicted to ship travel are accustomed to hearing the terminology "ship time," which to me means a total disrespect for international time zones in the name of convenience for ship management.

Daylight Saving Time

By virtue of the fact that the Amazon is located in equatorial climes, daylight saving time (*hora de verão*) is not part of our lifestyle, as it is in the rest of the country. In the beginning we were also included (October to February), but the commotion created locally was great enough that we were finally liberated from the seasonal event. There is, nevertheless, a variation of half an hour or so in daylight hours even here in the Amazon—but not enough to warrant setting clocks back a full hour. Provincial lifestyles were perturbed greatly during the one year we participated, and most Santarenos came to ignore "government time" all together. Today we probably would not even be aware of daylight saving time in the rest of Brazil were it not for television programs. For those of us dealing with air traffic, we dare not forget such details.

The Fastest Time Ever Recorded

The shortest time ever recorded by scientists is said to be the time between a traffic light change and the guy behind you blowing his horn. Where? Rio de Janeiro. The second fastest recorded time in the world is the time between a traffic light turning green and the gunning of bus motors behind you. The place is Santarém, of course.

Appendix F – Further Reading

Amorim, T.S. 1995. *A Dominação Norte-Americana no Tapajós-A Companhia Ford Industrial do Brasil.* Santarém: Gráfica e Editora Tiagão.

Barata, F. 1952. *Arqueologia- As Artes Plásticas no Brasil.* Ediouro.

Bates, H. W. 1863. *The Naturalist on the River Amazons.* New York: Penguin Books

Bernard, H. 1992. *Insight Guides- Amazon Wildlife.* Singapore: Hofer Press.

Bogan, J.J. 1996. *Hammock Variations— Essays, Poems, Proverbs, Travelers Tales, and a Film about God's Own Bed.* Rolla, Missouri.

Caufield, C. 1985. *In the Rainforest: Report from a Strange, Beautiful, Imperiled World.* Chicago: University of Chicago.

Cavalcante, P.B. 1988. *Frutas Comestíveis da Amazônia.* Belém: Museu Paraense Emílio Goeldi.

COMTUR, 1998. *Inventário da Oferta e Infra-Estrutura Turística de Santarém.* Prefeitura Municipal de Santarém. Instituto Cultural Boanerges Sena - ICBS

Davis, W. 1997. *One River - Explorations and Discoveries in The Amazon Rain Forest.* New York: Touchstone.

D'Abrea, B. 1984. *Butterflies of South America.* Vitoria: Hill House.

Dunning, J.S. 1987. *South American Birds.* Newton Square: Harrowood Books.

Dutra, M. 1998. *Ramal dos Doidos.* Santarém: Instituto Boanerges Sena/Gráfica e Editora Tiagão.

Emmons, L.H. 1990. *Neotropical Rainforest Mammals- A Field Guide.* Chicago: The University of Chicago Press.

Falcone, A. E. n.d. *Amazon Surgeon.* n.p.

Fonseca, W.D. 1984. *Santarém-Momentos Históricos.* Belém: Falangola Editora.

Forsyth, A. and Miyata, K. 1984. *Tropical Nature: Life and Death in the Rain forests of Central and South America.* New York: Charles Scribner's Sons.

Franco, E. 1998. *O Tapajós Que Eu Vi (Memórias).* Santarém: Instituto Cultural Boanerges Sena/Gráfica e Editora Tiagão.

Galvão, E. 1973. *Exposições de Antropologia - Museu Goeldi.* Belém. Gráfica Falangola Editora.

Gentry, A.H. 1993. *A Field Guide to the Families and Genera of Woody Plants of Northwest South America.* Chicago: University of Chicago

Goodman, E.J. 1972. *The Explorers of South America.* Norman: University of Oklahoma Press.

Goulding, M. 1989. *Amazon: The Flooded Forest.* London: BBC Books.

Goulding, M. 1980. *The Fishes and the Forest.* Berkeley: University of California Press.

Goulding, M., Smith, N., Mahar, D. 1996. *Floods of Fortune- Ecology & Economy Along The Amazon.* New York: Columbia University Press.

Hagmann, G. 1998. *Taperinha- Um Breve Histórico.* Monograph. Santarém

Harter, E. 1985. *The Lost Colony of the Confederacy.* Jackson: University Press of Mississippi.

Hilty, S. 1994. *Birds of Tropical America - A Watcher's Introduction to B ehavior, Breeding and Diversity.* Shelburne: Chapters.

Hilty, S., Brown, W. 1986. *Birds of Colombia.* Princeton: Princeton University Press.

Kricher, J.C. 1997. *A Neotropical Companion: An Introduction to the Animals, Plants and Ecosystems of the New World Tropics.* Princeton: Princeton University Press.

Lotschert, W. and Beese, G. 1989. *Collins Guide to Tropical Plants.* London: William Collins Sons & Co. Ltd.

Maas, P.J. & Westra, L.Y. Th. 1993. *Neotropical Plant Families: A concise guide to families of vascular plants in the Neotropics.* Germany: Koeltz Scientific Books

Machado, J.P. 1989. *Marajó.* Rio de Janeiro: Editora Agir.

Mee, M. 1988. *In Search of Flowers of the Amazon Forests.* Suffolk: Nonesuch Expeditions Ltda.

Meggers, B.J. 1996. *Amazonia - Man and Culture in a Counterfeit Paradise.* Washington and London. Smithsonian Institution Press.

McIntyre, L. 1993. Magnum Bunkum. *South American Explorer.* Number 32:38.

Nery, S. 1901. *The Land of the Amazons.* New York: E.P. Dutton & Co.

Neves, W.A. 1989. *Biologia e Ecologia Humana na Amazônia; Avaliação e Perspectivas.* Belém: Museu Paraense Emílio Goeldi.

Onis, J. 1992. *The Green Cathedral: Sustainable Development of Amazônia.* New York: Oxford University Press.

O'Connor, G. 1997. *Amazon Journal, Dispatches from a Vanishing Frontier.* New York: Penguin Books.

Plotkin, M.J. 1993. *Tales of a Shaman's Apprentice.* New York: Penguin Books.

Prance, G.T. and Lovejoy, T.E. 1985. *Key Environments: Amazonia.* Oxford: Pergamon Press.

Prefeitura Municipal de Santarém, 1997. *Plano Municipal de Agropecuária.* Santarém: Gráfica e Editora Tiagão.

Ridgely, R. S. and Tudor, G. 1989. *The Birds of South America- Volume I - The Oscine Passerines.* Austin. University of Texas Press.

Riker, D.A. 1983. *O Último Confederado Na Amazônia.* Manaus: Imprensa Oficial do Estado do Amazonas.

Rodrigues, R.M. 1989. *A Flora da Amazônia*. Belém: CEJUP

Roosevelt, A.C. *et al.* 1991. *Eighth Millennium Pottery from a Prehistoric Shell Midden in the Brazilian Amazon. Science*, vol. 254, pp. 1621-1624.

Roosevelt, T. 1994. *Through the Brazilian Wilderness.* Mechanicsburg: Stackpole Books,

Santos, R. S. *Tupaiulândia (Santarém) II Volume.*

Schauensee, R.M. and Phelps, W.H. 1978. *Birds of Venezuela.* Princeton: Princeton University Press.

Sick, H. 1984. *Ornitologia Brasileira.* Brasília: Universidade de Brasília. Vol. 1-2.

Sioli, H. 1985. *Amazônia: Fundamentos da Ecologia da Maior Região de Florestas Tropicais.* Petrópolis: Editora Vozes.

Shoumatoff, A. 1986. *The Rivers Amazon.* San Francisco: Sierra Club.

Smith, N. 2002. *Amazon Sweet Sea: Land, Life, and Water and The River's Mouth.* Austin: University of Texas Press.

Smith, N. 1998. *The Amazon River Forest - A Natural History of Plants, Animals, and People.* Oxford University Press

Sterling, T. 1973. *The Amazon- the World's Wild Places/Time Life Books.* Amsterdam: Time-Life International.

Tocantins, L. 1982. *Amazônia- Natureza, Homen e Tempo*. Rio de Janeiro: Editora Civilização Brasileira S.A.

Veríssimo, J. 1970. *A Pesca Na Amazônia*. Belém: Universidade Federal do Pará.

For more specific details on Santarém and the region, I recommend that you continue your research at Instituto Cultural Boanerges Sena (ICBS) at Travessa 15 de Agosto, 1254. It is a private library and research center, owned and administered by Cristovam and Ruth Sena, who for many years have dedicated themselves to the preservation of books, newspapers, photographs, videotapes, paintings and other historical documents pertaining to the region. In 1998 ICBS took on a new professional role in the community, that of publishing books written by people of the Amazon. Cristovam is a forester by vocation and, in that role, has worked as an extension agent for EMATER in the State of Pará for many years. He is recognized as one of the foremost authorities and speakers on the Amazon and is a consultant for many governmental and private organizations.

Literature Cited

1.   Roosevelt, A. C., R. A. Housley, M. Imazio da Silveira, S. Maranca, and R. Johnson, "Eighth millenium pottery from a prehistoric shell midden in the Brazilian Amazon," *Science* 254 (1991): 1621-24.

2.   ———, A.C., M. L. Costa, C. L. Lopes, M. Michab, N. Mercier, H. Valladas, J. Feathers, W. Barnett, M. I. Silveira, A. Henderson, J. Silva, B. Chernoff, D. S. Reese, J. A. Holman, N. Toth, and K. Schick, "Paleoindian cave dwellers in the Amazon: The peopling of the Americas, " *Science* 272 (1996): 373-84

3.   Neves, W. A. 1991. *Origens, Adaptações E Diversidade Biológica Do Homen Nativo da Amazônia.* Belém: Museu Paraense Emílio Goeldi, p. 42.

4.   Goodman, E.J.   1972.   *The Explorers of South America.* Norman: University of Oklahoma Press, pp.12-13.

5.   Goulding, M., Smith, N., Mahar, D. 1996. *Floods of Fortune- Ecology & Economy Along The Amazon,* p.21

6.   See Goodman, *The Explorers of South America*, p. 79

7.   Ibid., pp. 120-123

8.   Fonseca, W.D.   1984.   *Santarém - Momentos Históricos.* Belém: Falangola Editora, p. 10.

9.   Machado, J.P.   1989.   *Marajó.*   Rio de Janeiro: Editora Agir.

10.   Tocantins, L.   1982.   *Amazônia- Natureza, Homen e Tempo.* Rio de Janeiro: Editora Civilização Brasileira S.A., p. 93.

11. Davis, W. 1997. *One River - Explorations and Discoveries in the Amazon Rain Forest*. New York: Touchstone, pp. 353-354.

12. Harter, E. 1985. *The Lost Colony of the Confederacy*. Jackson: University Press of Mississippi.

13. Fonseca, Santarém - *Momentos Históricos*, pp.98-99.

14. Meggers, B.J. 1996. *Amazonia - Man and Culture in a Counterfeit Paradise*, p. 191-192.

15. Emmons, L.H. 1990. *Neotropical Rain Forest Mammals- A Field Guide*, pp. 44-94.

16. Plotkin, M.J. 1993. *Tales of a Shaman's Apprentice,* 7-8.

17. See Goodman, *The Explorers of South America*, 67-68.

18. Rodrigues, R.M. 1989. *A Flora da Amazônia*, 168.

19. Bates, H. W. 1863. *The Naturalist on the River Amazons*, p. 172.

20. Roosevelt, T. 1994. *Through the Brazilian Wilderness*, p. 320

21. Bogan, J.J. 1996. *Hammock Variations— Essays, Poems, Proverbs, Travelers Tales, and a Film about God's Own Bed*. Rolla, Missouri.

Index

ICOMI, 193
Iguanas, 82, 90. 112
INPA, 116, 123
Instituto Cultural Boanerges Sena (ICBS), 221
Intestinal parasite, 163, 164
Iquitos, 15, 16, 50, 57, 68, 70, 93, 108, 235
Itaituba, 54, 87

Jaguars, 76, 119
Jambu, 24, 25
Jauari palm, 127
Jenipapo, 35
Jesuits, 17
Johnson Wax Company, 87
Johnson, Curt, 88
Johnson, Fisk, 88
Johnson, Herbert, 87
Johnson, Sam, 87, 88
Jute, 54

Kapok, 152
Kew Gardens, 18
Lá em Casa, 24, 30
Lago Verde, 80, 88, 201
Leal, Diógenes, 211
Linhão de Tucuruí, 195, 227

Macapá, 35, 57
Maçaranduba, 139, 140
Macaxeira, 26, 41
Macedo, Edivar, 47
Macedo, Sávio, 47
Macedo, Luzia, 47
McGladdery, Sharon, 11, 106
Machado, Antônio, 45, 46
Magnusson, William, 116

Overal, William, 122

Pacu, 143
Papaya, 125, 145, 227
PARATUR, 92
Parintins, 42, 46, 57, 81, 1667, 224, 226
Pata da vaca, 158
Pato no tucupi, 24, 294, 229
Pé de moleque, 41, 229
Pedroso, Jocivan, 163
Pedroso, Luiz Manoel, 134, 139
Pião branco, 157
Pião roxo, 157
Pimenta de cheiro, 29, 30, 39, 229
Pimenta de malagueta, 30
Pimentel, Paulo Sérgio, 46
Pimentel, Zilma, 46
Pineapple, 31, 35, 150, 212
Pinto, Domingos, 172
Pinzón, Vicente Y., 15
Piranhas, 82, 119, 172, 174
Pirão, 24, 229
Pirarucu, 229
Pizarro, Francisco, 153, 157
Pizarro, Gonzalo, 15, 157
Plotkin, Mark J., 152
Poço Branco, 83, 97, 106. 233
Ponta Negra, 181, 230

Quebra pedra, 157

Rede Globo, 220
Rhome, R. J., 22, 82
Ribeiro, Eduardo & Eunice, 109, 142
Richardson, David, 80, 165
Riker, Robert, 22, 201

The Author

Some people get infatuated with Brazil at an early age. Steven Winn Alexander (Gringão) was one of them. He turned on to the country and the people at the enlightened age of eighteen when he dropped out of college to visit a Brazilian girlfriend he had met at the University of Montevallo. Based on his own personal experiences over the decades, he legitimately warns Brazilian enthusiasts to never live for more than a year in country, unless they are willing to put down steadfast roots. Returning to the United States to complete an undergraduate degree at Berea College in Kentucky, Steven never outgrew his obsession to return to Brazil. Upon graduation he joined the U.S. Peace Corps and was assigned to the State of Minas Gerais, where he lived from 1962-1964. On completion of his tour, he joined the teaching staffs at the University of Wisconsin-Milwaukee, Arizona State University, and the University of Florida, Gainesville— all Peace Corps training centers. On following the path of his trainees, he found himself back in South America from 1965-1967 as Associate Peace Corps Director in Brasília, the newly established capital of Brazil.

Quite happy in Brazil, Steven admits to having undergone a moment of inexplicable madness when he accepted an invitation by the U.S. Agency for International Development to study at the School of Public Health at the University of North Carolina, Chapel Hill in return for a two-year obligation in then, South Vietnam. Having surfaced from this interlude, he eventually ended up in Alaska with the U.S. Public Health Service for a period of eight years. People in Santarém often kid him about having come from Alaska to the Amazon, certainly two extremes in climate. Another question frequently asked of him is, why? Steven is fast to reply that he had never in his life thought of living in the Amazon. As a matter of fact, he had never heard of Santarém, that is, before meeting Harry Owens, Jr., a former Public Health Service physician associated with Fundação Esperança in Santarém. Breaking up a profound love affair with Alaska was not easy, but ultimately he accepted Esperança's invitation to head up the community health program, arriving in Santarém in March of 1979. The question of leaving public health for eco-tourism is yet another intriguing question asked of Steven. He replies that the transition was, in fact, an easy one, mainly due to the heavy travel schedule in the region over his five years with the Fundação Esperança. You might say he got to know the region very well. When his job with the health organization terminated in 1984, he decided to stay in Santarém in private business. Ecology and community had helped set Steven's irretractable roots in what he now refers to as "God's Country."

Steven Alexander and his wife, Áurea Lúcia Dias, are proprietors of Amazon Tours (Amazon Turismo Ltda.) in Santarém. They are also owners of Bosque Santa Lúcia, a 109 hectares (261 acres) forest reserve located at Poço Branco, on the outskirts of Santarém. Their future plans include an environmental education program at the site. They have two children, Steven David (1981) and Arthur Daniel (1984).

Steven is recipient of the Padre João Felipe Bettendorf Medal for Distinguished Services to the Municipality of Santarém, an honor conferred to him by Mayor Joaquim de Lira Maia on June 22, 1999— on occasion of the 338th anniversary of the city. In December of the same year he received the title of Honorary Citizen of Santarém, an award presented by the Santarém Chamber of Councilmen/women.

CPSIA information can be obtained
at www.ICGtesting.com
Printed in the USA
LVHW051245191220
674610LV00003B/702